Praise for *Four Blue Stars in the Window*

"A beautifully written book showing how a strongly-knit family coped with the Great Depression and World War II. Reminiscent of John Steinbeck's immortal *Grapes of Wrath* but with a more elevated and heroic tone."

— Walter Boyne
historian and author of
Clash Of Wings: World War II in the Air

"This story hit home with me. I was amazed at its accuracy and history. I was able to compare different events with a biography of my own grandfather, who happened to live in Wisconsin during the same period. It was truly a gift and I shall refer back to it often."

— Eric Robinson
USCG Ret. Machinery Technician 1st Class

Four Blue Stars in the Window

Four Blue Stars in the Window

ONE FAMILY'S STORY OF THE GREAT DEPRESSION,
THE DUST BOWL, AND THE DUTY OF A GENERATION

BARBARA EYMANN MOHRMAN

BERN STREET
PUBLISHING

OMAHA, NEBRASKA

Paperback ISBN: 978-0-9884174-1-0
Kindle ISBN: 978-0-9884174-2-7
ePub ISBN: 978-0-9884174-3-4
LCCN: 2012919951

Author's photo courtesy of Leslie Webber Photography.
Design and Production by Concierge Marketing Inc.

Printed in the United States of America

10   9   8   7   6   5   4   3

To My Family

Dave, Jill, Scott, Kristin, Austin, Kade,
Jamie, Clare, Kendall, Charlie, Harrison, and Rowan.

And above all, to my father.
Forever and always with my gratitude and love.

Author's Note

Memories fade after sixty-five years. Recollections differ slightly. Personal perceptions alter the accounts just a bit. I have done my best to research and re-create each event authentically as it actually happened and in the words of those who lived through them.

I began to work on this book when I learned that my cousins did not know the exploits of the Eymann boys during World War II. I started by interviewing my uncles, aunts, and cousins to gather the story.

Then the project took on a life of its own. I read scores of history books on the Depression and World War II. Websites provided background. I scoured personal log books, scrapbooks, newspapers, family pictures, and memorabilia of the Eymann family. I toured the *USS Cassin Young*, a WWII destroyer, located in Boston. I was fortunate to meet and interview Eigo Tanaka and get a Japanese perspective of the Kamikazes during the war. I attended a reunion of the *USS Lindsey*.

At the *Lindsey* reunion I met Merle Martin, a radioman who was on the ship both at Iwo Jima and Okinawa. I am indebted to him for allowing me to interview and tape his account of that horrible day. I was and still am moved by his account of his experiences. After sixty-five years his voice quivered with emotion as he told his story.

I was honored when he told me I was the first person with whom he ever shared his experiences. A complete list of interviews is at the end of the book.

There are thousands of towns like Oakdale across the United States. And there are thousands of American families that faced similar hardship. Each town helped carry our nation through the Depression, the Dust Bowl, and World War II. These towns—and these families, mine among them—make our nation great.

Eymann Family

Chriss Eymann, born May 20, 1889,

Hattie Mae Retzlaff Eymann, born May 4, 1896

Children:

Cleona Eymann Sharples (None, pronounced Nōne) May 31, 1915

Deloris Eymann Bates Forslund (Tude), born September 26, 1916

Alvin Eymann (Turk), born September 10, 1918

Hans Eymann, born January 27, 1921

George Eymann (Chub), born March 3, 1922

Kenneth Eymann (Ton), born May 14, 1923

Betty Eymann Rittscher, born December 18, 1924

Stanley Eymann (Mick), born May 30, 1930

Marlene Eymann Smith (Deets), born January 25, 1933

Donna Eymann (Wella), born July 1, 1936

Contents

The Oakdale Cemetery.

The Cemetery, 1999

T he rays of the sun angled gracefully through the gentle mist surrounding the cemetery. In these early morning hours the graveyard at the top of the wind-swept hill was still, quiet, and peaceful. I turned the wheels of my car off the paved two-lane highway and onto the narrow gravel road leading to the entrance gate.

Just beyond the gates stood a stoic, gray statue of a soldier, which loomed large and solemn against the backdrop of headstones. The figure had been weathered over time by the frigid winters and blistering summers of Nebraska. Near the statue lay buried a Civil War veteran. In his place of honor, the warrior seemed to stand guard over the others who found their rest among the peony and iris bushes and low-hanging evergreen branches so plentiful throughout the cemetery.

Black marble benches had periodically been placed among the headstones—their seats inviting the occasional mourner to rest and meditate in this eerily beautiful field of death. A vast array of people must have, at one time or another over the years, spent time sitting, thinking, reminiscing, and grieving, for the bench surfaces looked worn and hollow. It always intrigued me to ponder the millions of memories that had surely been relived in the minds of the visitors through the years.

My car crested the entrance hill and followed the dirt path leading to the graves, bumping gently over the rutted road. I stopped the car, opened the trunk, and grasped the items I needed to do my work. As I made the short walk to the far west corner of the cemetery, I was propelled toward this familiar section because I know it as well as I know the back of my hand. This corner section contains the plots belonging to my family. Each year, for as far back as I can recall over the last fifty, I have come to this location.

In my family, the month of May always found us preparing for our annual Memorial Day trip to decorate graves. My father kept a triangular-shaped flower garden tucked into the corner of our backyard. He was truly a magician with this small patch of beauty because glorious colors burst forth every spring in anticipation of fulfilling their May duty as memorial bouquets—the highest honor any flower could achieve.

My father's peony bushes stood in the center—sturdy, green, full, and healthy. These bushes bore the most fragrant, gorgeous flowers each year, gigantic and richly vibrant with deep maroon, delicate pink, and fresh white blossoms adorning this carefully cultivated plot of land. Mingled among the peonies were taller, narrow, spiky, green plants of iris. Atop their pointy spikes burst graceful white, yellow, and purple blossoms. The pungent yet sweet scent of the growing flowers wafted through my backyard playground. The flowers had but a short life blooming no more than a few brief spring days. As the special day neared, my father would cut the flowers at their zenith leaving their long, lonely stems and ample green leaves intact.

His job was then finished, and my mother took over the organizational aspect of the preparation. She knew by heart the list of graves to be decorated. She would designate the kind of bouquet we would leave on each grave. Close relatives received the largest, most beautiful arrangements, and distant or vaguely disliked relations were relegated to perhaps a mere long-stemmed iris.

So it was each year. My father tended and cultivated the flowers. My mother readied them. She set the glowing tributes in water and packed them into the trunk of the car early in the morning we were to leave. The night before our seventy mile journey from our Columbus home to the Oakdale cemetery, the cool, damp basement of our home smelled sweet and tangy with the flowers waiting to be loaded. The moist air of the basement cradled the delicate flowers and kept them fresh.

When my teenage years struck with a vengeance and I began to rebel at the requisite trip to the cemetery, my mother promptly put me in my place.

"In my day," she reminded, "all of the girls and women would gather wildflowers from the meadow. We all dressed in our Sunday best complete with hats and white gloves. Standing on the bridge we would hold a solemn ceremony to recall the sailors lost at sea by tossing our wildflower bouquets into the river."

When faced with this exceptional display of devotion, I would irritably pull on my tattered bell bottoms and get in the car.

Those floral scents were not the only aromas of Memorial Day. Early in the morning the kitchen had bustled with activity as my mother fried chicken and frosted the creamy coconut cake we took along with us. The actual day of delivering the flowers was punctuated by a family picnic. The picnic was sometimes held in the city park, in an open field, or near the bank of the river. Once in a great while we went all the way to Ta-Ha-Zouka Park in Norfolk.

This picnic was the culmination, celebration, and reward for the sometimes tiring work of cleaning and decorating the graves. We children would run, play, swim, and eat the tasty treats lovingly prepared by our mothers and aunts until night fell.

Our parents would load sleepy children into cars for the ride home. The bittersweet irony of remembering the dead at the cemetery and reveling in life at the picnic haunts me now although as a child I thought everyone celebrated this day exactly as we did. It both shocked and horrified me to find out many did not.

Eymann family picnic in the 1950s.

It is only now, with reflection, I realize that in the process of making and delivering these home-grown floral arrangements, I have gradually learned the history of my family. These excursions not only paid homage to departed relatives, they were, in fact, a lesson in the oral history of the Eymanns.

As a child in the 1950s, I learned the names of family members who had died well before I was born. As a youth in the 1960s, I learned more of the scandalous family activities. Finally, as an adult, the complete truths were laid bare, and I learned the stories of worry, sorrow, divorce, war, abandonment, and shame.

After fifty years, it amazed me that I could still walk directly to any of the family graves although if asked to give directions to a stranger I would be hard pressed to give an explanation of their whereabouts. A torrent of emotions overtook me. It was not until I lost a cousin, an uncle, and a parent to this cemetery that I truly understood the meaning behind this day I had celebrated all of my life.

Laying down my store-bought bouquets, I offered up a tiny prayer that my father would forgive my inability to grow the bountiful blossoms he did. Walking thoughtfully, I stood beside a grave marked only by a flat gray headstone. Beneath the shadow of the pine tree I knelt and placed the colorful cluster of spring flowers near the stone. My eyes rested on the name etched there: Chriss Eymann.

As I read the name and numbers carved in stone, I felt a cold shudder of regret. A crisp ripple of pain passed through me because after all this time, and the circumstances of his death, I was still unable to speak out loud the words written there. Chriss Eymann was my grandfather.

Next to his marker lies the headstone of his devoted wife, my grandmother Hattie Mae Eymann. I lingered there briefly, turned, and moved purposefully to the other plots nearby leaving both footprints in the mud and my other floral tributes near ornate headstones.

The sunshine glistened and shimmered among the tree branches over the brass markers tucked closely beside several graves. Against the green backdrop of waving grass the markers still stand proudly aloft as a bright reminder of military service. Attached to them and twirling in the omnipresent Nebraska wind are small American flags.

The morning had brought more visitors strolling with hands full of flowers and carrying pails of water. Unlike the groups of mourners who passed these markers oblivious to what lay beneath them, I know their stories. They begged to be told. I imagined whisperings of truths that longed to be shared.

For a few minutes my thoughts turned to the children that Chriss and Hattie Mae brought into the world. The five boys and five girls were, at the same time, both a delight and a handful. None, (pronounced Nōne) the first born in 1915, was the obedient, responsible oldest child—a daughter. Tude, the next girl born, was independent and just a bit sassy. Turk followed Tude. As the oldest boy, Turk was quiet, a risk taker, the definitive leader of the pack. Hans came next, and from the time he was born he was the hothead of the family, quick to anger. The sweet, kind, good-natured child they called Chub was born after Hans.

In a matter of months Ton came along, the thinker, the inventor, and the family problem solver. Betty, a beautiful girl, followed her brother. The last boy to be born came next, Mick, the fun-loving jokester of the bunch. Finally Deets and Wella, forever known as the "little girls" came onto the scene during the depths of the Great Depression. Their names are intricately carved into the headstones along with the names of the women and men who married into the family—Nadeen, Claude, Lucile, Doris, Marian, Edgar, Kenny, and Adolph. Some of these markers record both a date of birth and of death while others provide only a birth date.

This World War II generation of my family was one of the few who were not careless with their youth. By necessity, the brothers (my father among them) chose deliberately how to spend their hours, cautiously doling out their precious time among the required toil of farm work, games of baseball and basketball, swimming in the Elkhorn River, hunting, school work, and the inevitable pursuit of the opposite sex.

Their rite of passage proved to be the sad and troublesome game of war planned by leaders but acted on by youths who knew the exact cost of sacrifice they were called upon to make. And this, as with so many other facets of their lives, was governed by the chance of being born, raised, and coming of age in the most trying of times this nation had to offer.

Turk, Hans, Chub, and Ton all marched off to war serving their country at the same time. My grandparents kept their sons' pictures affixed to the wall above the Philco radio. The pictures showed the boys fresh faced, uniformed, with mouths set in quiet determination. Daily, the family gathered by the radio listening to the strange-sounding names of places they recognized only through letters home after battles were finished: Tarawa, Leyte, Iwo Jima, Okinawa. How quickly these words became part of their everyday life. Each day became a torture with new fears and worries as my grandparents waited for word of their four sons. The victories came, but too slowly, and even then were marked by the count of bodies washed up on those foreign shores.

After consulting my watch I realized I had been standing, lost in thought, for the better part of an hour. I shook my head to regain my composure and reconnect to the real world, yet the voices from the past called, begging me to remember. I gave the flowers one last adjustment and turned toward my car.

As always, I was pulled by my ever-present obsession with time and punctuality. I was expected for a family dinner in town shortly, but as I opened the car door and eased myself into the seat, I took one last look over the graves and the symmetrical line of flags pulsating in the breeze. I passed slowly again through the red-brick-flanked gates and turned down the winding gravel road toward the tiny Nebraska town of Oakdale.

Modern day Oakdale is a forlorn place with an almost abandoned look to it. There are more stores on Oakdale's Main Street that are boarded up and closed now than stores that are open for business. A few small homes, some with carefully tended lawns and others with weed filled yards, comprise what remains of the village in the northeast section of the state, not far from Norfolk.

Yet, in 1872, Mr. I.N. Taylor and four others proudly founded this first town in Antelope County at the junction of Cedar Creek and the Elkhorn River. The men took the easy way out and named the city for the abundance of oak trees growing there. They forked over the sum of three dollars and twenty-five cents per acre to the Omaha and Northwestern Railroad and Oakdale was born.

By 1873 a flour mill prospered, famous for the production of My Kind of Flour. The city flourished with nine hundred inhabitants, churches, a library, a bowling alley, and even a pavilion for dances and Chautauquas near the baseball diamond.

Life was good until the stock market crash of 1929. The 1930s hit Oakdale like a ton of bricks. Banks failed, the mill went into bankruptcy, and rail service declined. Yet Oakdale persevered with what the *Pen and Plow* newspaper called "a strong pioneer spirit of working together when things needed to get done."

I decided to risk being a few minutes late to drive past the field where the old farmhouse still stood, dilapidated and in ruins. Near the turn-off from the highway to the farm I could read the modern, green population sign: Oakdale Population 362. Yet in a 1940s picture of the farm the population sign is visible and read 561.

The shutters of my grandparents' house hung askew and what little remained of the paint looked like dried up curls that continuously flaked off leaving only bare gray boards exposed to the harsh elements of the open prairie. Some parts of the roof were missing and there seemed to be no rhyme or reason as to why other parts remained intact.

The year before when I drove my mother by the old place she noted, "One good wind and it will all blow away." Of course she was right and all the more reason for my deviation of plans to take a last look, just in case that wind came. All that remained of the barn were the old boards lying on the ground rotting in the dirt.

And yet, there is something valuable here. The Elkhorn River wends its way through the old farm still on the same course as always; the land remains constant. I drove slowly around the dirt driveway that encircled the house and barn. I could picture Chriss and his sons working in the fields struggling to make the land produce enough to feed the large family. As I looked over the expanse of river, I imagined the carefree hot summer days of swimming in the river and the frosty cold days of winter sledding and ice skating.

The images of their faces lingered in my mind as the Nebraska wind swirled around me. Some members of this family chose the path they would follow while others were forced to follow the path that had been set before them. Who could have foreseen the unexpected consequences and the rippling effects that the collision of these paths would cause? Who would make it through to the other side and who would be lost forever? As I pressed the accelerator and drove toward town, I found myself remembering a different time, a time long past, and a place where the future I have lived was yet to happen.

Part I

Main Street circa 1939, Oakdale, Nebraska.

So This Is Oakdale

Swiss Family Eymann, Spring 1930

He would often dream of Switzerland. He saw the soaring mountains rising over the surrounding verdant foothills of the snow-covered Alps. He smelled the fresh, clean air fragrant with the scent of wildflowers, clover, and grass. The alpine air represented childhood to Chriss Eymann.

His boyhood home lay tucked into the sloping foothills of the Alps. The immaculate, small, white and red chalet appeared neat and well cared for with cattle grazing at the base and smoke rising in white curly wisps from the chimney silhouetted against the cerulean sky. For the first thirteen years he was on earth, this was his home. This orderly, quiet life was all Chriss knew. Those mountains were his home, his work, and his playground. In his dream he could not only see but feel the warm comfort of the wood stove and the heat from the animals kept under the house on the lower-level earthen floor.

Samuel, his father, who at sixty years, should have been well beyond the age of wanderlust, decided to uproot the family to find a better life in America. He said, "It is there we will make our future, together we will buy land and farm it and make it prosper," he explained to the children.

Although much younger than her husband, Samuel, Anna was reluctant to leave her family, her land, and her language, yet she agreed to follow Samuel on this adventure. Anna and Samuel packed up most of their fifteen children and not much else in order to sail to America. They had arrived at Ellis Island in March of 1902 alongside millions of other immigrants clinging to the same ideas and dreams. Chriss was thirteen years old.

The sizable family made their way to the middle of the vast new nation neither speaking the language nor having relatives to assist them on their way, settling finally in Oakdale, Nebraska.

In 1902, Oakdale was a mecca for German-speaking immigrants. Many farm owners needed hard-working men. German-language churches thrived there and thus Oakdale provided an upright, honest way of life that appealed to Samuel. So it was here they stayed, in the land of plenty, amid green, softly rolling prairies. The stocky, bearded, hard-working Swiss immigrant aided by a multitude of sons to send into the field and the blonde, robust, capable Swiss woman who was his partner in life.

Like Chriss, some of his brothers and sisters stayed in Oakdale with their father, but several of the children missed their homeland more than they could bear. Annie, Gottfried, Emil, and his father's namesake, Samuel all returned to Bern after a short stint in Oakdale. They could not understand and were unable to adjust to this big, wide open, flat, and, at times, strange and difficult country.

"Things are too fast for me here," Emil explained to Chriss before he left to board a ship that would take him back to Switzerland. Chriss was also old enough to miss his country. He missed the sweet, soothing sound of his language being spoken around him. He missed the quiet order and peaceful simplicity Switzerland offered.

Chriss recalled that Samuel, however enchanted he was with his new country, was Swiss at heart and instilled in his children a loyalty to family, a philosophy of live and let live, a respect for all human life, and a peaceable manner of solving problems. Samuel was a God-fearing man, strong in his convictions but realistic in his approach to life.

He insisted his children learn to speak English as soon as possible and as well as possible although German was still spoken at home. He immersed his children in both school and church to accomplish his goals, putting the children in a wagon pulled by horses and taking them to the German-speaking United Brethren Church where they received both a sermon in German so they could learn and a free English language lesson in their Sunday school class. It was the best of both worlds for him!

Samuel would lead his family into church and set them down in one of the pews near the front of the sanctuary. As the minister intoned, *"Wir sind alle brüdern,"* Samuel would nod his head in agreement scrutinizing the long line of children seated with him to ensure they were taking it all in. "We are all brothers," the minister repeated in English and this Samuel and his kin believed. Samuel was most certainly one of nature's noblemen, gracious and caring yet highly principled in his beliefs, which he embedded within his offspring.

Chriss could recall the day he set foot on American soil. Was it actually possible that almost thirty years had passed since he came through Ellis Island as that thin, quiet boy? But, of course, time had moved on and although the dream of owning his own farm had not come to fruition, his life had its share of satisfying moments.

By age twenty-two, Chriss was, if not tall, then at least handsome. He wore his dark brown hair a little on the long side. If he did not part it in the middle and smooth it back, it would fall slightly over his left eye giving him a roguish, foreign look. His skin was naturally dark, with a beautiful caramel color. After working daily on the farm in the blazing Nebraska sun, his skin took on a "brown as a berry" color that exuded health, vitality, and masculinity. He possessed a long, straight nose. People described him as kind because his mouth always seemed to be turned up into a smile.

Although he seldom spoke, people inevitably described him as pleasant. But it was his bright, beautiful, brown eyes that were

Chriss and Hattie Mae 1912

his best feature. Chriss had a straightforward way of looking at people that made them feel as if he would listen to them for hours and that they alone possessed every ounce of his attention. His movements were purposeful and he was often pegged as serious.

Unbeknownst to him at the time, his future was sealed at the United Brethren Church he attended in Oakdale. If life was a series of compromises, then Chriss had seen his share. But the day he saw Hattie Mae Retzlaff's dark flashing eyes and her sparkling, lively smile, he realized she was not one of them. They met at church. He was a mature twenty-two-year-old, and she was a laughing fifteen-year-old school girl.

If Chriss was described as serious, then Hattie Mae conversely was merry, playful, and just plain fun. She was amusing and witty. She loved to play practical jokes. One time, after tiring of seeing her sister wear the same favorite hat for days on end, Hattie Mae buried the hat in the sand near their home, causing her sister to fret and stew a few hours before giving her clues to find the hat. Hattie Mae was the first to organize the games the children would play and readily joined into the fun. So it was no surprise that many boys in Oakdale yearned for her attention. Her tiny yet ample figure, dark brown curly hair, and laughing brown eyes were the envy of many a Nebraska girl. The most attractive thing about Hattie was that she was not aware of the effect she had on others. She was carefree, happy, and beautiful in a fresh-faced, farm-girl way.

Chriss noticed her right away, but his shyness would not allow him to speak to her. His timidity got in his way. He began to watch for her at church picnics and events trying to get near her but never directly talking to her.

He watched her from afar until at last Hattie Mae walked right up and spoke to him, "Chriss Eymann, do you want to take your picnic supper with us under the oak tree over there or just look at us?"

To his amazement and wonder she had noticed this handsome, silent, hard-working young man and before he knew it Hattie

Mae had chosen him. They courted in the Oakdale manner of church events, baseball games, band concerts, and dances. And then, to his delight, as a sheer curtain of delicate snow fell outside, Hattie Mae married Chriss at the home of her parents on that wintry first day of December 1913. He was twenty-four and she was seventeen when they started their life together.

Now at forty-two years of age Chriss was short but wiry and fit from all of the farm work he did and his daily struggle to feed, clothe, and care for his own large family. His dream of one day owning a small, tidy farm was still just that … a dream. Yet life had unfolded around him in a loving way, and he was not at all dissatisfied with the lot he had been dealt.

He felt fortunate in these lean times to have work farming for George Hunter. Chriss was able to earn a wage working for George and in addition was permitted to live in the small farmhouse on the lower acreage where he was also allowed to farm a few acres of land to feed his family.

Chriss had a milk cow and two horses named Molly and Dan. Hattie Mae raised her chickens, and so they got by. After Chriss returned from his work on the Hunter farm, he began his work on his own acres. George had provided him with ample opportunity for hard work and the chance to make a living. Although his days were long and laborious, he was aware of how lucky he was to have the plot of land and strong sons to help farm. He was willing to work to the bone to keep it all going.

Cleona, their eldest child, arrived two years after they were married. Since then a new son or daughter was added to the family like clockwork every two years or less. After Cleona came Deloris, Alvin, Hans, George, Kenneth, and Stanley. Hattie Mae quipped to her sister Fanny, "All it took for me to get pregnant was for Chriss to hang his overalls on the bedpost."

Chriss could not possibly have worked for George and farmed his own plot of land without the help of his boys. The girls helped

Chriss and Hattie Mae Eymann Wedding Photo

Chriss harvests corn, circa 1930.

The young Eymann children, from left: Hans, Tude;
seated: None holding Ton, Chub, and Turk, 1923.

Hattie Mae with the cooking, cleaning, sewing, and canning. Although it was not quite what his father, Samuel, had predicted when he uprooted the family in Switzerland and moved them to Nebraska, Chriss's family worked well together to make life prosperous in America.

On this morning in 1931, Hattie Mae was already in the kitchen starting breakfast when Chriss rose from the bed. The early morning sky was awakening to the new day. There were fields to work and livestock to care for and to feed. Nothing in the Eymann home started without coffee and breakfast. As Chriss entered the kitchen, Hattie Mae was busily frying eggs she gathered from her hens and buttering the bread she baked with the butter she churned just yesterday. She was bustling to prepare everything for the large family she nurtured, fed, and cared for every day.

"Good morning, Hattie," Chriss said to his wife as his lips brushed across her cheek.

Although Chriss spoke English well by this time, he retained a strong German accent and his English had a lilting, pleasing, almost melodic tone. Each weekend at least one of his siblings made the trip to Oakdale from Omaha or the surrounding areas to visit him. They happily conversed together only in German. The children crouched behind the doors and listened to the funny sounds that German words made. They tried to imitate the words. *Guten morgen* sounded like "glooton moorgane" when the children spoke German, and Chriss and his siblings laughed back at the children and their pronunciation. They were happy to be together. Speaking their own language was a simple pleasure that reassured them of their more carefree origins.

Hattie Mae responded affectionately, "Good morning, you old coot! It looks like cold weather today." She continued to speak but worry has now crept into her voice, "Chriss, please remember we must pay down the bill at Taylor's grocery soon. I will take more eggs and butter into town to sell but we still owe more than they will bring."

There was never quite enough money to pay the entire bill and take care of the needs of the growing bevy of children. Chriss nodded his head and thought about his plan to someday get a loan from the bank to buy their own land and farm only for themselves. Then there will be money enough to pay for the groceries they cannot grow for themselves: sugar, flour, kerosene.

But this last year brought calamity to everyone. The stock market crashed hard, bringing far-reaching bank failures to even Oakdale, as well as unemployment and worry. It seemed each summer got drier and dustier resulting in crops being harder to raise. This was hardly the time to test his plan. His more immediate worry was just how he would be able to pay the bill he already owed.

Chriss walked now with a deliberate stride to the bottom of the staircase as he did every morning. He called out to each of the sleeping children by their nicknames as he summoned them to get up and begin their day. "None, Tude, Turk, Hans, Chub, Ton, Betty," he called out to each of them in his rolling voice. He didn't add the name of Mick since the newborn baby was still asleep in his crib. Although his voice was pleasing, the children knew he meant business. Soon footsteps were heard above the kitchen.

No one can remember where these nicknames came from. Some said they were German words and some thought they were simply sounds Chriss liked to say; regardless, when the children heard his voice, they were up and moving on the double. Chriss never had to call twice as the children were well aware of the consequences if they did not respond as directed. Each child, at some point in time, had been the recipient of a swift paddling that came from disobeying their father. That was to be avoided at all costs! Each child knew the discipline meted out by Chriss would be followed by a cuddle and a soft word from Hattie Mae. The parental balance was reassuring to each child.

Hattie Mae continued her conversation with her husband as he settled down to eat, "Chriss, school is almost over for this year. The boys will be able to help more around the farm soon. Maybe we could ask George for a few more acres to plant this spring and the girls and I could do some more canning for winter?" But as Hattie Mae spoke, her voice was overshadowed by the sound of children clomping down the stairs, books being packed up for school, and the playful teasing that goes on among siblings as they prepare for their school day.

Chriss went outside while the children ate. He hitched Molly and Dan up to the wagon. Molly and Dan had been with the family for a long time. Molly was a gray mare and Dan was the brown stallion. These animals not only pulled the plow to plant the crops in the field, they were also the family's only source of transportation and were, as such, extremely valuable. Although it was spring, the weather in Nebraska was anything but predictable. This spring day had brought cold temperatures.

"Time to leave!" Chriss called to the children as he hefted his body into the seat and grabbed the reins. All of the children, except Mick, clambered out of the house and piled into the wagon, grateful for the ride into town instead of the usual walk. Hattie Mae stood back on the porch, clutching the tiny bundle that was Mick in her arms. With only one little one at home, her days were quieter, yet she missed the help of the girls and comforting sounds of the children. When Chriss restated the names and affirmed that all of the small heads were accounted for and seated in the back of the wagon, Chriss yelled, "Giddy up," to the horses, clicked his tongue at them, and took off for the ride to the schoolhouse. He deposited his youngsters with a cry of, "Be good and learn!"

Then he was off to work at George's farm for the day. He turned around one last time as the horses trotted on the rutted dirt path toward Oakdale. He looked down the line of his children waiting to enter the schoolhouse. The reward of his life was the feeling of those small arms, now clasping school books, around his neck as he put them to bed each night. For today he decided to enjoy the feeling of satisfaction and peace. He would leave his other worries for another day.

Chriss milks the cows, circa 1935.

2

The Sled and a Risky Rescue, December 1930

C hristmas was over and again, as usual, every year each child got one present. Hattie Mae had fashioned and sewed each girl a new dress. The material for the dresses had come from the twenty-pound cotton bags of flour the family purchased. Hattie Mae had been saving the bags all year. To fancy up the dresses she had taken some old lace from the worn-out clothing of the girls and attached it to the dresses. Hattie Mae was clever, creative, and skillful and the homemade dresses looked just as good as store-bought.

This year the boys had also each received one item. Twelve-year-old Turk got a baseball glove, a basketball for eight-year-old Chub, and a bat for Ton, age seven. All of these gifts were surreptitiously provided by Harold Allen, the sports editor of the newspaper who believed mightily in the athletic ability of the Eymann boys. Harold and his wife, Beth, were childless and so had "adopted" the Eymann boys as their own.

But the very best gift this year had gone to ten-year-old Hans. He had received the real sled he had always wanted! It had come as a hand-me-down from their cousin but Hans didn't care. Up until this point the boys had fashioned their own sled by using their father's grain scoop to ride down the snowy banks and out onto the frozen river. They had to dodge around the trees with little or no way to steer the scoop and sometimes they didn't make it. When one of the boys hit a tree, it was good for a hearty laugh. Hans could barely wait to take his new sled out on the snow-covered hills near the frozen Elkhorn River to see how fast and how far it would go.

Several days after Christmas the boys decided the time was right, and they set out for the river banks dragging the sled behind them. Turk chose a steep hill to give the sled its initial trial. The hill led directly onto the snow-covered river where the boys figured it would slide a mile given the increased speed it would pick up coming down the hill.

The younger boys followed Turk's lead as they began to pull the sled up the hill but Hans protested, "Gol darn it, this is my sled and I'm gonna choose where to use it and I'm darn sure gonna go first."

Chub had grabbed the blade sharpener from the barn that they used to sharpen the mower blades and now he set to work making the sled runners as sharp as knives. Hans got on the sled first while Chub, Ton, and Turk attached a rope to the sled and started to pull, just to give the sled a good start. The boys took turns pulling and riding to see which boy could pull the sled the fastest and which boy could hang on the best while the others maneuvered through some pretty sharp turns to try to knock him off. It was bitterly cold after the winter storms had passed through but the boys hardly noticed the arctic weather.

They had a great time playing on this section of the river with the sled. However, the thing the boys did not consider was the fact they were racing over and over the same area of the river with the sharp blades of the sled. Each time they changed riders, Chub would re-sharpen the runners. The past few weeks had brought bitterly cold temperatures and snow but just prior to that the weather had been fairly mild for a Nebraska winter. Today was a cold but brilliantly sunny day. The boys, in their jubilant celebration of the sled, were blissfully unaware that the river was not frozen as solid as they thought, and with the repeated cuts

ELKHORN RIVER

The Elkhorn River near the Eymann farm, circa 1930.

from the blades of the sled, the ice had already begun to crack and break.

"My turn now," Turk called. Since he was the oldest he had given his younger brothers many rides, but he was now more than ready to test out the sled and show his siblings how sledding was really done. Chub, Hans, and Ton took hold of the rope, and running with all of their might down the hill they propelled the sled to the ice-covered river and let go of the rope as Turk careened onto the wintery river.

CRACK!

The boys heard the noise, and as they looked on in horror, the ice tore apart and the sled disappeared into a watery hole. Turk had been swallowed up along with the sled.

The three boys screamed bloody murder and Ton cried, "Oh, shit, what are we gonna do now?" Suddenly, the top of Turk's head bobbed up in the water and he yelped, "HELP ME! GET ME OUTTA HERE!"

Hans thought quickly, ran to the river bank, and grabbed some dead tree branches. He ordered Chub and Ton to lie on the ice. Chub anchored the human chain down by holding onto the large root of a bush on the river bank. In turn he held Ton's legs. Ton stretched his little body as far as he could to grasp onto Hans's feet. Hans lay on the ice with Ton clutching his feet as he reached his arms as far as he could to hold the branch out to Turk. The boys could hear the crackling and snapping sounds of the ice but they had to save their brother.

Hans yelled, "Turk, pull yourself up as far as you can and grab the branch. We will pull you as hard as we can." Turk managed to lift himself out of the watery chasm enough to grab the branch with his shivering, blue hands. Each of the boys struggled with all of their might to pull as hard as they could. Slowly, Turk's frosty body emerged from the water as the boys tugged him to the safety of the river bank.

But their trouble had just begun. When Turk landed on the dry river bank, Chub declared flatly, "Damn, we can't take him home like this. Mom will whip us for nearly killing Turk. What are we gonna do?"

Hans quickly came up with a solution. "We are gonna build a fire, warm him up so he gets his color back, dry his clothes out some, and then take him home. Turk, take off all of your clothes while we make a fire."

Turk's teeth were chattering so much he could barely speak but he gasped at this idea and said, "Are you crazy, Hans? I'm near dead already, and if I take my clothes off I'm gonna freeze to death for sure in a couple of seconds."

Hans wasted no time as he began to rip off Turk's icy overalls. "Ton, go and get that dry wood from up the bank a piece. Chub, get crackin' and light up this piece of tree bark. Get going!" Hans's voice was serious and firm.

The boys did as they were told and soon they had a small fire going on the river bank. Turk was stark naked and stood as close to the fire as possible turning from his front to his bare, blue butt like a steak cooking on a camp fire. Chub held the soaking overalls on the other side of the flame to dry them. Ton worked on drying his shoes and socks and Hans worked on his shirt.

As Turk began to thaw out, the boys heard him say, "God damn sled!" They burst into laughter but Turk swore such a blue streak at them they quickly quieted down and waited for him to warm up. When he was as dry as he was going to get and appeared to have a human color again, they put his partially dried clothes on him and trudged off toward home.

Suddenly, in the quiet of the freezing winter day Hans called out, "Shit, I forgot, we left that sled under the ice and that was my sled!" He cursed both his brothers and his bad luck with this year's Christmas present.

3

Let's Play Tarzan, Summer 1931

The boys had spent the hot summer day tending the irrigation ditches at the Hunter farm. In their overalls and bare feet the boys walked the rows of corn with their shovels. Their task was to divert water from the small canal that ran down each row of corn. When a row was totally wet, they would remove the dam they had built to allow the water to flow. Then they moved down a few rows to build another dam and repeat the entire process.

Acre after acre the boys walked the rows of corn removing any obstacle that prevented the flow of water to the precious stalks of corn. The work was hot and tedious, but the boys knew their father was depending on them to keep the corn irrigated and growing.

To make the work more enjoyable, the boys would grab handfuls of sheepshower grass that grew wild in the prairie fields of Nebraska. The boys would pop a handful of grass in their mouths and chew happily. This moss green grass was almost as good as eating a lemon drop candy. The grass had a tart taste that was refreshing on a hot summer day.

Finally their chore for the day was done, it was late afternoon, and the temperature in the shade bordered on one hundred degrees. "Let's go boys," Turk commanded his brothers as the tired boys returned their shovels to the barn. Hans, Chub, and Ton trailed after Turk but they asked no questions because they were certain their older brother would find some adventure for them this late afternoon.

At thirteen, Turk was already a risk taker, always on the prowl for a new experience, the motivator and instigator of this raggedy bunch of siblings dressed in bib overalls and no shoes. The younger boys knew they could always count on Turk for something interesting to do but they couldn't always guarantee it would be safe or they wouldn't get into trouble.

There was the time he persuaded the boys to dig into the side of the river bank to make the secret fort. Although the fort itself was a wonder to behold and the boys made frequent use of the fine facility, it was the things that happened there that were cause for worry. This was the secret location where the boys would take the dried out silk from the corn stalks and roll it in thin bark. Then they would attempt to smoke it. Of course, Turk and Hans knew it tasted terrible but they convinced Chub and Ton to give it a shot, whereupon Chub immediately threw up his lunch after ingesting the acrid smoke.

This was the clandestine location where, after hunger pangs decimated Hans's will, he "borrowed" a chicken from his mother, took it to the fort, built a fire, and barbecued it on a homemade spit. It was still pink inside after hours of cooking, but Hans could bear no more. He only regretted his decision a few hours later when the partially cooked and very poisoned chicken caused a revolt in his stomach and made him violently ill.

After fifteen minutes of a sweaty walk toward the river Ton piped up, "Where we headed, Turk?"

Turk replied in his casually disdainful voice, "Not really sure, but I'll know when we get there." This response seemed to appease all of the boys and they continued to string along after Turk's lead until they reached the river bank. Swimsuits? Who needed them? The boys stripped out of their dirty clothes and dove into the clean, cool water of the Elkhorn River.

The Eymann boys' shack on Cedar Creek.

After a few minutes of horsing around in the water Turk said, "Hey, do you guys remember when we got to see the movie about Tarzan?" Turk resumed his questioning, "Remember how Tarzan was swinging through the trees to rescue Jane? Well, take a gander up the bank a piece. See those willow trees? I bet we could do the same thing as Tarzan and pretend we are saving Jane! Let's go!"

The wet and naked youngsters eagerly scrambled up the bank and arrived at a grove of young trees about thirteen feet tall and eight or ten inches wide at the bottom. The trees were young but strong enough to support the weight of the slight boys. Each boy picked out the tree he wanted to climb and shimmied up the trunk until he reached the tip-top. Turk started the motion that set his tree swinging from side to side. Not to be outdone, Hans joined in. Chub and Ton watched for a while but finally caught on and began their own swaying motion.

The four trees swayed dramatically from side to side, and pretty soon the trees were swinging so far from right to left the boys were able to touch each other's hands. "Now," said Turk, "when you get close to the next tree, let go and see if you can catch the other tree so we can swing from tree to tree—all over the place. I dare you!"

That was all Turk needed to say and soon the boys were leaping and grasping from tree to tree as if in a choreographed ballet of movement. "AH-AH-AH," they screamed at the top of their lungs. After a few minor setbacks and falls, all four of the boys were successfully swinging from tree to tree, letting go, and grabbing hold of the next one in what now looked like a circus act.

Chub shouted, "Yes, Jane, here I am to save you!" All of the boys joined in to save Jane and the laughter echoed through the grove. Quickly, the game changed from Tarzan saving Jane to let's-chase-each-other. Now the boys were swinging the trees so violently in the effort to escape each other they almost touched the ground as each one tried to outdo his brother and capture his victim. The boys chased each other from branch to branch and tree to tree. It was not long until they were screaming and laughing so hard they were exhausted and fell like flies onto the bank of the Elkhorn River, oblivious to the effects of their raucous game.

When they finally looked up, they could see the trees had been well abused by their play. They hoped their father would never find out because he would skin them alive for mistreating the trees.

The brothers quickly grabbed their overalls, got dressed, and walked the rest of the way back home, worn out from their day's adventure. They knew, no matter the cost, whatever adventures were yet to come their way, next time would be worth it just as long as they were together.

4

The Baby, Fall 1931

From a food-scented breeze that wafted from the kitchen window oldest-sister None called out to her siblings, "Dinner's ready!" The boys were too far away to actually hear her voice from the barn. But her little sisters were tending the hens in the yard, and they could be counted on to relay the message out to the boys. None knew it never took too long for this brood to get the message that food was coming.

"All you kids wash those dirty hands, get in here now and sit yourself down at the table." None bustled about the warm kitchen maintaining her pace of work all the while holding baby Mick on her hip.

It was October and the kitchen was warm as they experienced the remnants of a wonderful Indian summer in Nebraska. She took the spaghetti carefully out of the wrapper. She knew this had to last the family a long time, so she measured out precisely how much each child should get. Earlier she had brought up a jar of canned tomatoes from the cellar that Hattie Mae had painstakingly canned in August. Those tomatoes along with the store-bought package of spaghetti would feed the kids tonight and for many nights to come. She could always open a jar of peaches for dessert. Momma had put up plenty of fruit from the summer crops, but None also realized that this supply had to last through the winter.

Turk moaned as he entered the kitchen and began to wash his dirt-covered hands, "Not spaghetti again! Seems like we have that pretty near every night lately!"

None's sharp reply was like a slap in the face to Turk, "Well, see here Mr. Smarty Pants, it sticks to your ribs, fills you up, and it's hot isn't it? Ya got something to eat at least so wash up, be quiet, and sit down."

Turk meekly did as he was told. The kids were accustomed to sixteen-year-old None taking charge of both the cooking and of them. She had, in fact, been the one who walked each of her siblings to their first day of school, made sure they knew what to do and what was expected of them, and then got herself on to her own day of school. Each Eymann child had at least one job to do to make the family function and that was hers. But Momma was always there in the kitchen with her. Tonight Momma was nowhere to be seen. Daddy neither.

Eight-year-old Ton entered the house amidst an uproar of voices as he and his brothers rough housed their way through the process of washing up and getting to the table. Ton looked around the kitchen. For a brief second he had forgotten what was happening in the house as he asked None, "Shouldn't we wait for Momma and Daddy to say the prayer?"

Tude gently reminded him in that firm older sister voice, "Ton, remember Momma's gonna have our new baby very soon? We are just waiting and by tomorrow we will have a new brother or sister to play with for sure."

The circle of tow-headed children bowed their heads to say their nightly dinner prayer and to include one for the new baby too but most of all so they could eat.

Momma's sister Fanny had been there most of the night before and through the entire day as had Daddy's sister Martha. None had done something unusual that day also. She had not gone to school because she felt she was needed more at home. None had shooed the kids from the house to school quickly that morning and then shooed them outside again after they returned from school. She wanted the house to be as quiet as possible for Momma. It did not take much encouragement from None to get her siblings outside in that sunny, crisp autumn air, but she had stayed inside to both take over for Momma, making sure the food was prepared, the house clean, and all the chores attended to, and to keep a close eye on the proceedings of the day.

She became particularly alarmed when Daddy came home and went straight into the bedroom. She kept a vigil as Martha and Fanny had taken turns periodically bringing water, towels, soap, and other items her momma needed into the bedroom. None had seen each child come into the world and frankly she wondered what was taking this one so long. But there is no timetable with babies being born and they came when they were ready.

She sighed and turned back to her work putting Mick in the high chair. Silverware clicking against plates was the only sound now as the children hurriedly filled their empty stomachs.

Then it happened. It was faint but the children cocked their heads, pricked up their ears, and stopped eating as they heard the sound of a baby's cry. None smiled; she was glad to finally hear the baby, but her smile did not last long.

All at once, there were loud words coming from the bedroom and the shirring sound of people rushing out and back in, doors slamming tightly. There was no second cry from the baby. Something was not right, None thought to herself while she spooned peaches into Mick's open mouth. She held her breath and waited for the sound of a cry, but when she heard crying, it was not from a baby. The mournful wail belonged to Hattie Mae.

More shuffling, more unexplained noise, and then nothing but a grim hush spread through the house like a misty fog. At first the children sat riveted to their chairs, looking at one another, not knowing exactly what they should do, waiting. They were uncertain of what they were waiting for but they knew they should not move. The pause was agonizing. Although it took no more than five minutes, the wait seemed to last for days.

Finally, Martha and Daddy walked slowly into the living room. The children seemed to take their entrance as tacit permission to move. They scurried to fill in the doorway between the kitchen and the living room as soon as they heard Daddy's footsteps halt. Peering from the crowded doorway they could see their father. In his arms was a very small bundle wrapped in the soft, yellow, well-worn blanket that had cradled each of them as newborns. Martha had tears flowing freely down her cheeks and a savage, desperate expression in her eyes. Daddy's face was downcast, and neither one spoke as they lay the inert, blanketed bundle on the table in the living room.

The seven children bunched in the doorway craned their necks to get a view of what was happening and, even more urgently, to make sense of it. They watched as Chriss bent down and gently removed the blanket. He carefully and lovingly kissed the baby girl's small alabaster cheek. Mournfully, he raised his head and with two hands he securely rewrapped the lifeless baby in the aging yellow blanket. Then he laid his head down on his folded arms next to the precious bundle and his body shook with sobs.

Martha began to cry copiously as she embraced his shoulders, and together they mourned over his tiny daughter. The children watched wordlessly from the doorway at this unexpected sight. Finally, as Chriss raised his head to gaze down at the angelic face of the deceased newborn, he methodically rubbed his hands over his neck in sorrow.

5

Play Ball! Summer 1935

T urk strode toward the baseball diamond, his bat slung over his shoulder and his glove clutched under his arm. As he walked by, women turned to stare at him. It wasn't that he was handsome in the classical sense of the word, no; it was the swagger of confidence coming from this seventeen-year-old young man that got their attention.

Although small in stature, his fit, muscular body drew others into his strength. His face was open and honest with a straight, longish nose, high cheekbones, and a mouth set in a purposeful line. Although Turk smiled little and spoke even less, he was admired by all who knew him. At times, he appeared aloof, like his father Chriss, until he turned on his charm at which time a broad smile would light up his face. At other times a mask of disdain and disregard returned to his inscrutable face leaving the world to wonder just what thoughts he was thinking.

In athletics he had no equal. No matter the sport he was cocky, cool, and capable. Some said "cocky and cool as Dizzy Dean."

On this particular July night Turk was on the baseball field and playing by far his best and most favorite sport. It was easy to see he felt completely at home on this field, and while others sweated and strained to shag the balls that whizzed by them, Turk seemed

Turk Eymann at work on the farm.

to gather them into his glove effortlessly with a grace that could only be described as God-given.

The night air was colored by the waves of heat radiating from the tramped down dirt of the baseball diamond. The heat appeared to have a life of its own, at times white hot and at other times the red-brown heat boiled up as a baseball shredded the dirt of the infield, missed perhaps by a glove gripped in a sweat-slippery hand.

Both the Oakdale and the Tilden teams took the field in what promised to be another barn-burning competition. Each time these two teams played, their entire towns turned out for the event. Game days meant family picnics and bitterly contested ball games. Civic pride and bragging rights were at stake as well as a good deal of betting. Win or lose there was a celebration lasting well into the night. There was never a tougher rivalry than the one between Tilden and Oakdale, and at least one serious fight broke out each time they played.

Tonight it was a late-arriving crowd, perhaps in order to down another glass of tea or lemonade to stave off the unbearable heat. Paper fans glued to sticks whisked to and fro in the hands of the ladies in the crowd. They were dressed in their coolest summer dresses, and the array of straw hats was as varied as the red faces of the supporters beneath them.

The fans separated into their distinct camps, one favoring Tilden and an equal amount favoring Oakdale. The Tilden followers had piled as many people as possible into each car making the ten-mile trip and were boisterously yelling their encouragement for their home team and favorite players.

The red-capped Oakdale team took the field first while their star pitcher, Jack Tavnor, slammed mostly strikes over the plate. The blue-capped Tilden boys diligently swung. Although a few bats connected to the zinging pitches, these balls careened skyward and were ultimately caught by one of the Oakdale outfielders. The Tilden side of the inning was quickly and efficiently dispatched.

Now it was Oakdale's turn to show what they could do in response to the pitching of Tilden's ace, Dot Warner. Several swings later success came as an Oakdale player connected smartly with the ball and sent it over the head of the third baseman and into left field.

The throng of Oakdale fans jumped to their feel cheering wildly. The Tilden supporters sighed deeply. The batter rounded second base. The third base coach gave the "keep going" sign, and as the runner slid into third base, the battered white ball was winging its way toward the outstretched glove of Tilden's third baseman.

Which one arrived first? Was it the foot of the Oakdale runner touching the base or was it the glove of the Tilden third baseman clamping tightly down over the ball and swooping his glove down to tag the runner? Collectively, the crowd held its breath as they looked over at the umpire. He raised his arms and then thrust them to either side of his body as he yelled, "SAFE." The Oakdale runner jumped up, keeping his foot securely on top of the base as he brushed the dirt from his hair and hands.

Suddenly, a maelstrom erupted from the Tilden side. The third baseman threw his glove down in disgust as the pitcher, coach, and shortstop all stormed the ump.

"He was nowhere near the base!" yelled one.

"Gol darn, are you blind as a bat, ump?" questioned another.

"What in the hell were you looking at because it sure wasn't the baseball game!" declared the coach.

Without warning, the furious pitcher lost all control as he gave the runner an unexpectedly violent shove. The thrust sent the Oakdale runner's butt down to the base. As the runner tried to pull himself up, the Oakdale players charged in to help him. Gloves were tossed to the ground, fists at the ready, running as fast as they could into the melee at third base. The Tilden players were in the middle of a dirt-filled punching, shoving, kicking riot.

One solitary player ambled away from this dust bowl of aggression, moving purposefully toward the Oakdale dugout.

Turk walked into the dugout, lowered himself to the bench, lay on his back, and crossed his arms underneath his head, cradling it like a pillow. He whistled a tune as he reclined on the hard bench never even glancing toward the ongoing ruckus of noise, fists, and bodies that surrounded third base.

Soon the coaches were able to pull the players apart and send even the most irate of them to the dugouts for a cooling-off period to gather their common sense again. As the bruised and bleeding Oakdale players entered the dugout, the center fielder asked Turk, "What were you doing in here?"

Without hesitation Turk replied, "I came in here to let you boys have some time to sort things out. My daddy taught us boys to do your fighting with your baseball glove and to save your fists for your bat. He always said actions speak louder than words so let your baseball skills do your fighting." With those words he grabbed his fielder's glove, slipped it back onto his hand, and headed out onto the field.

*Eymann family baseball glove and Turk's most
valuable player award from the national tournament
in 1936 signed by ten major league players..*

6

The Invention—Making Something out of Nothing, Summer 1936

Turk was combing his hair looking into the side mirror of the Ford when he heard the sounds of his younger brothers running out onto the porch of the old farmhouse. Turk had grown into a calm, cocky eighteen-year-old—independent, adventurous, and just a little on the wild side. What he lacked in stature he made up for in confidence.

His body was taut with muscles, and his grace was often displayed in his athletic ability as he played for several town teams. Although he bore an attitude of complete indifference, girls were drawn to him, and his time and attention were much in demand. He was anxious to be off on more adult adventures with his friends, but he greeted his younger brothers and talked with them for a few minutes before he left.

"Where you headed tonight, Turk?" Hans asked his older brother. Hans was eager to achieve the independence Turk enjoyed, and he wanted to hear all of the details involved. Hans's strong, athletic build also made him a natural for sports. His open, kind face glowed with startlingly blue eyes and a trusting smile. Yet that face could turn on a dime to red hot anger, and his brothers knew just how far they could push before Hans pushed back.

"I'm going to Marvin's place to pick him up and then we are heading to Neligh to the movies," replied Turk. "Are you writing a book or something?" he joked with Hans. "Why are you asking so many questions?" He turned to the younger boys, "What are you squirts gonna do?"

"Not much to do around here," Chub filled in the answer.

"Well, you guys stay out of trouble. See you later tonight," and with that Turk climbed into the car he had borrowed from a friend and raced off down the long lane that led away from the farmhouse.

"You stay out of trouble too," Chub shouted back at Turk, "and that will be lots harder for you than for us!" The boys laughed together at the small joke. Chub and Hans rested in the yard, but Ton disappeared into the barn. When he returned, he was carrying two lengths of wooden two-by-fours in his hand.

"Where on earth did you find those?" Hans questioned Ton excitedly. "Dad was probably saving those to use for some repairs."

Ton admitted he was digging around in the corner of the barn and uncovered the wood near the horse mower the family kept there. "Let's go back into the barn and see what else we can dig up," Ton suggested. "Maybe we can make something today."

Ton was the quiet one of the family who liked to take things apart and put them back together in new ways. He was never one to speak up, but when a problem presented itself, he was usually the one to solve it. How should they hook up the well closer to the house? How could he fix the motor on the mower?

There was nothing that Ton would not tackle, so it was natural the three youngest boys would be excited about what they could create together. They headed for the barn with Jix, their family dog, trailing at their heels. After an hour of excavating, they uncovered some unexpected treasures in addition to the wood: a scythe, some nails, and a bit more wood. Suddenly, a plan was brewing.

Finally, after much discussion, Chub proposed the best idea, "We sure found enough stuff to make something now. What about making a miniature mower? We could use it in the yard. What else do we need?"

Ton was way ahead of his brothers. As soon as he heard the word *mower* and knew there was the possibility of making something that just might work, he sprinted toward the few toys the kids kept in the yard. He spotted the coaster wagon that belonged to his sisters. They liked to put their homemade dolls in the wagon and pull them around the yard for a ride. The wagon was a hand-me-down from Mr. Hunter's children, and his sisters treasured it like it was gold.

But the boys thought dolls were just plain stupid. In their minds their project was much more important than pulling silly dolls around, so they wasted no time or thought. Ton quickly removed the four wheels from the wagon and brought them back to the growing pile of materials the boys had accumulated. The level of excitement had just increased tenfold!

All three boys worked diligently hammering the boards into a small, simple frame. The wheels were then attached to this frame chassis. They fit like a glove. The plan was perfect. They carefully attached the scythe and installed a crank to turn it. Ton explained, "This crank will keep the scythe turning. It will cut the grass as long as someone operates the crank and keeps it moving. That should be good enough."

Hans voiced the next problem by asking, "How are we going to make the chassis move?"

Chub solved the problem quickly by giving these orders, "Hans, you're going to pull it with a rope. Ton, you'll crank the scythe, and I'll steer the mower and make sure the pulleys and gears we attached to it work. Got it?"

The boys eagerly hauled the "mower" into the "shop" for one last going over. All seemed to be in perfect working order. "Okay, now is the time for a real trial," Ton declared.

The three boys hauled the mower out of the barn and toward the alfalfa field located close to the house. It was near summer's end and the alfalfa was still growing. The alfalfa would be harvested and baled for the animals to eat throughout the winter.

"Let's just test it out on the edge of the alfalfa field," Chub suggested. They all agreed on this course of action and set out enthusiastically to see if their invention would work.

"This is like pulling a twenty-pound weight through a mud puddle," Hans moaned as he pulled the mower with all of his strength. Somehow, with Hans pulling, Chub guiding, and Ton cranking the scythe, they began to cut the alfalfa.

"Gosh darn it if this thing don't work!" Chub yelled successfully from the rear of the mower where he could see the entire operation taking place.

Hans was sweating profusely, and Ton had to keep his eyes peeled to make sure the scythe did not break loose and cut them all to ribbons. "Sure as the devil if this thing don't beat all!" Chub proudly informed the boys, keeping them posted on the progress of their homemade contraption.

The boys were so pleased and proud of the fact that the mower could actually cut that they forgot where they were and just how much of the alfalfa they were cutting down. One half hour later they fell on the ground, exhausted, laughing, sweaty, and triumphant over what they had accomplished together.

Suddenly, Chub sat up and looked out over the field. He saw the many swaths and paths that lay mown down all over the field. It was not the orderly, systematic mowing that Chriss did. The stems of alfalfa he cut usually lay neat and ready to be picked up and baled. This mowing job was a helter-skelter mess of stalks. Hans and Ton peeked up over the destruction now too and a terrified look appeared on all three faces. They had cut down practically half of the growing alfalfa and had made circles and patterns in the grain with their mower.

"Oh shit!" Hans blurted out loud the words all three boys were thinking. "We are gonna be in hot water when Dad sees this!"

Chub openly stated the words they all dreaded, "What do you think Dad will do to us?"

They did not have to wait long to find out because Chriss arrived home from work shortly after. Chriss had taken the horses and wagon over to work today, and as he led them to the barn he called out, "Boys, come now and help with chores."

When he saw the boys walk from the direction of the field, he thought that odd so he quizzed them, "What were you boys doing over in the alfalfa patch? Get on over here now and tell me what is going on."

The three boys left the mower in the field and double timed it up to where Chriss stood waiting for them.

"Dad, we made our very own mower. We were just testing it out a little," Hans explained.

Chriss raced out into the field to check out the story the boys told him. He saw the two-by-four chassis with the scythe and pulleys. He saw the patches of mown down alfalfa lying on the ground. The boys surrounded the mower and all three tried to explain all at once and at the same time how they made it and how it worked.

A hint of a smile passed momentarily over Chriss's face when he saw the mower the boys had created and heard their complicated explanations. But just as quickly the smile disappeared as he told the boys, "Gosh darn it all, if you three aren't always into something, making something and causing me trouble. That alfalfa was the only thing we had to feed the livestock this winter, and you three mowed half of it down today! Get out there and pick up the alfalfa you cut down. We will dry it and bale at least some of it for winter. Tomorrow you will come with me to George's farm and work since you have so much energy and so many ideas. That should tire you three out and keep you out of trouble. Now get going and get to work. No dinner until you are all done."

The boys got cracking and did exactly as they were told to complete the job of gathering the cut alfalfa. When their work was done, they pulled their mower into the barn. If nothing else they could use the parts to create something else.

The curtains in the farm kitchen parted slightly as Chriss watched them pull the mower toward the barn. He could not help but feel a bit of pride in the boys. *Those boys didn't have much but they sure knew how to make something out of nothing, I guess we can't give them fancy toys or materials but we can give them something better. We can give them the opportunity to use what they have, make things, fix things, and learn to make do with what they have at hand.*

Chriss was still angry about the alfalfa, but as he looked at his three sons, in his heart he knew they were good boys and he was a lucky man.

Part II

Chriss Eymann uses a homemade planter/cultivator to work the fields, circa 1936. The homemade contraption was made with wheels and odd parts of other machinery.

The Depression and the Dust Bowl Years

7

Swarms of Destruction and Despair, Summer 1936

New York City and the stock market were a world away from Oakdale, Nebraska, but Chriss knew they were connected. He didn't absolutely understand or even have a clue what the stock market was all about, but he did know farm prices were affected by whatever happened way back there in New York City.

On the radio he heard the announcers talk about a stock market "crash." Again, he was not certain of what kind of crash this could be. It wasn't a crash like when a car hit something but it did more damage to his family than an everyday, ordinary crash could have. What's more, it was nothing he had any control over. Chriss farmed the large acreage for George Hunter but he also kept a few acres of crops close to the farmhouse he rented from George. These few acres meant the difference between eating and starving to death for his large family, so after a long day of farming for George, he and the boys tended their tiny acreage with great care.

Then the stock market crashed in 1929. The price of crops went way down, and the demand for their grain, corn, and livestock seemed to evaporate overnight. This presented a genuine problem to the farmers in Nebraska and needed to be fixed. The only way farmers could see to get out of debt and be able to pay off their loans to the bank was to plant more crops—as many crops as possible on the amount of land they owned.

George Hunter demanded that Chriss increase his planting but with prices falling daily the farm still could not break even. But for Chriss there was no more land to plant. He could work with only the few acres George allowed him to use. He and his family had to make do with whatever they could harvest from their land to eat and to feed the livestock they kept for eggs and milk.

Even though things were bad on the farm in Nebraska, Chriss heard they were worse in Oklahoma, Texas, and even Kansas directly to the south of them. The drought that was gripping the mid-section of the country had dried almost everything out. Chriss listened while George talked about the conditions he had seen while traveling through Oklahoma. He described the drifts of dust piled against the houses, covering roofs, and sweeping through the air in gigantic clouds. He told about the farm fields as Chriss listened with a growing apprehension in his stomach. These were not farm fields any longer but rather fields of dust with nothing, not even a stick of native grass, to hold down the soil. These barren fields spread for miles and miles, George went on, no crops, not even weeds to keep the dirt in place.

And then the unrelenting drought. No rain for months on end. Nothing but burning, desert-like weather with no relief in sight. George explained how people could not even walk outside without their mouths and lungs plum filling up with dust and how they would sometimes die of "dust pneumonia." Babies and old people were the most affected by this insidious disease. When George related to him that things were so desperate people were abandoning their farms and allowing them to just dry up and blow away, Chriss felt something bad was coming their way too.

Folks in Nebraska were feeling the effects of the dusters too. When the hot, dry Nebraska wind blew the dust into Antelope County, the women would shut the windows and soak towels with water to place around the sills. Even this did not keep the dust from penetrating their homes. When the dust was red, folks said that was just some of Oklahoma covering up good Nebraska soil.

The past few summer growing seasons had been bleak, but the Nebraska fields were still green with crops. The farmers had weathered the lack of rain and dust blowing in and although farming was tough, they were making do. Then it hit. It was not the dust from the south that attacked and destroyed the Nebraska fields. It was not even the drought. Instead it was the grasshoppers.

All of those grasshoppers in Oklahoma, Texas, and Kansas had nothing left to eat. There simply was not one particle of vegetation left on the ground for them to consume. So they left in swarms and bunches, not unlike some of the discouraged farmers, looking for food, something, anything to eat. Chriss started to hear stories from other farmers but never believed the swarms would find their way to Oakdale.

He was out working in the fields that July in 1936. It was another torrid, dry, dusty day just like all of the other summer days he had endured for the last two years. Chriss prayed he could outlast the drought long enough to harvest some of the crops this year. With no moisture the fields were not producing healthy crops, and those that did remain had little chance of living until the fall harvest.

He heard the swarming before he saw them or maybe he just sensed their presence. Their frenzied movements stirred the air, and he could perceive a faint, dull buzzing noise in the sky. At first, it was just the sensation of sound and motion. Something unusual was in the air that upset the horses and made the hair on the back of his neck stand up. Something was amiss here for sure.

Chriss peered at the sky to the west and then he saw it—the swirling, churning, teeming dark cloud. The cloud mass was moving toward him and the farm with relentless purpose. The flow of darkness spread and stretched across the sky for miles. What had seconds ago been bright daylight was now bathed in darkness as if it were the middle of the night.

At first sight he could not discern what exactly comprised the cloud. Was it a monster thunderstorm moving in? Was it hail? Perhaps it was the beginning of a tornado? But as the darkness approached him, he could hear a distinct zzzzzzzz reverberation radiating from the pitch-black cloud, and he knew it was not simply a weather system moving in. This was a living assemblage of insects headed right toward him.

Chriss rapidly turned the horses from the field and directed Molly and Dan into the barn as the mass descended onto his acres of crops. With one hand holding the horses' reins, he batted away hoppers from his eyes and clothes. It was a losing battle. He felt his way toward the barn rather than saw his path. Inside he could hear a deafening noise but could not see exactly what was happening outside because any view he possessed through the slats of the barn were obscured by the pulsating throng of insects.

The air was thick and totally filled with their presence. They alighted on the crops and covered the growing stalks of corn completely as they sucked the air out of the Nebraska sky and ate and ate and ate. This feeding frenzy seemed to last for hours while Chriss hunkered down inside the barn with the skittish animals. Chriss sat in the hay powerless to do anything to intervene in the tragedy unfolding around him.

Finally, the sky brightened a bit. Chriss struggled to open the barn door, pushing against the millions of insects coating the outside structure of the barn. He slowly pried the door open enough to cautiously slip his thin body outside. Try as he might to close the door quickly the grasshoppers slipped and slid into the barn landing on the hay and the animals sheltered there. He pushed his way outside further stepping on thousands of grasshoppers in front of the barn doors. Scraping grasshoppers out of his eyes, he turned toward the plot of land where he had planted alfalfa to feed the livestock, corn and beans to feed his own family, and all the food that would help them survive the winter months ahead. He could not believe what was before his eyes.

The bulging swarm of insects had settled on his crops and stripped them to bare stalks. In some cases the crops were stripped right down to the dirt. Nothing remained in the field that only a short time before had contained the life-sustaining food the family would need to survive through the next year. Yet there remained thousands of insects on the few bits and pieces of green that were still left.

Chriss ran at the field and began to hit them and fight them off with his hands. His face stung from the blows of the pelting grasshoppers. They neither knew nor cared that he was there as they continued their orgy of eating. He looked to the east. He could see the back end of the black cloud moving on to find full, green fields of crops to feed their persistent hunger.

He made his way through the mass of insects both in the air and at his feet toward the Model T that Turk's friend had driven to the farm that day. The boys had taken George Hunter's truck to town. Chriss had to get to town and find his boys. Chriss had watched the boys enough times to know how to start the car. He approached the front of the car to pull the choke and crank the lever. He swatted the hoppers away as he primed the carburetor. This task done he made his way to the door. What he saw astonished him.

Grasshoppers lined the door handle, the driver's seat, dashboard, and floor of the car. Chriss tried to rid himself of the pests, but he finally just sat down on top of them hearing a liquid, squishing sound as his overalls met the seat. The key was still in the ignition. He tried to turn it, but the grasshoppers swarmed over his hand and the key making the task difficult. Chriss extricated himself from the insect-infested front seat, mucked his way to the front of the car. He would at least try to crank it to life. Nothing ... no response from the car.

He pulled back the hood to look inside. The engine was coated with layers of insects. Every inch was covered with their fat, green bodies. He checked the radiator and could see that it too was completely clogged with the greenish-brown invaders. He quickly closed the hood and decided the car was a lost cause. He would walk to the road and on into town.

He reached into his pocket and took out his handkerchief. After scraping the hoppers away from his eyes, nose, and mouth, Chriss tied the handkerchief firmly around his head to cover his mouth to try to keep the insects out and still breathe. His feet crunched over the pests as he walked up the hard pan dirt road that led to the highway. He hoped to flag down a passing car, but if not he would make the walk.

As he stepped onto the highway, he could not see any part of the road that was not coated with the hoppers. After a few minutes of walking, his boots began to slip on the mushy slime of insects covering the roadway under his feet.

Defeated, Chriss sat down on the side of the road. The plague of grasshoppers was diminishing now as there was nothing left for them to eat. They had taken their fill and then moved on to find greener pastures. He looked around. All that remained in every direction were devastated fields crisscrossed by gravel roads. There were no crops to be seen, no leaves on trees, nothing was left. The only thing he could see in his few acres was a bed of dirt and even that was still covered with teeming insects.

What should he do? What was the family going to eat this coming winter? How would they feed their animals? In his despair, Chriss could not even fathom the dilemma they faced nor could he fashion an answer to his questions. He had never seen anything like it before, but he guessed the worst was yet to come and their problems had just begun.

8

The Darkening Storm, 1938

It seemed the good years had passed them all by. The happy times had been fleeting and now were almost impossible to recall. Life had always revolved around the seasons, the weather, and the whims of the gods. When the grasshoppers came, it was simply another unlucky fluke, a joke of the gods. But the grasshoppers invaded and stayed.

The Eymanns knew things were just as bad in other places. The hobos who rode the trains into Oakdale also found that Hattie Mae had a soft heart. She never turned away anyone who approached her door asking for food even if all she had to give was a small pancake. "There but for the grace of God go I," she stated.

The sight of the ruined crops filled every farmer with true despair—Chriss among them. The farmers took the poisoned bran offered by the government programs. They covered the fence posts of their fields with the brown, deadly grains, hoping the pellets would kill all of the pests that alighted on the fields and consumed them. Although the dead and dying grasshoppers congregated around the posts, plenty still survived to devour the newly planted fields. Each time the farmers thought they were winning, the grasshoppers proved them wrong, eating their crops as confirmation of who was really in charge. Chriss had always been able to use his hands to fix his problems but not this time.

Chriss Eymann with work horses Molly and Dan.

The work of his body could not deliver his family from the nightmare of starvation with no hope of being able to earn a living. The inability to provide for his family tore through his heart, and robbed him of meaning in his life. People were selling all they had left at this point to provide for their families.

Turk was driving trucks to help feed the family. He would drive cattle from Oakdale to Omaha. One day Turk came upon some store-bought bread lying in the road. The loaves had fallen from a delivery truck. He stopped and gathered all the loaves he could and piled them in the truck. That night his siblings thought they had died and gone to heaven with store bought bread to eat for dinner.

Desperate to feed his family, Chriss had taken whatever jobs the WPA offered. At times, he worked on bridges and sometimes he repaired roads, all for a few coins a day. It wasn't much but it was something. He would have worked every day but it was not allowed for there were so many men who needed work to provide for their families. The work time was distributed to give something to as many as possible. What else could he do?

There was not a day that passed when Chriss did not try to find a solution to their problems, But between the grasshoppers, the red dust that blew in from Oklahoma coating the windows and house with a thin film of soil, and the daily battle to find paying work, Chriss had changed. His appearance was markedly different from the healthy young man who began farming for George all those years ago.

His once round cheeks had become chiseled so now his cheekbones were prominent as well as his jaw. The hollows under his eyes had become black with worry and apprehension for the future. Although still strong, his once muscular arms were raw-boned and scrawny and his thin body disappeared within the cavernous overalls he wore every day. His hair had a tinge of gray now as well as having receded on his head. His well-worn cap sat huge on his head.

Not only had his appearance been altered by the travails of the last years, his personality had changed too. His once ever-present smile was now nothing more than a haggard line cut into his face. His eyes once so bright had lost their luster. Chriss avoided the company of others whenever possible, preferring to remain by himself, with Jix, the family's pet dog, as his only companion. Previously he delighted in listening to others and giving his full attention to whatever story or tale they had to repeat, but now he wanted nothing to do with the dances and social activities of the small town.

Chriss found himself now with more time on his hands than he ever wished for. He would gladly have traded every second for a chance to work. But there was no work, nothing to do, no way to earn an honest living. The shame of his inability to provide for his family wormed its way into his heart and soul until he was unable to forget it and unable to release the power it held over him.

Chriss sat stone still on a tall-backed wooden chair in the kitchen. He looked neither right nor left but stared straight ahead into space. He did not feel the rigid boards or the ramrod straight back of the timbered chair he sat upon. He was looking for a future, for answers, for guidance, for deliverance.

From the corner of his eye, he detected the slight rippling movement of the curtain that covered the window. The flimsy, flowery material fluttered wildly in the breeze. Over the course of months and years the bottom of the curtain had become tattered by the constant battering of the Nebraska wind. He scrutinized the tendrils of fabric as the curtain whipped back and forth in the brisk gusts of air. Chriss found himself sitting more and more often in the kitchen chair. There was nothing to do and nowhere to go. This billowing, pliable forgetfulness of watching the curtains had become a comforting habit for Chriss. It belonged only to him. Jix sat at his feet, guarding over Chriss. No one was able to penetrate the shell that covered and hid him during these times. Family, friends, and the immediate world around him were excluded and could never share in this private haven.

What at first had seemed a comforting escape, over the course of days and months had become instead a jail that Chriss sealed himself within. He would sit in the chair for hours not speaking just staring straight ahead. Sitting alone and silent became the framework of his life. He was completely isolated from the outside world. During these times he was detached and removed from the life of the family. No one knew what he was thinking or feeling. He had been transformed from a healthy farmer to a specter of his former self.

9

Saturday Night, Spring 1939

H attie Mae gave a weary sigh and wiped her hands on the red-and-white-floral apron she always wore tied firmly around her ample waist. She had worked feverishly, just like every other day on the farm—cooking, sewing, tending children, caring for her hens, cleaning house, and washing dishes. Although her life was hard scrabble around the farm and there was never a lack of things to accomplish, it had been a good day with the children.

"Oh right," she corrected herself, "they are certainly not all children anymore!" None, Tude, and Turk were all out on their own now although the girls still came often to help her with the work. Hans, Chub, Ton, Betty, and Mick had been joined by Marlene whom they called Deets and shortly after that by baby Wella. The loss of the baby had been rough on Hattie Mae but it appeared to be more painful for Chriss. They were both consoled by the arrival of the two little girls and even though times were tough, they were managing. Hattie could honestly say she was content as long as the kids were well behaved, did well at school, kept out of trouble (for the most part), and were clean. Clean, now that would be her next chore.

Saturday evening had arrived. For the Eymann family this night meant both money and entertainment were coming their way. Hattie Mae kept a hen house near the family home where

A happy time. The Eymann family attends the 1939 State Tournament to watch Ton and Chub play baseball. From left: Edgar Sharples (None's husband), None Eymann Sharples, Tude, Chriss holding None's children Russell and Shirley Sharples, Hattie Mae, Betty, Turk with girlfriend Kay seated in front of him, and Hans.

Ton and Chub Eymann at State Baseball Tournament.

she raised a flock of hens and, of course, a couple roosters. Those hens were her pride and joy! The hens provided meat for the family, which they usually enjoyed only with the advent of company. But those hens laid eggs, and just like the fairy tale, to Hattie Mae and her brood, she treated them like they were made of gold. Those fresh eggs, at times still warm from the hen, scrambled up into many a breakfast or dinner for her children. But those white ovals were also a precious commodity she could use as barter at the dry goods store. Hattie Mae always wore a smock-type dress with a large apron in the front. That big apron served as a dust rag, kid nose wiper, and the place where she deposited the eggs she gathered from the hen house.

Each and every Saturday night the entire family packed up and took their supply of extra eggs to the Union Store to sell them or to exchange them for items they needed and could not grow or make for themselves. Without Hattie Mae's fussing and guarding over her chicks, the family would never have been able to acquire sugar for the pies she baked from the fruit they grew, flour for the family's bread, kerosene for the lamps, and other items the family had grown to love and depend upon.

Hattie Mae truly loved that strutting, clucking, feathery throng of birds. Holding the edges of her apron up to form a bowl out of the fabric, Hattie Mae tossed some grain out to feed the plumed flock. "These hens are worth their weight in gold," she mumbled to no one in particular as she cradled the gathered cloth of the apron with one hand and tossed the grain out with the other. The hens made a beeline for Hattie Mae, cackling and striking to grab the first bites away from the other birds. She watched them greedily fight over the bits of grain.

She surely did have affection for them, but she did not bat an eyelash as she grabbed up a couple hens to fry for dinner on an evening when company was coming to call. Hattie Mae was, at heart, a realist who understood exactly what it took to survive and was willing to do whatever it took. She would quickly choose a couple chickens and, in the blink of an eye, wring their necks.

Without hesitation she would plop them into the boiling water she had previously prepared on the wood stove.

As the feathers boiled off, she would snatch the simmering chicken out of the kettle and with deft fingers that even a butcher would envy she chopped up the chicken, rolled the parts first in milk and then in flour, dashed a bit of salt and pepper over the coated chicken, and finally plopped them into the cast iron skillet she used for frying.

Hattie never measured anything and all of her work was done on the kitchen table. This huge oak rectangle was all she needed to accomplish her work. Delicious smells emanated from Hattie Mae's kitchen. Although the nights on which company came were few and far between, they could be certain there would always be the best fried chicken they ever ate at Hattie Mae's table.

However, no company was expected this Saturday night. Instead, Hattie Mae wrapped the eggs and placed them carefully into baskets to be transported to town. After this chore was completed, her next job was to round up the children to be transported to town along with the eggs. Saturday night was special to the families of Oakdale for many reasons, not the least of which meant that it was bath night.

Everyone got cleaned and spruced up on Saturday night. The older boys took care of themselves. Sometimes, after a hot, sweaty day of working in the fields, the boys simply jumped into the Elkhorn River to cool and wash off. But Hattie Mae insisted that each Saturday night the younger children have a proper bath with soap and plenty of scrubbing. There was no arguing and no way out. The clang, clang, clang as Hattie Mae dragged the large tin tub up the rickety porch steps and into the house meant only one thing to the children. Bath time!

Hattie Mae pulled the tin tub into the kitchen and positioned it near the wood stove. The tub's proximity to the wood stove was infinitely more crucial in icy December than in hot July, but this spring the weather had remained on the cool side and the

Hattie Mae with her hens.

children were grateful for the warmth of the old reliable stove. To Hattie Mae's way of thinking order was order and it didn't matter if it was twenty below or one hundred degrees, the tub was always placed in the same spot.

After hauling the tub inside, Hattie Mae headed out to the well with her worn wooden-handled bucket. The first well for the farm had been located across the road. Hattie Mae had to walk clear down the long dirt driveway, across the highway, and back in order to get water. The day Ton had created and cobbled together a well and a pump nearer to the farmhouse had been a joyful one for her.

What had been a major chore was now a bit easier, but Hattie Mae still made several trips to the well, dumping a few buckets of well water into the tub to fill it up. She then took some of the hot water kept in the reservoir of the wood stove and added it just to warm the bath water temperature a bit.

Chriss chided her that she was forever spoiling the children, adding warm water to the bath, or allowing the girls to skip the evening dishes to play baseball with their brothers. But she knew their lives had enough hardship already, and she was glad to do these small things to give them, what she considered, a bit of luxury and comfort. She brought out the bar of homemade lye soap and placed it near the tub along with a supply of well-worn towels.

"Mick, you first! Get on in here and be quick about it so your little sisters can, at least, take a lukewarm bath," she called to her youngest son. The rule was that the oldest child living at home went first when the water was the cleanest and toastiest. It was one of the small perks of being the oldest in this large bunch. After Mick came Deets and Wella. As soon as one was done, the next one jumped in until all were clean. Most times Hattie Mae plunked Deets and Wella into the tub together so they had a little time to play in the water. This ritual was repeated on a weekly basis.

When all the children were bathed, hair combed, with clean dresses, shirts, and overalls on, it was time for Hattie Mae to change into her "town" dress. This consisted of her taking off her apron, smoothing the wrinkles out of the dress she was wearing, and putting on her only pair of shoes and the only hat she owned.

The older boys then hauled the tub out into the yard. Nothing was wasted as the boys poured the used bath water onto Hattie's newly planted garden. As she herded the children toward the door, they chattered excitedly about the evening ahead of them and the possibility of a candy treat. Chriss pulled the wagon up to the house, led by trustworthy and faithful Dan and Molly. Lastly, the precious cargo of eggs was meticulously loaded into the wagon with the help of the boys. The Eymann family set off for the few mile trip into town.

The Union Store was divided into two distinct sections. All the dry goods were located on one side and all the groceries on the other side. First, Hattie Mae brought her eggs in and set out for the rear area in the store. Here she would set up shop and sell her eggs to the townspeople who did not keep hens. With this money she would make her way to the other side to buy flour, sugar, and the staples the family could now afford. She wisely put some of the eggs aside to use as barter for the items that were essential to her but that she did not have enough money to purchase.

For Hattie Mae these minutes of selling her eggs provided not only financial compensation but also companionship. This was the night all the farmers in the area and the townspeople came together. They gossiped and joked together and caught up with each other's lives in general during this time. All of the inhabitants of this region were in the same boat. No one had an abundance of anything, so it was comforting to share troubles and enjoy conversation together. They could commiserate with each other about their struggles. Plus … it was free.

Although these Saturday night transactions were vital to the well-being of the families, the children loved to come for different reasons. As darkness began to fall, Mr. Hansen, the owner of the Union Store, would hoist up a sheet between two trees in back of the store. While their parents were buying, selling, and visiting, the children would plop down on the wooden benches Mr. Hansen had constructed from planks of wood set on top of kegs of nails or empty buckets. They were excited to see the shoot-'em-up Western movie and were agog with wonder at the action. Although the movie was in fact very old, to the kids it was brand new. Many times, they were treated to free popcorn made by Mr. Hansen's wife.

But if the children were especially fortunate, their parents maybe had a penny or two to spare for them. The kids bought as much candy as possible with their coins, thoughtfully considering which kind of candy was the best bargain and provided the most pieces. Was it the licorice snaps or the chick-o-sticks? Maybe it was the cherry lumps or candy buttons or possibly the Boston Baked Beans or Bazooka bubble gum? Any candy would be a supreme treat and they would happily munch away as they kept rapt attention on the movie.

The entertainment of the movie for the children and the convivial social time for the adults was nothing, however, compared to the action that took place later in the night upstairs above the store. As the night wore on, the melodic sounds of a banjo, guitars, and fiddles and the rhythmic percussion of drums warming up could be faintly heard over the buzz of friendly voices in the store. When the market of buying, selling, and bartering was concluded, the novelty of meeting and greeting had worn off a bit, and the movie was at an end, everyone headed to the upper level for the best part of the evening. No matter what age, one or one hundred, everyone took part.

The band performing above the store was a rag-tag bunch of men from Neligh who got together at Bill Good's house to rehearse. Bill's house was chosen for this practice because of the trap door to the cellar. The main entrance to the cellar, where Bill kept his beer, was located outside the house. Unfortunately for Bill, his neighbors were overly strict and inquisitive and would have certainly disapproved of any beer drinking.

To circumvent the neighbors' watchful eyes Bill installed a trap door to the cellar through the kitchen floor. Now no one had to go outside to get the beer. Instead the men would simply open the trap door and lower Bill's eldest daughter Jeanette down into the cellar. Jeanette would grab as many beers as her hands could hold, whereupon the men would pull her back up. They then proceeded to make music and drink beer until the wee hours of the morning.

This informal troupe played almost every Saturday night for their friends and neighbors to enjoy. No money was taken. They simply played only for the pleasure of watching their friends savor the music and have a good time.

Listening to Bill Good and his band, these people were able to forget their troubles for a few minutes and be entertained. Everyone danced including the children. Bill's youngest daughter,

Nadeen Good in a high school photo.

Nadeen, would often join her Dad on stage and sing along with him as he played the banjo.

Eventually, as the number of dancers on the dance floor swelled, the youngest children were sent to the cloak room to listen and dance so they wouldn't be underfoot of the adult or teenager swaying with his special sweetheart. The children would twirl and spin until fatigue overcame them, and then they would dance just a little bit more. At the point they could not lift their feet any longer, they simply gave up, lay down on the long wooden benches provided for rest periods, and drifted off into a weary slumber with the music still reverberating inside their dreams.

It was at one of these Saturday night dances that Ton took notice of Nadeen. He was then a gangly sixteen-year-old to her youthful thirteen years. She was "on stage" singing soulfully in harmony with her father. Her long curly black hair was held back with a shiny barrette. Her round, sincere brown eyes shone brightly as her silky voice poured out the melody. She was wearing a black-and-white polka dot dress her mother had sewn along with white bobby socks and black saddle shoes.

Ton kept his eyes focused on her from the back of the room where he sat with his brothers and their friends—all Oakdale High School basketball players. He tried to make sure the other boys did not catch him staring at her because he wanted no part of the razzing and teasing that his brothers would give him, yet his eyes constantly sought out the beautiful girl singing on the homemade stage.

Ton did not know Nadeen Good yet, but he hoped he soon would.

10

The Crystal Lamp, Winter, 1939

The panes of her bedroom window were frosted over with a thin layer of ice that created a pattern of webs and arches. Nadeen lay in her bed imagining the window to be made of stained glass like in pictures she'd seen in books at school. She lay there unable to sleep in the murky, cold darkness. She was waiting for the dreaded sound she now heard all too often.

The crackle of tires on gravel caused her to sit up in bed. As she raised herself from the warm covers, she could see the dim headlights of the car as they shone briefly through the flour sack curtains that hung beside her bedroom window. Silently, she grabbed her terrycloth robe from the foot of the bed and inserted her feet into slippers waiting beneath her bed.

This had become her pattern over the last few weeks. It did not happen every night, but the mystery car showed up to drop off her father on a regular basis. Nadeen inched her way carefully through the parlor. Although she had become increasingly more adept at this journey and was well acquainted with every nook and cranny of the house, the darkness altered her perception of these familiar objects and increased her caution. As always, she pulled back the curtain. She realized what she would see but she still placed her face close to the freezing pane of glass. This night was bitter cold. The pane was covered with a lacy layer of frost.

Nadeen Good's father, Bill, and his brothers (from left):
Dots, Bill, Lester, and Ray Good.

She warmed the glass first with her breath and then rubbed some of the frost away with the sleeve of her robe.

Tonight, across the narrow gravel driveway, she could see the now familiar black car. She knew the car carried her father and someone else. She had never been able to clearly discern who the other person was but assumed it was one of the band members.

At first, she reasoned Daddy was coming home late after playing at some dance or event farther away from home than usual. Nadeen was accustomed to the smoky, sweet smells that lingered on his clothing after these events. Daddy loved to dress up for his performances. He would pull on his best black slacks and leather shoes saved especially for these occasions. His shirt was clean, starched, and ironed stiffly, but Daddy liked to wear a blue sweater over the shirt because the fleecy blue fabric softened his look. Most times he pulled on his black jacket, depending on the season. But always the jazzy beret covered his brown hair. He never left home without it. The clothing, worn only for his musical appearances, always retained the smells of the night, and Nadeen was used to them. A triangle of light peeked through the window lighting the darkened living room just a bit. There in the corner was her father's banjo. He had not played at any dance.

Tonight Nadeen observed the car as she had many other nights. The windows of the car were steamed over from the warm breath of the inhabitants. She waited. She waited so long that her feet started to get numb from the cold floor until finally she saw the car door open.

The night was freezing but extremely clear. Maybe it was due to the temperature—because her daddy walked briskly from the passenger side of the car, around the hood, and on toward the house, not stopping to speak to the driver of the car. As he approached the gate of their yard, he stopped and turned back toward the car. The window of the driver's side rolled down as he waved and called something to the driver, but the words were taken away on a gust of wind. Nadeen could not hear the words, but she was dumbstruck by what she was able to see.

Framed inside the unobstructed window she saw curly blonde hair, smiling blue eyes, and the rosy cheeks of a beautiful woman. The woman called something back to Daddy, and although Nadeen couldn't make out what they were saying, there was no mistake as to their intent. She watched her daddy sprint back to the car window, bend down, and kiss the woman on her red-stained lips.

Nadeen backed herself away from the window. The only thing she wanted to do right now was to forget everything she had already seen. She took several steps backward, pivoted in the direction of her room, and escaped to the life she knew before the scene unfolded outside.

As she began to run, her outstretched arm hit a crystal oil lamp, knocking it to the floor in a spray of glittering shards and piercing noise. Her mother Myrtle's bedroom door flew open as she stood amidst the debris.

"What on earth?" her mother muttered as she saw the mess on the floor. But as she gazed over at Nadeen her eye was distracted to the window. The warm, circular spot where, just seconds before, the heat of Nadeen's face had melted the ice provided an unimpeded view of the car, her husband, and the blonde woman. Anger flushed over her mother's face first, followed closely by fear as she watched her husband kissing the curly blonde head inside the car.

"Momma, Momma, I am so sorry. I will never get out of bed in the middle of the night again!" Nadeen pleaded. But as the words came out of her mouth, Nadeen was not sure exactly what she was apologizing for. Was it for the shattered lamp or was it for her shameful father? It no longer mattered as she watched her mother melt to the floor into a heap of tears and anguish.

That night the scale of her childhood tipped, swaying miserably and decidedly to the wrong side. The balance in which she held her life was off center, topsy-turvy, and twisted into nothing she could recognize.

11

Antelopes at Play,
Winter 1939

The gymnasium was stifling hot. It appeared the entire community of Oakdale had come out to see their local high school basketball team play arch rival Neligh for a bid to the state tournament. The gym was a mad house of anxious, screaming fans all gathered for this important game. It was Friday night and both teams were prepared to do battle.

Harold Allen's pencil practically flew across the pages of his notebook as he set himself on the bleachers ready to watch the Oakdale Antelopes play for a coveted spot at the state basketball tournament. As the reporter for the newspaper, he was well acquainted with the players and their families.

"Well, folks, it was nineteen below this morning," he later wrote. "But that didn't stop Coach G.L. 'Pop' Kistler from leading the Oakdale Antelopes to their first state tournament bid tonight. The Antelopes have been winning their games with consistent regularity for several years and haven't lost a regular season game scarcely since the channel for the Elkhorn was dug, way back when.

"The scrappy, well-tutored Antelopes display a fine brand of sportsmanship and behave in a gentlemanly way both on and off the court. However, the truth be told, the team has a lack of height and they look like the Singer midgets out there. Many basketball squads have a short and a long but Oakdale will have only one long 'Lanky Link Lingenfelter' and four shorts including Hans, Chub, and Ton Eymann and Tav Tavener on their squad.

"Many spectators like to watch as they put their heart in the game, keep their training, and are natural athletes. This is unlike the boys from Neligh who were observed to practice some poor training. In fact, this reporter was surprised to learn that basketball practice had even started there as some of the young aspirants were still puffing their cigarettes outside of the gym."

Although Chriss found it difficult to leave the farm these days, he never failed to attend the boys' games. He was among the Oakdale backers seated in the stands. Hattie Mae was there also but she made it a habit to never sit with Chriss.

She said, "He never sits still during a game and is constantly shouting out, so I prefer to sit with the other mothers in the bleachers to watch our boys."

Chriss watched with pride as Hans, Chub, and Ton took to the court wearing their brown-and-yellow Oakdale Antelope uniforms. The referee tossed the ball into the air, two opposing players jumped for it, and with that the game was under way.

It was a close contest with the lead being handed back and forth between the two teams several times. The score was tied as Chub threw up a long jump shot and scored two points for Oakdale to take the lead. Everyone in the gym heard Chriss's accented voice cheer enthusiastically as Chub tied the game. He had already scored ten points in the game and Chriss had yelped with joy at each basket.

Harold continued to pen his story, "Our boys in yellow and brown drew first blood in this contest with the state tournament on the line. It was nip and tuck. The game kept the fans on their feet though the prevailing style of ladies' short dresses averted some of the spectators' attention from the game."

Suddenly, Neligh streaked down the court with the ball as their agile forward connected with a short jumper to tie the game yet again. Hans brought the ball up the court, made a pass to Ton, and Ton went in for a lay-up. The guard from Neligh gave him a rough push to the floor and the crowd shrieked, "Foul" in opposition to the illegal shove.

Ton headed to the free throw line and launched the ball. It rolled around the rim and fell out. The Neligh boys grabbed the rebound and peeled off down court. There were only seconds left to play. Chriss shouted, "C'mon boys … get the ball!"

Neligh could not get near the basket as Oakdale closely guarded it, so the nifty Neligh guard took his shot from a far distance. The ball glided toward the basket but clearly missed the rim. From the free throw line, Ton snatched the ball and dribbled it swiftly up the court. Time was almost out! Five seconds remained.

The Oakdale boys drove for the win. Ton broke away from the pack and extended his arm to put up his shot, but as he shot, a Neligh boy caught up to him and loudly slapped his arm to foil the throw. Another foul! The Neligh crowd let out a collective moan and a worried hush fell over the Oakdale fans. The Neligh followers were all hopeful that Ton would miss the free throw just as he did last time.

Over the din of hundreds of conversations Chriss's voice could be heard, "Ton, you make this shot! You can make this shot! You done it a million times. Do it now!"

Harold Allen's pencil hesitated for a split second as all eyes focused on the slight young man standing poised to shoot at the hoop. The crowd drew in a breath and held it while Ton bent his knees, raised his arms, and without hesitation poured the ball into the net as the buzzer sounded to end the game.

Harold rapidly scrawled, "In the end, the Antelopes pulled the game out led by Ton Eymann, the forward who hasn't any too much weight at one hundred twenty pounds. Oakdale simply refused to let down. The boys made up for lack of height and weight by pouring in counters from all directions. It took exactly three rabbits' feet, two white elephants, and the crossed fingers of the entire local rooting section pulling for them when the slender and diminutive Eymann calmly potted two gift tosses in the last five seconds to secure the victory.

"The Oakdale Antelopes move on to the state tournament. This reporter, along with the entire population of Oakdale, is hoping they go all the way this year. Remember, if you are coming down to Lincoln to watch the game a single admission costs thirty-five cents and be sure to bring fifty more cents to watch the Antelopes in the finals. FIGHT GANG FIGHT! WIN GANG WIN!"

The jubilant team headed to the locker room to change. The elated Oakdale crowd slowly made their way to the exit all the while reviewing the high points of the game with friends and family. A defeated and dejected Neligh contingent exited in a somber, quiet line, only a few stopping to comment, "We'll get you next year!" Chriss accepted the compliments from the Oakdale fans as he waited near the gym door to take his sons home.

He spent these few minutes of solitude reliving the athletic accomplishments of his boys. Turk had been a star baseball player before he left for California. For the last two years he had been working in an airplane factory in that Western state. Before he left he had been offered an opportunity to play for a major league farm team. He would have done it but his family needed his help. Hans, Chub, and Ton all played basketball and baseball equally as well, not to mention they were on the academic honor list. Chriss would have it no other way.

"Always give your best, no matter what you are doing," he had drilled into his children. Chriss wished he could have helped Turk go on to that baseball career. Unfortunately, there was not much he could do. Times were tough all over. However, there was one thing Chriss took pride in being able to offer his sons. The boys could only play sports if the family could drive them to the games.

Chriss was able to find an old, run down car at a car dealer and for a modest amount of money he purchased the car for the family. The car was not in good working order, but Chriss knew his boys could tinker with it and bring it up to speed in no time. The car did not always work perfectly, but it was better than nothing, and no matter what broke down, the boys were able to repair it.

Chriss called out to the boys as they came out the locker room door, "Hans, Chub, Ton, I'm over here. Great game, boys! I sure did enjoy it and you all did your best and played well. Sure am glad it came out our way because it was a squeaker! Now, Ton, I knew you could make that shot. You done it a million times before. Don't be feeling bad about missing the first because you made it when it had to count. It's getting late. Ma already left for home with the little ones with her sister so let's get headed for home too."

The three jubilant yet exhausted boys piled into the back seat of the car while Chriss took the wheel. The Model T was sputtering a bit but the engine finally started with a bang. The country road was narrow and meandered through the rolling hills and sharp turns. The night was deeply dark with bitterly cold wind that had whipped and reddened their faces. Drifts of snow appeared at the edge of the road like white-capped mountains. The icy remnants of the winter storm of last week remained on the surface of the road. During the night's game the snow had started again.

White skiffs made the road treacherous, and as Chriss peered out his windshield, he had trouble deciding where the road began and ended as the snowy blanket was spreading around them. They were the solitary vehicle on the deserted country road.

Chriss listened to the chatter coming from the back seat as the boys reviewed the entire game, play by play. The boys gently but effectively ribbed each other for every missed shot, foul committed, and mistake made. Chriss kept quiet and concentrated on his driving. He was becoming more worried with each passing mile as he heard unusual, disquieting noises from the engine.

Hans had noticed the sounds too and asked, "Dad, the car doesn't seem to be working right. It sure is moving in fits and starts and pulling to the left. We can work on it tomorrow. Do you think it has enough gumption to get us home tonight?"

Chriss responded honestly, "Yes, son, I think it will be all right, but I am worried about making it up and over Devil's Drop."

The boys became silent. Although this section of road contained many gentle hills, there was one hill in particular the residents feared. It contained a very sharp incline and subsequent drop off. The townspeople had nicknamed it Devil's Drop because it had taken its share of automobiles down with it. All conversation had ceased as the boys watched to see what their dad would do. Devil's Drop was just around the next bend in the road.

Chriss ordered the boys, "Get hunkered down in your seats, boys. I am going to flat foot the gas pedal when we reach the top of the next hill. That way we will be traveling at maximum speed to make it up and over Devil's Drop."

Chub asked, "But, Dad, how will you keep the car on the road in this ice going down Devil's Drop?"

Chriss replied, "That's what you better get ready for, son. Good luck to us all."

Chriss followed his plan flooring the gas pedal at the top of the next hill, yet the car barely cleared the top of Devil's Drop. As slowly as they had climbed the hill, the faster they went down on the other side. Chriss released his foot from the gas pedal as the car began its descent, picking up speed as it rolled, slipped, and sputtered down. The boys clutched each other as Chriss maneuvered the car, constantly adjusting the steering wheel to keep it on the road as it traveled down at break-neck speed.

As the car left Devil's Drop behind and began its ascent of the next considerably smaller hill, momentum took it halfway up with no problem, but near the halfway point the car sputtered and the car slowed to a crawl. Chriss repeatedly pressed the gas pedal to try to inch and coax the car to the top but the engine had faltered. The car was all but stopped now and was soon rolling back down the hill.

Chriss yelled and ordered the boys, "Come on, boys. Hop out and give this old jalopy a push toward home or we are going to be spending the night in a snow bank."

The doors burst open while the car was still moving. The three boys scurried to the back of the car, and while the force of the car was moving backward, the boys pushed forward with all their might. Scrawny and short they might have been, but they proved strong enough to reverse the motion of the car and push it up to the crest of the hill. As the car began to descend rapidly, Chriss was able to restart the wounded engine. The boys grabbed onto the open flapping doors and slipped through them into the back seat. The car continued its limp toward home.

The boys slumped down—tired from the efforts of the game and the mighty push they gave the car. Soon they were sprawled out and snoring. Chriss drove on and for a moment his old vitality returned. His eyes shone brightly as he relived each and every moment of the night's game, confident his boys would be able to fix the car in the morning.

Eymann family holiday dinner, circa 1939.

12

Troublesome Times on the Prairie, Winter 1940

The house was unusually quiet as the girls prepared for school. Maybe, Nadeen thought, the silence was only inside of her, maybe she was the only one who felt weighed down. This feeling of uncertainty tugged at her heart.

Surely something would happen to change the direction their lives were taking. Something must happen to fix all the things that were now wrong. She couldn't put a name to exactly what those things were, but when she looked into her mother's distant eyes, she was sure of their existence.

Nadeen sat quietly at her usual spot at the table while her sisters, June and Jeanette, bustled about preparing for the school day ahead, unaware of the problems that faced them at home, more concerned with the problems of school and the daily activities. She listened as her sisters argued about a sweater one had borrowed and neglected to return. Her mother took no notice and made no comment as the girls' bickering continued.

Nadeen's mother, Myrtle, seemed to be deeply lost in her own thoughts until at last June yelled, "Momma, tell her the sweater is mine! She cannot wear it today because I want to wear it!" The only response from her mother was to set a plate of steaming scrambled eggs on the table with one word, "Eat."

The arguing was forgotten as the girls scooped steaming eggs from the plate. They had already passed on to other topics of the day. Who would score the highest on the math test? Who would be the queen of the dance? Who was currently keeping company with whom? Nadeen observed this drama unfolding with no appetite for either the food or the discussion.

Her sisters paid no attention to either her or to their mother until they called out, "C'mon, Nadeen, let's get going or we will be late." The girls gave their mother a quick kiss on the cheek and added, "Say bye to Daddy for us."

Gingerly, Nadeen approached her mother and gave her an unusually fierce embrace as if to fortify her strength. She whispered, "Momma, see you right after school. I will be home to help you."

Nadeen had decided that with the events of the early morning, she and her momma ought to stick together to ride things out. Their shared secret was tucked inside her heart and mind. Her mother's eyes misted over and she hugged her back. Nadeen wondered about Daddy but said nothing as she packed her books and walked out the door. She turned back just before the door closed. Her mother was seated steely eyed in the chair, gripping a hot, steam-filled cup of coffee. Nadeen winced at the sight of her mother, alone and adrift in her thoughts, but she pulled herself together and followed her sisters to school.

As the day wore on and she drifted in the normal sights and sounds of numbers and letters, Nadeen almost succeeded in convincing herself that what she had seen had been an illusion. It had been simply a bad dream or a nightmare. She tried to concentrate on spelling but her mind inevitably wandered over and over those nagging questions that lurked within her head.

Finally, the day was over. She met her sisters outside the three-story red brick schoolhouse to start their mutual walk home. As they rounded the last corner to her home she could see several strange cars parked on the gravel driveway.

June asked, "Is Momma having a bible study today?"

Jeanette replied, "I don't recognize any of the cars, but maybe Daddy is having a special practice for the band."

The older girls resumed their previous conversation as they ambled toward the house, but instead Nadeen slowed her pace. Evidently something big was happening because she could now see Uncle Ray, her daddy's brother, standing on the porch. His face was set in a tight grimace as he paced back and forth.

Nadeen began to run toward the house now. Suddenly the door burst open. Two policemen emerged from the house with their hands securely fastened around the shoulders of a man walking between them. His hands were cuffed behind his back. As they began to descend the porch stairs the man raised his head and looked into the distance. It was her daddy!

She ran faster than she had ever run in her life as she passed swiftly by her sisters. Their shouts and cries of "Daddy, Daddy!" could be heard down the block. But Nadeen's concern at that moment was not her father. It was for her mother. She tore through the crowd of people gathered on her front yard and porch and raced into the house.

Seated at the same chair where she had left her this morning was Myrtle. Her head was lowered to her chest and her shoulders shook with sobs as Aunt Lo held her hands. Nadeen and her sisters had always been close to Daddy's sister Aunt Lo. Aunt Lo's eyes met those of Nadeen, and the look of sorrow and heartbreak those eyes contained struck Nadeen as if someone had hit her with a baseball bat.

Aunt Lo quietly spoke into her sister-in-law's ear, "Myrtle, the girls are home now." Myrtle raised her head, turned, and looked straight at Nadeen as the door slammed behind her and the three girls reached her side.

A muffled cry of anguish rose to Nadeen's lips as she looked at her mother's ruined face. Her cheek was red and swollen, her left eye was as black as if someone had drawn a circle around it and colored it in with charcoal, a cut spread above her eyebrow and across her forehead. Her swollen lip was cut and bleeding as she dabbed at it with a handkerchief.

"Momma!" Nadeen shrieked. She threw herself at Myrtle's lap. As her head met the soft, worn cotton of her mother's dress, her sobbing and recriminations began. Nadeen's knees melted into the floor as the three girls encircled their mother with their arms and tears.

13

Humiliation, Winter 1940

Despite the horrible misfortunes of the day, an uneasy quiet had now settled over the wooden-framed white house. The onlookers and gawkers who had gathered outside the house near the gas station had moved on. Uncle Ray had driven off quickly after the police had taken Daddy in their car.

After Aunt Lo had helped calm the girls down, she assisted Myrtle to her room and settled her into bed. Aunt Lo brought a warm mug of tea with honey into the bedroom and returned to the kitchen a few minutes later.

"Girls," she called cheerfully and bravely to them, "what about some dinner?" The girls sat dejectedly at the kitchen table, sniffling and fighting back tears. No one felt like eating anything.

So, lacking any other ideas, Aunt Lo shooed them toward their bedroom saying, "A good rest cures a lot that ails you." The girls complied with Aunt Lo's order, if for no other reason than to escape the kitchen and the memory of what they had seen as they arrived home from school. In fact, it was reassuring to retreat to their room and pretend that normal still existed for them. Aunt Lo went home to her own family.

Rap, rap, rap came an unheralded knock at the front door. Jeanette, being the eldest, took charge by saying, "Who could that be?" as she swiftly answered the door, hoping their mother had not been disturbed by the noise.

As Jeanette pulled the heavy door open, there stood Uncle Ray, Daddy's brother, his hat in one hand and a determined look on his face.

"Uncle Ray," Jeanette murmured, "what do you want? Momma's asleep right now and Aunt Lo has gone home."

Uncle Ray's face clouded over at the mention of Myrtle. Chagrined but resolute in his mission, Ray stated his business.

"I just came from seeing your daddy over at the jail," he said. "He wants to see the three of you. I am here to fetch you girls over to the jail for that purpose. It's bad enough him being dragged away from his home in handcuffs and on display in front of all those nosy, pompous, self-righteous neighbors and all over such a silly misunderstanding. Well, no matter, hold your heads up, all of that will be worked out in time. He is alone and he wants to see you. Go on now, get your things and come on."

Nadeen's body trembled with revulsion, rage, and indignation over her daddy's demand and Uncle Ray's insistence. Never, not in a million years would she go to the jail. June and Jeanette began to whimper as they grabbed their shoes, but Nadeen's mouth was set in a firm line of resolve.

She crossed her arms over her chest, firmly planted her feet, and blurted, "I am not going over to no jail!" Her sisters stared at her in wonder over her newly found courage. Uncle Ray looked at her with a confused and anxious look on his face.

The impasse might never have been resolved until … clip, clop, clip. The measured plodding of Myrtle's shoes could be heard making their way over the oak floor. Everyone turned to behold the injured and subdued yet dry-eyed Myrtle advance toward the group.

In a whisper of a voice she stated, "Nadeen, no, you must go with Uncle Ray. Go on now and do what he asks. No matter what has happened between us, he is still your daddy. Go you must and go you will."

Without waiting to hear a response or argument from anyone, she painfully and wearily turned, slipped back into the bedroom taking her troubles along with her and closing the door with a hushed click.

What passed over Uncle Ray's blue eyes could only be called sorrow, and he respectfully tipped his head to Myrtle. He said, "Let's go now, girls. Do what your momma says and don't let's give her any more problems today. Seems to me there's been more than enough heartache for one day or even for one lifetime in this house."

The three girls filed out of the house, their silhouettes visible in the gathering dusk. Uncle Ray ushered them into his car and walked around the hood to get in the driver's seat. Nadeen pressed her tear-stained face against the car window. She saw the curtain flutter a bit. She caught a glimpse of the bruised and battered face looking sadly from the window. The curtain dropped back into place as the car drove away. She would never forget the resigned yet unflinching look on her momma's face.

As relentless as her feelings were against her father, her heart broke at the sight of him. His hands were tightly clasped behind his back, held firmly in the cold, gray metal handcuffs. Tears flowed freely down her face, dropping on her already moist blouse. She watched him shuffle from the door of the cell over to a small wooden desk and chair. His face, thin and ashen gray, was tightly drawn over his high cheekbones. His eyes glinted defiance and his mouth was drawn into a thin, tight line above his strong chin. Even under these dire circumstances, his face remained handsome. He displayed no emotion, neither anxiety over the situation he found himself in or remorse over the tumultuous events that had unfolded that day.

Uncle Ray guided her by the elbow as he propelled Nadeen and her sisters to the area where her father was now seated. Bill's unwavering gaze reviewed his daughters' faces as if to gauge their questions, emotions, and thoughts; but he said nothing, nothing at all in response to the three tearful visages in front of him or to the ragged sobs of breath they released from time to time.

Uncle Ray finally broke the silence. "Bill, what are they telling you now? Is there anything we can do or get for you?"

At this point the girls were relegated to being a mere presence in the room as Daddy and Ray discussed important matters. Daddy slowly shook his head as he leaned forward to answer Ray's inquiries. Nadeen listened intently but heard little more than the ticking of the clock on the wall and the raspy, shuffling, dry noise of papers being moved around in the office. This unnerving quiet was shattered suddenly by Nadeen's wounded cry, "Why, Daddy, what happened, what did Momma ever do to you, what did us girls do to make things so bad?"

Bill's eyes flickered over her and softened, but only for a second, as the slow shift of his head back and forth came as his only reply to her questions.

Uncle Ray shushed her and motioned for the girls to wait for him near the door. As they inched toward the door, the girls held hands and attempted to stifle the sobs, knowing every eye was directed on them, watching them, pitying them. Nadeen did as she was told this time, but she purposely hung back behind her sisters to be closer to the conversation between Daddy and Ray. She strained to make out the words flowing between them but only caught snippets of the conversation: "A few weeks … jail … Blanche … California." Ray mumbled an unintelligible reply as he pressed something into Daddy's hands.

"C'mon now, girls," Ray called, "I'm going to take you three back home now. It has been a very long day for everyone. Tell your Daddy goodbye now." With their heads bowed and eyes to the floor the girls said a sad, final goodbye.

Ever obedient and more than ready to escape the misery and humiliation of the jail, the girls followed Uncle Ray to the exit, but Nadeen turned back, one last time, to peer into the steely blue eyes of her father. Cold stubbornness and nerve mixed with a stiff upper lip glared back at her and took her breath away.

At that moment, she understood. She realized the old Daddy she knew and loved was never coming back and had been, in fact, replaced by this new model, prepared to take the consequences for the choices he had made and to move on to a new life ... without them. She knew then it was her duty to protect and care for her mother. Never again would she let her guard down

The feelings of safety, security, and the warm comfort of a normal family circle eluded her now. The composition of her circle had shifted, changed, and now excluded her daddy. It occurred to her it was now her job to tighten up that circle, to draw in the vacant space where Daddy had been but was no more. She would keep this circle of women that included her mother and sisters stable, solid, and intact. This wheel of women was now her primary concern—no, her only concern in her life. She would use all of the strength she possessed and work with all of her might to keep them safe and together.

14

The Jalopy of His Dreams, 1940

The engine was in the back seat and there were dents on the fender but Hans finally had his car. For months now owning a car of his own had been his dream and now that dream was finally a reality!

Hans had been doing fill-in farm work where anyone needed help and had been driving a livestock truck to make some spare money. Of course, most of his money went to help the family, but he had managed to save a bit. Hans had been searching and had finally found a car, if it could be called such, at the car lot in Norfolk.

When the dealer saw him looking at the car, he approached Hans with a deal that was too good to turn down. If Hans would buy the car, as is, no guarantees, and definitely not in working order, he would sell it to him for substantially less than it would normally cost. Hans jumped at the chance to buy this car. He knew he could count on his brothers to help him get this machine humming in no time. Now all he had to do was convince Chub and Ton to get to work on it.

"Hey Chub," Hans bellowed out the back door, "Do you want to go with me to Neligh to meet some girls?" Eighteen-year-old Chub was tinkering on a small motor and he looked up immediately at Hans, incredulous about the offer. Hans usually

Chub Eymann at the Eymann farm, circa 1940.

went to Neligh with his friends and definitely did not invite his younger brothers to go with him. With his brilliant blue eyes, gorgeous smile, and clean-cut looks, Hans had a way with girls and he knew almost every girl at Neligh High School.

Chub knew he would be in like flint with the girls if he were with Hans. He replied quickly, "Sure, Hans, just let me clean up."

Hans held up both palms to Chub and responded, "Not so fast. There is one small problem."

Chub questioned back, "What's that?"

"You and Ton just need to meet me down at the garage at four o'clock this afternoon," was his only reply and with that he walked away.

At four o'clock sharp Ton and Chub strolled into the garage and asked if anyone had seen Hans. "Sure, he is inside," they explained with smirks on their faces. As Chub entered the garage he saw the saddest excuse for a car he had ever seen.

Ton, Tude, and her son Carl at the Eymann farm, circa 1940.

There before him sat a dented, ancient car with cracked windows, its original black color faded to the gray of an early morning sky. As the boys approached the car they could see the engine parts in a box in the back seat.

"What in the sam hill is that?" Chub laughed and asked.

Hans was quick with a rejoinder, "Well, that's the car we are taking to Neligh tonight to meet girls." Hans went on to clarify, "And you and Ton can only come with me if you get this car to work so I suggest you two get cracking!"

Chub and Ton exchanged worried glances. They both knew they could do it and had the huge advantage of being in a garage with all the tools they would need and extra parts to use. Truthfully, the two boys could not wait to get at the car. So, while Hans supervised and drank a Coke, Ton and Chub got busy. The boys rolled up their sleeves, removed the box of engine parts from the back seat, and went to work on the car. In a matter of just a few hours the boys felt the car was ready for a test. Hans was astounded that they actually pulled it off so quickly, and he was more than willing to put it to the test.

Hans took his place behind the steering wheel. As the boys wiped their oily hands on a rag, Chub called, "Okay, Hans, start her up and take her out."

Hans's face was beaming with pride. This was his moment of glory. How long he had waited and saved for this moment. He started the engine … it purred to life … he put the car into gear to drive through the garage door and out onto the street eager to show the entire community of Oakdale his smooth vehicle. His very own and he was driving!

He stepped confidently on the gas, and as he did, the car drove unexpectedly—backwards. BAM! CLUNK! SPLAT! The rear bumper collided with the tool bench and everything on it flew up into the air.

Hans slammed on the brakes, opened the car door in one swoop, "GOD DAMN YOU TWO!" he shrieked, "WHAT IN THE HELL HAPPENED?"

Hans's anger erupted into a sputtering fit, "I asked you, what in the hell did you two do to my car?"

Ton and Chub were doubled over with laughter. "Oh, Hans," Chub pleaded, "calm down. It's easy to see what happened."

Hans stammered back, "It may seem simple to you but I want my car fixed and ready in an hour, got it?"

Hans's demands were crystal clear and the boys got to work to remedy the problem. The first time they installed the gear they must have set them in the reverse order so instead of Drive, the car went into Reverse. It was a simple fix of re-installing the gears correctly. The boys worked diligently because they wanted to get to Neligh yet that night. The car was ready to go in less than an hour. The boys washed up and set off for Neligh.

The car was quite a sight—and not in a good way—but it worked. The number of dented areas on the car outweighed the smooth surface area but Hans was proud as punch. Ton and Chub were simply happy he included them in this adventure, and they were pleased to have had the opportunity to work on a real car.

Neligh was a short drive from Oakdale. They bought bread, braunschweiger, and sodas and parked their car close to the movie theater in downtown Neligh. From this prime location they were able to watch the array of girls as they passed on the sidewalk in front of the car on their way to the movies. The boys called out and whistled at the best-looking girls.

As the movie began the number of girls passing slowed to a few stragglers and late comers. They boys decided it was time to move on to greener pastures, but just as they prepared to leave they spotted Susan. She had spied their car too and stared at them intently as she walked.

Everyone knew that Susan was sweet on Hans and wanted nothing more than to go out with him. Hans was not so eager to go out with Susan so he hushed his brothers in hopes she had not seen them lurking in the car. Susan proceeded up the street while the boys observed her in silence. Suddenly they heard, CLUNK! Susan had been so preoccupied with watching the boys, she neglected to watch ahead of herself. She slammed head first into the lamp post.

The boys now erupted into peals of laughter and giggles and they hollered out to her, "Haven't you ever seen boys before?" Susan picked herself up, dusted herself off, and ran toward the theater in humiliation.

"Show's over boys, time to move on," Hans bossed them. "We got a party to go to." With that the boys drove off in the car of a lifetime.

15

Baby Brother, 1940

Two bright brown eyes peered out from behind the flower bush in the front yard. Mick was playing one of his favorite games, the spying game. At ten years old his skin was continually browned by the Nebraska sun until in August he looked just like one of the walnuts he had seen in the store. His brown eyes were always curious and inquisitive, and he wanted so very much to be like his older brothers. He gazed at them intently as they approached the black Model T that had just driven into the farm. He imitated their mannerisms and their way of speaking. He watched as Harley Johnson, a friend of Hans, moved smoothly out of the driver's seat and stood beside the car talking with his older brothers.

"What ya gonna do today, Hans?" Harley asked.

Hans replied, "Ton, Chub, and I have to finish the chores yet."

Harley suggested, "Let's go on down to the river when you are done. I heard the girls from Tilden are coming out to the river today to cool off." The boys nodded their heads in agreement and proceeded off to the barn to finish their work.

Although the bushes were hot and bug infested and the leaves tickled his nose, Mick stayed put, hidden amongst the green camouflage. He waited and watched as the boys left the barn and disappeared together down the path leading to the Elkhorn

*At the Eymann farm, (back row, from left) Chub, Betty, and Hattie Mae;
(front row, from left) Mick and Jix, Wella, and Deets.*

River. He waited patiently until they were out of sight. When he felt sure they were gone, he crooked his head and listened intently. Way off in the distance he could faintly hear their shouts and splashes from the river. He sneaked quietly out and tiptoed over to the big black car.

Mick daydreamed for a few minutes about the car he would have when he was older. He ran his hand over the sleek body of the automobile and imagined what his car would look like. But he would need to learn to drive. Mick realized there was no time like the present. He easily convinced himself that with his brothers and Harley gone he should try out this car now.

Mick inched over to the crank in his overalls and bare feet. He had watched his brothers start a car many times, and he was fully aware he must do something with the crank first before he could actually drive it. He pushed down hard on the crank but it wouldn't budge. Next he pulled up with all of his might. He was pretty sure he felt it move slightly so he tried the pushing again by laying his entire body on the crank.

Mick possessed what his mother called "one huge stubborn streak." He was determined to get this car started now. Nothing … no movement. The crank was just not going to work for him today. Maybe if his sisters were home he could convince them to come out and help push the crank but that will have to wait for another day.

Mick was so disappointed but he was not down and out. He could still do some practicing with the steering wheel. He opened the door and crawled up onto the driver's seat. He squatted up onto his knees so he could peer out of the windshield. He put his hands on the steering wheel and pretended he was sailing down the hilly road just outside Oakdale. He made-believe the car was full of his friends and they puffed on cigarettes and horsed around together just like his brothers did.

Mick soon grew tired of this imaginary scenario and jumped into the back seat. He decided to play a game to see how fast he could jump from the front to the back and then from the back to the front. He amused himself this way for a while but was soon bored of this game also. The car had grown hotter with the windows rolled up sitting in the hot sun. He was sweltering in the stifling car but refused to give up the enjoyment of being alone in the automobile. His face was crimson from the heat and the exertion of his jumping game. He laid his head down on the soft cushions of the seat and before he realized how tired he was, he was already fast asleep.

It was the shouts, yells, and whoops from the wet boys fresh from their swimming escapade that awakened Mick. His heart was pounding and he was in a full panic. If his brothers caught him in Harley's car, they would wallop his butt good and proper.

His immense brown eyes gazed over the edge of the back window and although he could hear the boys, he could not see them yet. Maybe there was still time to escape. He looked again. The coast was clear. He opened the door only a few inches as he heard the voices drawing closer and closer. He pushed his body through the open slit of the door and then with all of his strength he slammed the door closed and ran for it, as fast as he could, back toward the house. But as he rounded the back of the car, he ran smack dab into Hans.

"Whoa, buddy, where you off to in such a hurry?" Hans grabbed Mick by the straps of his overalls and held him up above the ground so they were at eye level.

"I was runnin' back up to the house because I heard Mom call my name. I was just playing over there by the barn, trying to get away from all those girls for a while," Mick blurted out his story. Mick hoped Hans would buy his lie because he knew if Hans found out he was in Harley's car he would kill him—or worse, he would laugh at him with his friends.

"Hey, Eymann, wanna go in to Oakdale for a while and shoot some baskets at the schoolyard?" Harley suggested to Hans.

"Sure, it's hotter than hell out here and I'm thirsty but Harley what do you think … how about we take the squirt with us?" Hans motioned to Mick as he, Harley, Ton, and Chub hashed out their plan.

Mick looked up at Hans in disbelief and amazement. His older brother actually wanted him to go! Mick could not believe his ears. He may, in fact, be able to ride in the black car. He was too keyed up to say a word but simply nodded his head.

"Wanna go, Mick?" Chub and Ton both questioned him. Harley motioned for him to get in the car. Harley easily cranked the Model T and eased himself into the driver's seat. They set off down the drive toward the highway and town.

Mick rolled down the window. He felt the wind whipping his cheeks and the heat of the sun radiate off of his face. He had never been as happy as he was right now. He made-believe he was the one driving the car. But, truth be told, he was more delighted to just be with his big brothers.

Mick helps out on the farm. Mick and Chriss milk cows together, 1940.

16

The Motive for Hunting, Fall 1941

"You are slower than molasses! Get your shotgun, get in the car, and let's get on down the road," Hans commanded Ton.

It was autumn in Nebraska and that meant one thing—pheasant hunting. Not only did the boys enjoy this outdoor activity, for them it was more than a hobby. The birds they bagged would provide meat for the family.

Hans had been working as a farm hand and driving trucks since finishing high school. In addition to buying the junk heap of a car with his work pay, he was able to help out his parents with some money. They were all fortunate that Turk had found a good paying job at a McDonald–Douglas Aircraft factory in California. Turk sent money home on a regular basis. The boys' contributions kept the family afloat in these lean times.

Hans, with his blonde hair, laughing blue eyes, and athletic build had turned into quite a ladies' man and with the car his brothers often rode on his coattails to meet girls. Hans had a trigger quick personality though. One minute he was laughing and joking, but the next minute something would set him off and he would lose his fiery temper letting loose quite a string of obscenities.

"You just hold your horses," Ton responded. "You are just anxious to get to Neligh and kiss your girlfriend. It don't have

Chub and Ton ready to go pheasant hunting.

nothing to do with getting there early to hunt pheasants," Ton good naturedly kidded Hans. Ton was now a lanky teenager. Like his brothers he was a stellar athlete in basketball and baseball. He excelled in academics but there was a marked difference between him and his brothers. Ton seldom spoke and when he did he had a small stutter to his words. Most of the time it was imperceptible to others but he tended to speak only when it was vital for him to do so. His blonde hair and blue eyes also made him attractive to girls but he was shy, so much shyer than any of the other boys, so he usually kept his distance from the action. He had an economy of speaking that added weight to his words and made others listen to him when he did talk. Yet Ton was always up for hunting, sports, or any activity with his brothers.

"Either way and that is none of your business anyway. Now, get going!" shouted Hans as he started the motor of the car. "If you want to come along, you better get in now!"

Ton tossed his shotgun in the car, let Jix jump in, and hopped in the passenger seat. The car took off with the two boys and Jix installed at Ton's feet. No good hunting was ever accomplished without a hunting dog and Jix was one of the best.

The boys didn't argue anymore on their drive to Neligh. They talked over the day's plan for hunting and the good field Hans had heard about and gotten permission to hunt about ten miles from Neligh. Ton was right. First Hans had to stop to pick up Pat, his current girlfriend, and then the three of them would head out to the fields. Hans turned off the highway and drove the short distance into Neligh to Pat's house. But there was a hitch in the plans.

"Hey there, Hans," Pat smiled and greeted him with a peck on his cheek. She turned and said, "Hey, Ton." Both boys returned the greeting but their attention was diverted to the porch where a raven-haired girl sat on the porch swing.

Pat explained to the boys, "This is Nadeen, my neighbor. She is going to come with us because I promised her some company today while her family is gone. Also, my mom told me the only way I could go with you boys today was if she went along with us. Kind of a chaperone of sorts."

Pat's plan to take Nadeen was a good one. Now her mother had no reason to worry because Pat wouldn't be alone with Hans, and Nadeen could keep her company in case the boys got too caught up in a really good day of hunting.

Hans shrugged his shoulders. It didn't matter to him but the birds were a waiting. "Let's go get some birds," he called.

But Ton could not take his eyes off Nadeen. This was the girl he had seen at the dance singing with her father on stage. Her bright smile was open and honest. Her brown eyes looked kind and innocent. Her dark hair curled out from under the white bandanna she was wearing in the latest style. She had grown up since he last saw her at the dance above the store. He had just graduated from Oakdale High School, and he wondered immediately how old she was. Suddenly, Ton was thinking the day may turn out to be a lot more interesting than he originally thought it would be.

"C'mon then, ya'll. The birds aren't gonna wait for us forever," Hans reminded them. Hans gentlemanly opened the door for Pat and motioned for Ton to help Nadeen into the car.

Pat and Hans chatted away about events that had happened since they saw each other last week. The girls sat in the back seat while the boys took the front. Hans spoke with the girls over his shoulder as he drove his car down the dirt lane. Ton sat still as a stone with not much to add to the conversation. From the corner of his eye he checked out Nadeen. She was chatting with Hans and Pat and looked happy to be there in the car with them but she too was checking Ton out on the sly.

Hans stopped the car near the edge of the road close to the chosen field. The boys climbed over the barbed wire to get into the field but paused to hold two strands of wire up and two down creating a space for the girls to slide through.

Hans took charge immediately, "Ton, you and Nadeen walk ahead with Jix and scare up the birds. Pat and I will follow and do the shooting." Hans figured this would give him some extra time to be alone with Pat and he would get to do the shooting too.

Slowly, pushing their way through the brown, dry field and the remains of crops, Ton and Nadeen started to look for pheasants as they went.

After a few minutes of unnerving quiet, Ton finally got up the courage to begin a conversation. He asked, "Do you go to school in Neligh?"

Nadeen replied quickly, glad to have something to break the ice at last, "Yes, I go to Neligh High School. I am a sophomore but I have two older sisters who have graduated already. I want to graduate too and get a job like them. I want to move to Lincoln with my mother right after I am finished."

Nadeen realized she had blurted out much more information than she planned on sharing, but now since the dam had broken, the two began to compare notes on people they both knew, the sporting events she had attended, the music and food they liked, and their families. They had become so engrossed in their discussions and revelations they sat down on a log to rest for a bit and continued their mutual discoveries.

Suddenly, a voice boomed out, "What in the hell are you doing? I told you to scare up some birds, not get smoochy faced with a girl and sit your butt on a log! Get your lazy ass up and get moving! Pardon the language, Nadeen, but Ton you know better! You been hunting all your life and this is definitely not hunting. Now get your good-for-nothing, lazy ass up, you pretty boy talker. NOW!"

Ton and Nadeen jumped up at Hans's harsh diatribe. Nadeen blushed having been caught sitting on the job, and Ton murmured his apology to the deaf ears of his older brother. Pat was standing behind Hans, bent over with laughter.

The two boys took off to do some serious hunting with Jix in the lead. Ton was hoping this would make his brother forget his lapse of outdoorsmanship. Pat approached Nadeen as the boys were already far ahead of them in search of pheasants.

"Well, well, well, what do you think of Ton?" Pat questioned Nadeen.

Nadeen thought for a minute and then replied, "He is really nice but pretty shy." All the while her gaze was directed into the distance as she watched the boys disappear over the crest of the next hill.

Ton glanced back several times to get a last look at Nadeen, but he had to be careful not to incur the wrath of his brother. For the next few hours Hans kept him busy with shooting, fetching, and then gutting and cleaning the birds they had shot. But all the while Ton was pondering what he would say to Nadeen on their ride back to Neligh that would impress her enough to go out with him.

The hunting day was finished. The boys had bagged five pheasants. The four made their way back to the car followed by a jubilant but tired Jix. The game and guns were loaded into the car and they drove back to town. While en route the four reviewed the day. Hans and Pat made plans to attend a movie the following weekend. Hans was hoping that Ton would ask Nadeen too but he was still too timid to take that step.

Finally, they arrived back at Pat's house. While Hans assisted Pat from the car, Ton opened the door for Nadeen. He got his courage up and as he helped her from the car he said, "Would it be all right if I come and visit you sometime?"

Relief flooded his face as she answered, "I would like that but you would have to talk to my mother first." Ton assured her he would come by next week to talk to her mother and then after a few more minutes of gentle teasing between Pat and Hans plus a few stolen kisses the boys drove off toward Oakdale.

Hans opened up with, "Ton, you got yourself a new girlfriend? She sure is pretty. What do you think Ma will say? You gonna see her again?"

Hans teased his baby brother so he was more than a little surprised when Ton looked him in the eye and seriously replied, "Hans, today I have met the girl I am going to marry."

Those words shut Hans up but he still chuckled a bit all the way back to the farm.

The Eymann family kitchen. From left; Hattie Mae, None, Chriss, Tude, and Nadeen.

Part III

*A blue star mother, Hattie Mae displays her four
sons' military photos and blue stars above the
Philco radio in the front room, 1943.*

Darkening Clouds

17

Day of Reckoning, April 1942

S pring arrived in Nebraska. The farmers faithfully returned to their fields preparing to plant a crop they hoped would thrive and bring order to their world—a world devastated by drought, dust, grasshoppers, and now war.

The hordes of grasshoppers and occasions of blowing red dust had retreated into the past. The farmers lived now trusting that the worst days were behind them and life would soon return to the normal rotation of planting, caring for, and harvesting their crops.

Chriss rose before dawn to prepare for the very long day ahead of him. Although he was relieved and blessed to be able to work the fields for George Hunter, his mind was preoccupied with how he would get all of George's planting done and his own on his small section. From this tiny area he must make the land grow enough to feed his family. The last few years had been burdensome and trying. For Chriss it was not only the lack of food and work that weighed on him, it was the effect it had on his family.

Chriss worried mightily about Turk taking off for California by himself. Even when he knew Turk was working at the aircraft plant, he wished Turk were back home on the farm. The money Turk saved and sent had been the salvation of the family and

Chriss was grateful. Yet he missed his son and felt his absence, not only in the fields but in his daily life. Somehow, if Chriss could just work harder, he could pull his family out of this abyss they found themselves in. Then Turk could come on home and they could buy the farm they desired.

Hans and Chub were also working on other farms to help out with the expenses and make ends meet. The boys never complained about what they had to do, but with them off working, Chriss had even more responsibility to farm his plot. The younger boys helped as much as they could, but they were all still busy with school, chores, athletic events, and school work.

The one thing Chriss was certain of was that his children would get an education. Learning came before all else. Although the children were required to return home to do their chores as soon as they finished their school activities, Chriss would never be one of those men who took his kids out of school to work. He would make do as best he could. He prayed fervently to God each night that this year the crops would produce the most bountiful harvest, there would be no hail or tornadoes, and that the dreaded grasshoppers would not return. These thoughts and desires dominated his mind.

But one thought terrified him more than any other. War had been declared and the preparations for war had begun in earnest. Chriss fretted constantly about the rift between his religious beliefs and his loyalty to his adopted country. For the life of him he could not understand why people had to fight to solve their problems. *Wir sind brüdern!* We are brothers!

There were only so many hours in a day to get everything accomplished, Chriss thought, as he pulled himself out of bed, slipped into his overalls, and headed to the kitchen. Of course, Hattie was already there stoking the stove, starting coffee, and making the beginnings of breakfast. They exchanged good mornings.

Hattie watched Chriss closely. In the last few years she had noticed the times Chriss sat absently looking out into space.

She had observed these times becoming more frequent than she would have liked, but there was little she could do about them. Hattie sensed that Chriss was more troubled today than usual because he was staring straight ahead and had not said more than the two words of good morning to her.

To distract him she turned on the radio in the wooden cabinet. How proudly and prominently it was displayed in the living room! When Tude and her new husband, Al, had given them the radio, they were both surprised and pleased. The house had no electricity but the radio operated from a battery. Everyone knew the use of the radio must be monitored, and they were all cautious and conservative about the amount of time they listened because they did not want to run the battery down. No one wanted to be without the radio nor did anyone want to have to haul it to town to be recharged.

Today, however, Hattie was concerned about Chriss's mood so she turned on the radio to cheer him up. WJIG from Norfolk was the only station they were able to pick up, but it was enough for them. Hattie was hoping for some good music, but, unfortunately, only reports of the war in Europe came over the airwaves.

"*Ach, mein Gott,* not more words about the war!" Chriss complained. His normally soft voice became harsh as he commanded Hattie, "Turn off that radio. I don't want to hear any more about the war!" Hattie obediently turned off the radio and busied herself at the stove.

Chriss was silent for a while but inside he seethed with anxiety. He worried about his new country. He blurted out suddenly to Hattie, "Some of my relatives still live in Germany and have faced problems and difficulties every day. They have suffered so much! No one here understands the power Hitler holds over them. I want to stay out of that situation. I want America to care for America. I wish we could all just get along and live and let live."

Chriss did not finish his eggs but instead grabbed his hat and headed outside to get some chores done before heading over to Hunters for his day of work there. As he approached the staircase, he hollered out the nicknames of each child. His routine had never changed even though None, Tude, and Turk were all living outside of the house now. "None, Tude, Turk, Hans, Chub, Ton, Betty, Deets, Mick, Wella," he yelled.

As the name *Turk* escaped his lips, he smiled. He had just remembered that Turk had arrived home for a visit late the night before. Turk's pal had kindly picked him up from the Union train station in Omaha and brought him back to Oakdale. He heard the children stirring upstairs as he walked out the door into the cold Nebraska spring morning.

Gradually the children trailed down the stairs including Turk. The younger children had been asleep when he arrived home so they were excited to see him. They hugged his legs and crawled all over him. Turk responded to them with playful tickling that produced peals of laughter from the little ones.

Turk disentangled himself from his brothers and sisters and looked at his mother as he began to speak. He started, then stopped, gathering his courage, and then haltingly said, "Mom, Hans and I have talked and we are signing up for the Navy together. We will both be leaving later this month."

Hattie looked directly into Turk's intense eyes. She knew her stubborn and proud son very well and she knew she would not be able to talk him out of this. She also was aware how very tough this would be on Chriss and for the entire family because they depended on Turk and Hans for many reasons. She was worried about what Chriss would say to the boys and how he would react to the news they were enlisting.

She sighed and said, "You must break the news to your father very carefully, son. Have you thought about what you will say to him? It will take a lot of convincing for him to let you go."

"It's not his choice. I am a loyal American and I know my duty. As soon as those sneaky Japs attacked Pearl Harbor, I knew this is what I must do. The men of this country are volunteering by the thousands to pay them back for what they did in Hawaii. My aim is to sink the Axis. Daddy taught us actions speak louder than words. Hans and I plan to take action," Turk finished his explanation breathlessly.

"And what, my son, is your duty to your father, to your family? I know you want to do what is right but are you sure leaving us is the right thing? Have you thought through the teachings of the church? Son, I know you must do what you think is right, but please think of these things before you speak to your father."

Hans had joined his brother in the kitchen. His blue eyes were serious and downcast at the prospect of the chore ahead of them. Both boys gave their mother a quick kiss on her cheek and set out to find their father in the field. They spotted Chriss, and as they neared him both boys kept their eyes glued to the ground. They were keenly aware of the hurt and anger they might be raising in Chriss but were equally as committed to serving their country.

Hans said, "Turk, let's get this over with. We just have to spell it out to him that we are enlisting. We're doing it together. He just has to understand."

Chriss had spotted the boys and waved them over to where he was fixing some fence. "Morning, Dad," both boys said at the same time.

Chriss smiled widely when he saw Turk and Hans but he kept his emotions in check as he said, "Morning, boys, glad to see you up and around, Turk! Hans, I know you are working today over at the Smith farm, but maybe you and Turk could help get this field ready to plant corn in a couple weeks. It is already April, you know. I have a couple other chores to keep Turk busy today too."

Hans nudged Turk and since he was the oldest he began speaking, "Sure, Dad. But Hans and I need to tell you something first." Turk took a deep breath as his father scrutinized him. "We are enlisting in the Navy this week. We will probably leave later this month for training." Turk's voice trailed off quietly as he and Hans watched Chriss for his reaction.

Chriss said nothing. His brown eyes never wavered from the boys. He peered intently at them, waiting for more words, an explanation, anything to help him understand what had happened here.

Hans took over, "Dad, we are Americans. You know what the Japs did at Pearl Harbor. A sneak attack and they are in a pact with Germany and Italy too. Turk and I are going to do whatever it takes to help Uncle Sam win this war!" Hans searched his father's face for a reaction.

It took some time for Chriss to gather himself and put the sentences together in concise English. He finally began, "My sons, you know where I come from, you know the language I speak, you know many of our relatives live in Germany now. Can you think of going there to fight them? Why must people fight over their problems when we are all brothers and our differences should be worked out together? Don't Japanese and German people breathe the same air we breathe and walk the same earth? We are all more alike than we are different. Violence is never a solution to a problem. Why can't we seek to get along rather than kill?"

"But, Dad, you taught us to let our actions speak for us," Turk pleaded with his father. "This is a situation that requires action and right now! We cannot allow American lives to be lost and not take action against the killers. It is our duty to go. We are going to avenge every sailor who died and to protect our American soil and families. It is something we must do. It was not us who started this fight, but I refuse to walk away from the challenge of defending my country. It cannot be helped that Japan is an ally to Germany. It is my duty to serve."

He went on, "Dad, Hans and I want to fight this war together. I promise I will take care of him and watch over him every minute."

Turk tried to answer his father's questions but mere words were not enough for the things Chriss had on his heart and mind. No answer was required at that moment anyway because Chriss had already turned his back to the boys and walked away. His eyes looked down at the fields waiting to be planted. If the boys could have glimpsed his face, they would have seen the tears starting to form in the corners of his eyes. His head slumped to his chest, his shoulders sagged from the weight of the decision the boys had made. The world was suspended over him, like a black cloud.

Pacific Letters,
October 1942–March 1943

Dear Hans,

I hope you and Turk are getting some good training out there at that base in California. One thing I know for sure is that your weather is better than here. It's fall in Oakdale but it feels like winter with the hard freezes we have already had. You two are probably lolling on some beach talking to girls while we do our chores in winter coats.

Well, I knew it was coming sooner or later but I sure wished it had not happened so soon after you and Turk left home. My induction notice came today. Mom brought it to me and just looked at me with those troubled, brown eyes. Dad was sitting at the table eating lunch when I opened it. We all knew what it was but he didn't say a word either. He just got up from the table and went out to the barn. I guess there just aren't any words that can actually describe what each of us is feeling. I know I am not like you guys though. I am gonna wait until the last possible minute to show up at the recruitment center, even if that means I have to go into the Army.

I feel as if the weight of the family is on my shoulders right now. I am needed, especially now during harvest, to work at George's farm and also to harvest our crops. There's plenty to do even with Ton and Mick helping out. Dad works every day but, honestly,

Chub Eymann, 1943, at Tude and Al's house
after he completed Army basic training.

some days he just isn't up to it and instead sits in that chair. I am torn between wanting to help my country and wanting to help my family. I know you felt the same way only you thought you could count on me staying here. It didn't work out that way and my only hope now is that Ton will stay at home to farm.

Oh well, the die is already cast and I am to leave for basic training within the week. We all miss you two goofs! We know you are smart and will do well in training but try to keep out of trouble too. I will write more after I arrive at basic training.

Your brother, Chub

October, 1942

Dear Tude,

How's things in Omaha for you, Al, and little Carl? I am on my way to Fort Leavenworth, Kansas, where I will officially become a soldier in the United States Army. I have never been away from home so everything is all new to me. I am hoping I will get to do my training somewhere close to Nebraska so I may be able to make it back for leave.

A bunch of us guys from Oakdale are riding the train together so that makes the trip more bearable but I am already missing home. I miss the sweet smell of alfalfa, the cedar trees along the bank of the Elkhorn, homemade fishing poles and long summer afternoons, my dog Jix, and everybody I love. Guess I better buck up because that's the Army life now for me!

Ever your brother, Chub

December, 1942

Dear Mom and Dad,

Here we go again! After those few weeks in Kansas I got shipped to San Francisco. I never had been to any place like that before and I did certainly enjoy the couple of days we spent there. But now they are telling us to get ready to ship out. It was really getting cold in Kansas so when we left we wore our wool uniforms which, I can tell you, are surely not needed here in California.

Today we boarded the troop transport ship—what a sight that was! I bet you could fit six thousand men into that thing. Everybody keeps asking the same questions. Where are we headed? Where are we going to be stationed? But no one tells us anything right now. So here we go on this huge ship to who knows where? I will let you know where I am as soon as I find out myself!

Your loving son, Chub

January, 1943

Dear Mom and Dad,

Heavenly days, you will never guess where I am headed … Hawaii! They finally came around and told us. They also passed out some lighter, cooler uniforms to wear as we were beginning to suffer in the heat with those wool duds. I was relieved to get the new uniform but I am not exactly thrilled to hear where we are headed. Hawaii is way too far from home! Who knows when I will be able to get back for a leave?

But, they don't ask you what you want to do in the Army, they just tell you what you're gonna do. Your job is to do it and keep your mouth shut! I have orders and I am going to be assigned to the Medical Hospital Ship anchored in the harbor in Hawaii. I have no idea what I will do there. I am not a medic but at least now I know a little more about my duty. The food on this tub is terrible! Whoever said Navy food was good has never eaten any that is for sure! All we get is beans and spam and spam and beans. The cooks try to doctor the spam up by buttering it and layering it with everything imaginable but the guys always know it is spam. They pick up their trays, walk over to the trash and, splat, into the garbage goes the spam. I sure miss the food from the farm. Fresh, red tomatoes and ears of golden sweet corn are all I dream about.

You will not believe it when I tell you about the area where we sleep on the ship. There are rows and rows of bunks, almost like hammocks, stacked three or four high. So you actually have to roll yourself out of bed and roll yourself back into bed if you don't want to clunk your head on the guy above you! I will write more after we arrive at our destination.

Your loving son, Chub

February, 1943

Dear Mom and Dad,

Our ship finally made it to Hawaii. I was glad to get off that vessel and have my feet on dry land for a change! I know now that I made the right decision to not enlist in the Navy ... the food would have killed me before the Japs did! We docked at Pearl Harbor and it was truly a terrible sight to see. Some of the ships are still lying at the bottom of the harbor and there is damage everywhere you look. Out at Hickam Air Force Base you can still see the bullet holes in the buildings. It gives me the shivers to think about the chaos there was back on that December day of '41. Glad I missed it!

The first thing we had to do as new arrivals was go for six weeks of basic training. They had us doing target practice with rifles, as if I had never hunted before in my life, that was an easy training for me. The part I don't like is the 6:00 a.m. jog but I am getting used to it. We run through the sugar cane fields close to our barracks. I have never seen anything like those tall canes! Our barracks are really just small cabins that were built for the workers in the macadamia nut fields nearby. They are rustic but comfortable.

I made it through basic with ease and now I finally have been assigned my duty. I am to be the driver for the command car. Can you believe that? I had to travel thousands of miles to actually get a car to drive! The command car is a massive four-wheel-drive vehicle. Our commander is responsible for running the hospital ship docked just off the coast here. They transport the wounded soldiers from the battles in the Pacific to this ship, patch them up as best they can, and then send them on to hospitals in the States. I feel this is a very important job and I intend to take it very seriously.

Your Army son, Chub

March, 1943

Dear Ton,

Hot damn! I am the luckiest devil in the Army! My duty now is to drive the hospital ship commander here in Hawaii. I am on call but all I have to do is drive him wherever he wants to go. I take him to the ship in the mornings and then pick him up around noon. He usually tells me, "Let's go down to the beach." When we get there he says, "I want you back in two hours." And with that I am a free man! This is really a tough life! Ha!

I take my camera and the jeep. I drive around the island until I find something I want to investigate. Hawaii is beautiful, tropical, and really original. There is nothing back in Nebraska like the plants and flowers I see here. There are two motels near the beach. Otherwise it is pretty much palm trees, sand, vegetation, and the ocean. A wide open, wild, and unique place! Driving the company commander is a glorious job! Don't tell Mom and Dad but the commander drinks a bit. He keeps a swig bottle in his briefcase, and as we are driving to the beach he pulls it out and takes a few swallows. The other day he asked me, "You want a snort?" Of course, I said no because I was driving but I told him, "Oh no sir, I don't drink." This is pretty much our routine every day.

I am enjoying this Hawaii duty while it lasts, but even with the hot sun, warm waves, and beautiful women I am homesick. I sure hope I get a leave to come home sometime very soon. Give Jix a good pet for me. Tell everyone hey and take care.

Your brother, Chub

19

California Dreaming, Spring and Summer 1942

Turk looked around at the brilliant sunshine that drenched the San Diego Naval Base as he, Hans, and myriads of recruits waited in the bus. The bus had paused in front of the entrance under the black wrought-iron arch. On either side of the arch were identical white-washed sentry posts. The armed sentries posted inside of the small structures protected the mobilization process going on within the base. California, and San Diego in particular, was vigilant for Japanese spies, some disguised as tourists, who might try to take photos of the war preparations.

The San Diego Naval Base stretched for as far as Turk's eye could see, jutting out into the Pacific with the leviathan ships berthed in the docks preparing for their duties in fighting the war. Turk scanned the crystal-clear blue sky, and as his gaze surveyed the area he could see the tall palm trees swaying lightly in the sea breeze.

As the bus entered the actual grounds of the base, Turk saw the highly maintained green hedges surrounding the buildings and the carefully tended flower beds. His eye took in row after row of barracks, all recently completed, that allowed as many as twenty-five-thousand recruits to train at the facility. The blocky, stark-white barracks all looked the same but Turk noted all were drenched in that glorious California sunshine and the winds from the ocean made this both a comfortable and beautiful place. He could see pride written everywhere as American flags furled in the gusts and uniformed men hurried between the buildings in their efficient and sincere efforts to win the war.

This base was to be his home for the next few weeks as he and Hans trained to be radiomen. At this point in the war the Navy knew how to test and train the recruits that entered their service. Hans and Turk had been tried and tested to see where their abilities could best be used. Both boys were going for radioman training. Their job would be to ascertain positions and to guide the strategic bombing for the pilot of their aircraft. It did not hurt their cause that both boys were slightly smaller in stature and weight than many other recruits and so were able to fit in the miniscule door at the rear of the Avenger aircraft and plant their narrow butts on the tiny wooden seat in front of all the radio equipment. The boys entered the base confident in their ability to learn and knowing they would graduate at the top of their class.

Chriss had always insisted that his children do their best no matter what they were doing—athletics, school, or work. Farm boys grew up knowing how to create, repair, and make do with the materials on hand because they had to, there was no other choice. This practical know-how and honing of their skills made the boys eager learners and excellent problem solvers. What some of the recruits from the big cities struggled to figure out, the boys saw as old-fashioned common sense.

The days passed quickly. The Navy was not one to waste time or to accept less than anyone's best effort. The recruits were kept busy from dawn until dusk, and for the first couple weeks they were not allowed to leave the base. There were drills to do and marches to take, and each recruit felt it was crucial to the war effort to learn his job to the best of his ability. If everyone just did his job correctly, then maybe they could help end the war sooner rather than later and they could all go home. Days were long and hard. The trainees were ripe for a leave by the time one finally arrived.

*Turk and Hans attend radioman/bombardier training in
California, 1942. Seated in front row, Turk is second from the
left; Hans is third from the left.*

Everyone had heard the stories of what San Diego was like
but each one wanted to see for himself. Turk and Hans were no
different. That first night of leave found them raring to go. Hans
couldn't wait to find some place to dance. Back in Oakdale he
was known to cut a pretty mean jitterbug and he surely did love
to dance with the girls. Turk was more of a loner and his aim was
to get out and have a beer and a cigarette with nothing much else
on his mind. Wearing their best dress whites they headed out for
that initial night on the town.

The streets of San Diego were teeming with life. It would have
been impossible to underestimate the impact that twenty-five-
thousand young men added to the life and livelihood of the city.
But no one could have imagined the changes that would mark
the city in the year 1942. Not only were there thousands of

servicemen adding to the population of the city, there was also an influx of defense workers.

The blitz-boom of San Diego was on and the streets were alive day and night with youthful exuberance. There was always something happening outside in the near-perfect weather no matter what day it was or what time. The release of the training-weary recruits with the after-work-shift liberation of the plant workers resulted in a carnival-like atmosphere of merrymaking and revelry.

Turk and Hans walked into this metropolitan street fair ready to do their part. Hans headed with his buddies straight to the dance clubs that were located near the base. He wanted to dance the night away with some good-looking girls and forget that he had to return to the military regimen. Turk, on the other hand, headed to a nearby tavern, ready for a beer and some quiet time where no one was giving him orders and where he could just sit and think for a while.

Turk decided his best bet was the tiny bar near the USO club. He headed there knowing others in his situation would be there, so if he wanted company, he could have it. If not they would leave him alone with his thoughts. Turk was reluctant to admit it but he was homesick. This certainly was not his first time away from home, but this time he knew he could not return to Oakdale and its green fields if he wanted to. In fact, he was sure he would not see Oakdale for a few years with the war going full blast. He was prepared to do what he had to do but still … he missed home and the farm.

Turk opened the door of the club and ambled over to the bar to get a drink. He sipped his beer in the quiet pleasure that came with no demands on his time. The bar was boisterous and full. Soon the recruits were in fine form, and in the corner some fisticuffs started to fly as the alcohol flowed. Turk's peace and quiet was gone, so he made his way through the crush of sailors to the door and out on the street. He figured he could walk a ways further and maybe find a less jam-packed place to down a beer.

As he left the bar near the USO club, he glanced back. Standing in the doorway silhouetted against the fading evening light was a girl. She was wearing a cotton candy pink dress and pink high-heeled shoes. Jauntily perched on her head was a beret as white as Nebraska snow. Her sable hair swung as she turned her head upward, and Turk heard a peal of laughter erupt from her lips. She appeared to be waiting in the doorway for someone, so Turk tried to appear nonchalant as he walked over to check her out.

"Turk, Turk Eymann?" he heard someone call his name. This stopped him dead in his tracks. He was trying to ascertain where the vaguely familiar voice was coming from. He looked around only to find it was from the girl standing in the USO doorway. He was absolutely certain he did not know any girls in San Diego.

But there it was again. "Turk Eymann, it's me, Kay, from Oakdale, don't you recognize me? I can't believe you are standing here in front of my eyes," she exclaimed.

Now Turk knew why that voice was familiar to him but he was looking directly at the last person he ever expected to see today. Kay was wearing a defense plant badge on her dress and her mahogany eyes were shining brightly. Her smile lit up her face as if the San Diego sunshine powered it. Turk's eyes popped open widely as he stared straight at his high school sweetheart, the love of his life that he had not seen for two years. He could not believe the change in Kay from school girl to working woman!

"Kay, what are you doing way out here? I did not know you were in California!" Turk stumbled with the words.

Turk and Kay had dated all through their high school years but had parted company that summer after graduation. Turk headed out to California to work, and the two had not remained in contact. Truthfully, he could not remember their quarrel or what exactly caused the break-up. At that moment he only remembered how much he had been in love with her, how beautiful she was, and how very glad he was to meet her again, tonight, so far from home.

"Why, Turk, you have always been handsome but look at you now in that uniform with that California tan!" Kay gave an exaggerated whistle and beamed back her pleasure at seeing him.

"My cousin talked me into coming out to California after we graduated. I was heartbroken when we broke up and there was no reason for me to stay in Oakdale, so I came here to work," she explained. "We both got work at the aircraft plant. We have a tiny little place here. I make enough money to pay my bills and send some home. San Diego is an exciting place to be right now. I want to help the war effort but I also want to enjoy life and this is a great place to do that! I heard from some friends back home that you and Hans enlisted, but I never heard where you were stationed. How long have you been here? What are you training for?" Kay plied Turk with questions.

Turk quickly suggested, "Kay, this is my first leave. I don't really know my way around here and I want to make the most out of the free time I have. Why don't you show me around a little bit before you and your cousin go home? Maybe we could spend some time together tomorrow too? We can catch up and I promise I will answer all of your questions. What do you say?"

Kay's smile was radiant. "You bet, Turk. It is so miraculous to run into you like this. I will get my cousin and we can all go together. I don't know about you but sometimes I just get so homesick. Just seeing your face reminds me of home, ball games, picnics, parades … it makes me happy to see you, that's for sure!"

Kay backed away and then returned shortly with her cousin. Turk offered an arm to each girl and the three walked down the busy Friday-night-frenzied streets of San Diego together.

20

The Secret Plan, August 1943

The orders arrived in the daily mail on August 7, 1943. Ton walked into the house holding the induction notice in his hand. He looked at his mother and said, "Well, it finally got here, Mom. I knew it was just a matter of time. I have to report for active duty on August 20."

"What are you going to do, son?" her uneasy question hung in the air between them. She had already sent three other sons to the service: Hans and Turk were already on board the *USS Sangamon* in the Pacific, and Chub was serving in the Army in Hawaii. She was aware that the odds of all of them making it home alive were stacked against them. She listened to the radio daily now for each and every report from the war. Her boys were all in action in the Pacific Theater. So it was vital to her to listen to the names of the far-away battles so when she did get word from them she would understand what they were going through. Her fears were raw-boned and real.

"I'm gonna enlist in the Navy like Turk and Hans. I hear they have the best food of any branch of the service," Ton declared.

Hattie responded with a weak smile, "I guess that is as good a reason as any. Ton, we will have to find your father and give him the news." Ton nodded his head slowly in agreement.

Chriss had disappeared into the fields of waving corn. He was working harder than ever. There were many days now when Chriss stayed out in the fields until darkness overtook the daylight and everyone was asleep. Sometimes he went from the field directly into the cellar, without talking to anyone. The dank subterranean room had become his refuge. Hattie guessed this was the only way he would not have to hear the war reports that he both wanted to hear and, at the same time, wanted to avoid. The harsh reality of losses in battle and what his boys were experiencing hurt him almost physically. This was happening more often now since Chub had left home.

Ton wondered what kind of reaction Chriss would have to the news that he also was leaving for the service. There were the practical matters to worry about: Who would help with the farm work? Who would work extra for money for the family? Mick was yet too young for all of that and was still in school. Ton pondered the way his father had grown increasingly despondent with the departure of each son, and he was truly concerned with how his leaving would affect Chriss and the family. But he had no choice about leaving. He had been drafted.

Along with several other Oakdale boys, Ton drove to the local draft board office in Neligh. He signed the enlistment papers and learned he would soon be on his way to Navy training. There were a few things on his mind that he knew must be done before he left and his time was very short. The most important was to talk to Nadeen. The two had been inseparable for the last two years, and everyone knew they were extremely serious about each other.

He decided to drive to her house while he was in Neligh. The weather was scorching. Nadeen was sitting outside on the porch of her house fanning herself with a paper fan. As he drove up, he could see Myrtle, her mother, peering at him from behind the kitchen curtain. Although she had given her permission for Nadeen to keep company with Ton, she was vigilant and watchful as the matron of the family with the

Ton and Nadeen, dating in Spring 1943.

sole responsibility of raising her daughters. Bill had gone to California with Blanche after the divorce. She was alone now to take care of and provide for her family.

When Ton walked Nadeen to the door at night after a date, the porch light came on immediately and Myrtle popped out of the front door to greet the young couple and usher Nadeen inside quickly.

"Nadeen, I just signed the papers for the Navy so I will be leaving in a couple weeks for training," Ton broke the news to her right away rather than avoid what they all knew was coming. Of course, they had discussed the induction often.

Almost every family in the area had someone serving in the military, and it seemed all the young boys were now gone or were soon to leave. The dances had dropped off. There were few men left to dance with and nobody felt much like dancing anyway. Life had changed quickly and concern with the progress of the war was on everyone's minds.

Nadeen looked at Ton with fear and despair. Although she had been expecting these words for the last few months, her heart skipped a beat when she actually heard them. She took a few moments to speak and had trouble with the words. Intense emotions and raw fear coursed through her body.

"I will write to you as often as I can and I will come home on leave every chance I get," Ton further explained. "Please write to me too and if you can just wait until the war is over, we can be together and get married. Let's just right now make a plan for a wedding for the month after I get out."

Tears moved slowly down Nadeen's cheeks but she smiled and said, "I knew you would be following your brothers. I know for sure you will come home safely. I feel it in my heart and soul. This will turn out all right and the war will soon be over. Ton, I will wait for you but not here. As soon as I graduate, I am going to take my mom and move to Lincoln. That way we can be closer to my sisters. There are more and better paying jobs there than here in Neligh, and I can make more money. First, I have to take care of my mom but I promise I will save as much as I can for our future together."

Ton nodded his head and agreed with her plan. "I know that censors review all of the mail because the letters we get from Turk, Hans, and Chub have black marks through some of the words. It will be almost impossible to let you know where I am."

Nadeen nodded her head because she knew this was true.

Ton continued, "We need a secret plan. I have an idea. When you get to Lincoln, buy a map of the Pacific. I will write my letters to you with a secret code that will tell you where my ship is located. The censors will never be able to figure this one out."

Nadeen listened intently to his idea, open to any suggestion about keeping in touch.

"You know my handwriting is pretty awful, right?" Ton stated honestly. Again she nodded her head in agreement. "Well, the first thing you do when you get a letter from me is look at how I sign my name. I will sign all of my letters with my real name, Kenny. If the K has a curl at the top, there will be a code within the letter that tells you where I am. If the K does not have a curl, then there is no coded message. Got it?"

Together they devised a complicated system of using words in lines one, five, three, six, two and four of his letters. Ton felt this complex system would evade the censors. Nadeen wrote it down so she would not forget.

"Got it," she replied. She was thrilled that he had thought out a plan to keep in good communication with her and posted on where he was. Even though they would be separated by thousands of miles, she could feel close to him. She could follow the progress of the war through the radio broadcasts and understand the battles he was involved in. She was worried, anxious, nervous, and scared as hell. But, like most of the people they knew, everyone was preparing to go to war and win it. They were absolutely convinced this was the right thing to do and was necessary. But, for now, the future was uncertain and unknown.

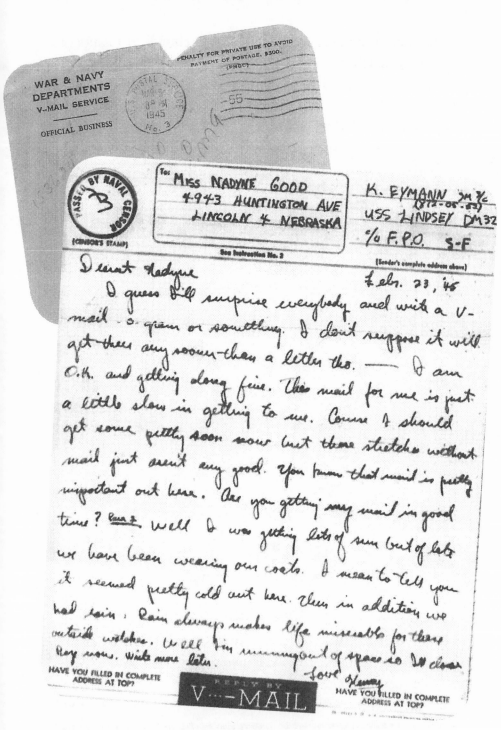

*V-Mail message from Ton to Nadeen using the secret code. The envelope
has been decoded and gives his location as I-W-O J-I-M-A.*
[Nadeen briefly spelled her name the way it appears in this letter.]

Ton's hand clasped Nadeen's as he reached into his pocket. "Nadeen, there's one more thing I need to do before I leave," he told her. Within his hand was a delicate gold bracelet with a shining golden heart at the center. Nadeen watched as Ton slipped the bracelet on her wrist.

"Here is something to remember me by," he explained to her. "I didn't have enough time to have it engraved but maybe when you move to Lincoln you can take it in to a jewelry store and have my name put on it. That way you won't forget me while I am gone."

Nadeen flung her arms around Ton's neck and hugged him tightly. Ton brushed her dark hair away from her face and looked at her intently as if he was trying to memorize each and every curve and angle. He kissed her, turned away quickly, and hopped back into the car. As he drove away, through the open window, he gave her a thumb's-up sign, waved, and was gone.

Nadeen spending time with Ton's family. Edgar, None's husband, pushes Nadeen into a hug with Betty while Deets and Wella watch, 1943.

Betty and Nadeen became best friends, 1943.

21

Darkness Falls, Fall 1943

The long and difficult days on the farm filtered into each other with little to distinguish one from the next. The fall harvest had begun in earnest, and while Chriss still worked at the Hunter place, the bone-crushing fatigue that plagued him made it impossible to accomplish as much as he would have liked on his own farm. He was glad for Mick and his help.

Each night, he arrived home, shoulders slumping, fatigued in body, mind, and spirit. He mentioned again and again to anyone who would listen that particular day in April of 1942. Chriss told people the day his sons left for the service was the worst day of his life. How could anything be worse than your two oldest sons leaving to fight a war? But Chub was drafted a year later and then the floor dropped out from under his feet as Ton enlisted in the Navy. Now all four were gone, fighting a war. Who knew where they were and if they were safe or in harm's way? He struggled to manage the anxiety he felt but most days, it was easy to see that it overpowered him.

He continually asked, "Why must my boys fight? Why can't people just be peaceful and get along?"

Chriss pulled open the heavy wooden cellar door located on the rounded dirt mound just outside the house. An aroma of dampness and mildew rose from the darkened cellar below. Jix hopped down to the floor of the subterranean room first. Chriss backed down the rickety timber ladder into the dark, moist cellar where the family kept all of their canned tomatoes, beans, and the fruit jellies Hattie put up every year.

The smooth dirt floor was damp as he let his body slump to caress its coolness. He laid his head back against the wall and stared ahead. Jix rested his head on Chriss's leg, and, without thinking, Chriss absentmindedly petted the dog's ears. As others used their energy to interact with the world, Chriss spent his strength turning his thoughts inward.

When it appeared to others that Chriss was simply staring into nothingness, it was then he could see them. He withdrew into himself and was consoled by these moments, mere snippets of past days. Turk's determined face as he swung the bat, Hans chatting away seated on the three-legged stool as he and Chriss milked the cows, Chub's grand smile as he bagged his first pheasant, shotgun slung over his shoulder, and Ton, tools in hand, working on some new project. How difficult it was for him to contemplate the days ahead without the boys at home. It was more than he could bear to consider about where they were and what they were doing.

He listened to every radio account of the war's progress now— the announcer charting a course through the battles of the Pacific. Each day he vowed he would not listen to the radio anymore, but like a moth to a flame he was drawn to the box that spewed out war information. Listening intensified the pain but he could not bring himself to miss the broadcasts. When he heard of the American soldiers and sailors lost in each brutal encounter, he asked if his sons were still alive. He simply could not stomach the idea that one or all of them might not make it home alive, and he was gripped by the paralyzing fear of the unknown.

That power of the unknown was fierce, wicked, and vengeful. The unyielding might of this power battled for control over Chriss's mind. He fought against this power on a daily, if not hourly, basis. Yet it was clear to all that he was waging a losing battle in this epic struggle. With every ounce of willpower he possessed, Chriss carried on his own unseen battle to maintain control of his own mind. The toll this effort extracted from him was immense.

His scrawny body was emaciated, his face drawn over his cadaverous cheeks. The shy smile was gone and replaced by tightly sealed lips that never smiled and seldom spoke. Often times, from the look in his eyes, it was evident that although his body was present, his mind was not. Chriss had evolved into a frightening shadow of his former self. He had faded from the outside world into a world where he was the only inhabitant.

Each time a visitor came to the house nowadays, Chriss would, with immense pride, bring out the massive athletic album he and Hattie had meticulously kept over the years. He had scissored out articles from the local newspaper, kept pictures, badges, and emblems of all of the teams the boys played for, and, of course, the prized photos taken by Al, his son-in-law.

There were pictures and articles of Turk playing baseball. Turk could have played for that professional team if only they could have spared him from the farm, Chriss lamented. But they needed the money he contributed, so he stayed to work. Hans, Chub, and Ton all had their own pages with pictures, articles, and mementos of their playing days. Chriss sought solace in the book, remembering happier, less complicated times, the times he enjoyed so much. When he looked through the pages of the books, the boys were still there with him.

But, today, no company was there to divert his anguish. He sat on the chilly, damp cellar floor alone but for his now constant companion Jix. In the darkness with arrows of light filtering in through the slatted door he looked at the jars of food arranged on make-shift shelves of board and blocks. The amethyst, magenta, and amber jars of jelly held his attention, and for a while he thought of summer ... trees budding and blooming, the sweet smell of the alfalfa, and the summer breeze. His gaze moved on to the moss-colored jars of beans and the vibrant crimson jars of tomatoes. Such work for Hattie. So much time spent canning. But the jars would feed his children this harsh winter.

His fingers ruffled through the animal's soft fur. His mood darkened yet he never cried. There were no tears. There was no feeling left in his body at all. With each loss and disappointment, all nerve endings had been severed and sealed. He was sure no feelings would exist in him again. He despaired of the boys ever coming home.

He stirred and moved, slightly disrupting the peaceful slumber of Jix. He glanced again at the vividly colored jars. He could not remember the last time he ate or even wanted to eat. But finally his eye landed on the brilliant yellow jar of peaches that Hattie canned during the summer months.

He stood, grabbed the jar, and settled back into his spot. Jix resumed his previous position. He opened the jar and ate some of the peaches methodically, without giving a thought to the texture or taste. It was simply something to do for him. He glanced down to look at the pet resting on his leg. The boys had raised Jix from a puppy to a trustworthy dog, and he had been their sidekick in hunting, swimming, and other adventures.

Jix now went everywhere Chriss went, following him and shadowing his every move. He followed him to the barn in the morning, he was in the field waiting for him in the afternoon, and in the evening and the nights when Chriss could not find peace and rest eluded him, Jix was there too. Chriss had taken to spending nights in the cellar and Jix had followed him there. Chriss was grateful for his undemanding company. Jix looked up at Chriss with eyes that seemed to say, *I understand and I know what is happening with you. The boys are gone but I am here. I won't leave you alone.*

Work was the other constant in his life. His family would starve without his farm work. Everyone cooperated to get him through the day. Hattie, Mick, and even the little girls did their part. They had all taken on more of the chores that enabled Chriss to function, at least in part.

Through this night the unrelenting melancholy did not abate. Chriss could not bring himself to physically climb up the flimsy ladder. He was emotionally unable to climb the ladder. He didn't want to try anymore. He laid his head down on the cool, packed dirt floor of the cellar. He closed his eyes and tried to sleep again. He did not want to think about the danger his sons were facing.

Chriss was beyond all efforts everyone made to reach him and talk him back, away from that far-away place where he retreated. It was not for lack of trying. Family members, friends, and neighbors had approached him to attempt to talk him out of his dark moods but none had been successful.

In the end he still had Jix. He leaned over and patted his head, ruffling his fur again. Jix only looked at him with his trusting brown eyes. Chriss didn't pretend to understand how or why but he knew Jix was well acquainted with his inner demons. He closed his eyes.

Jix laid his head on the floor and rested his right paw on Chriss's arm. Silently the two of them drifted off to sleep together.

22

Pollywogs and Shellbacks, Winter 1943

Both Hans and Turk had heard the stories from the veteran seamen who had already served in the Pacific. Out here in the middle of the ocean men were classified as two things: you were either a shellback, someone who had crossed the equator, or a pollywog, a novice seaman crossing the equator for the first time.

It mattered not whether you were a lieutenant or the lowest class of seaman; you were either a shellback or a pollywog. Pollywogs had yet to prove their worth as seagoing men and to experience the court of Neptune Rex. Scuttlebutt had it that today was the day the court would happen.

Hans peered out over the sun-filled deck of the *USS Sangamon*, an escort carrier, at the sailors who were gathered there. Each side of the deck was lined with shellbacks watching in gleeful anticipation of the entertainment to come. Hans poked his head above the crowd of men to try and see what all the commotion was about.

"What in tarnation is going on here?" he murmured out loud.

Turk was somewhere in the midst of the group of men who were huddled together trying to preserve their dignity but knowing it was useless. Hans maneuvered himself forward to get a better look. Uncomfortable and unsure as he was, he

Hans Eymann aboard the USS Sangamon *serving
as a radioman/bombardier on an Avenger, 1943.*

Turk Eymann aboard the USS Sangamon *in the South Pacific, 1943.*

wanted to get a bird's-eye view of the proceedings about to take place on deck.

Before the pollywogs had been brought up on deck, they had been forced to strip down to their skivvies. Hans heard Turk mumble a complaint but all of the men went along with the order and shed their clothing. While disrobing, Hans looked around. He was surprised to see even the lieutenants stripping to their tidy whities along with all of the other aviators and sailors. Rank held no privilege here. From the top-ranked officer to the lowest sailor, if this was his first trip across the equator he was in the same boat as the others.

A voice rang out, "Temporary command of this ship has passed to King Neptune. Slimy pollywogs prepare to face the court of King Neptune. I will escort you pollywogs on deck to face the charges brought against you by the shellbacks on board. Form a line, no talking and make it snappy."

"What charges could there be against us?" a brave soul yelled out from the crowd.

"Pollywogs are not allowed to speak until spoken to, so shut up," the shellback shouted him down, "just know you must be prepared to defend yourself and face your punishment."

The near-naked pollywogs lined up and trooped obligingly up on deck.

Hans found himself surrounded by men and wondering what would happen next. As he inched his way forward, Hans could clearly see the royal court. King Neptune wore a long white mop on his head that gave him the appearance of wet hair. His flowing white robe was cinched around his waist with a long scarf. It had the look of recently being a bed sheet. The homemade crown that topped the "hair" was adorned with jewels that had been cut from the fabric of old clothing. He held his three-pronged trident authoritatively in his hands. A black beard had been drawn onto his face.

To his right stood his "queen." Queen Amphrite was also dressed in white wearing a robe fashioned into a skirt. On her chest "she" wore a black bra that had been stuffed with regulation Navy socks. Her hair was made from what appeared to be dark-colored shorts that had been frayed and cut into long waves cascading about her head. She too wore a golden homemade crown with jewels. Her cheeks and lips were painted bright red and her eyes were rimmed with black eyeliner. "She" almost looked like a real woman.

Next to her but standing a few feet behind was Davy Jones and his band of men. Hans could see some of them sported eye patches and sashes wrapped around their waists. They wore frayed leg pants. There was even a sailor with a peg leg. A Jolly Roger flag whipped in the ocean breeze completing the motley pirate troop.

Each pollywog was brought before the king and issued a trumped up charge. As the shellbacks pulled Hans before the King, he was charged with being in King Neptune's domain without asking permission. Others were charged with spitting in the food of a shellback. Hans listened carefully as they pushed Turk forward to face the king. He was charged with the dishonor of being a pollywog.

Each man pleaded for mercy from the king for crimes committed, but it was clear no matter the defense the sailor provided for his crime, they were all going to be found guilty. Each pollywog tried to formulate a defense more creative than the last. It was no use. King Neptune found them guilty as charged and the punishment phase began.

The shellbacks lining the deck jumped into action amidst much laughter and shouting to begin the punishment. Each pollywog was required to kiss the royal baby who was a very plump shellback wearing only a diaper. His rotund stomach was greased except for a miniscule area in the center. As Hans bent over for the mandatory punishment of kissing that tiny area, another shellback whacked his butt with a paddle of wood sending his face directly into the smeary mass of grease on the large belly. As he backed away a shout went up, "All pollywogs kneel!"

Hans's knees hit the deck along with all of the other men. Suddenly he felt a strong stream of seawater pelt his bare back as the men were sprayed down. Another shout and the shellbacks formed two lines each facing the other with a narrow space between them. The lines went all the way up and down the deck.

"Pollywogs, King Neptune orders you to lie down on your back for the royal blessing."

Hans and the other men quickly laid on their backs as the royal chaplain blessed them by painting the men with a permanent purple dye. Hans was sure it was a pretty comical sight as he heard the raucous laughter from the shellbacks.

He heard another voice ring out, "Pollywogs, I am declaring a change in punishment." King Neptune intoned, "You pollywogs are ordered to the Royal Barber!"

Each pollywog stood in line to take his turn in the Royal Barber's chair where his hair was lopped off in uneven fashion with some tufts still standing here and there on each head. As soon as Hans was released from the chair, he was given to a shellback who ordered, "Time for your medicine from the Royal Dentist."

The pollywogs were ordered to open their mouths and take a dose of medicine, which was in fact a shot of Novocain. His eyes watered from the stinging and foul tasting shot. There was some hacking and coughing from the pollywogs while the shellbacks roared with laughter and approval of the punishment.

Retreating and recovering from the Royal Dentist's remedy, the pollywogs were then taken to the front edge of the deck. King Neptune ordered, "And now for your last punishment. When you have successfully made it through the gauntlet, you shall all be received into the royal order of shellbacks. Good luck!"

The pollywogs—shorn hair, red eyes, and wet skivvies—got down on their hands and knees to make their way through the gauntlet as quickly as possible. Hans was never sure but he thought he could smell rotten potatoes, coffee grounds, slippery eggs, and egg shells amidst the other garbage they crawled through. The pollywogs made their way as quickly as possible trying to avoid the intermittent paddling from the shellbacks who lined the course. It took a while to traverse the slippery, slimy path across the deck, but at the other end a shellback lifted each man up, clasped his arms around the former pollywog's shoulders, and welcomed him into the lofty atmosphere of being a newly minted shellback.

Later, as Hans showered the slop from his skin, he considered the reason for the ceremony and the day. Out here there was no shore leave, no bars, no girls. There was nowhere to go. It did not matter what your hair looked like or what colors were painted on your body. The only thing you had was each other ... brothers bound together by this war and the experiences they would endure.

He chuckled to think about seeing Turk get paddled by the shellbacks. Hans had stowed the Crossing the Line certificate the officers had handed out to the men with his gear. He wanted to remember this day when times got tough. Suddenly he realized that was at the heart of the whole matter and the purpose for the day. The ceremony had given the men a chance to take a breather, have a laugh, and share a joke, and to take a break from the fearful existence of being on a war mission. There was a special camaraderie among the crew now. They were all shellbacks and together they were off to face the enemy.

23

Home Away from Home, 1943–1944

S igning his name on his enlistment papers had swept Ton into the whirlwind of activity that had become a way of life in the Navy in 1943. Everywhere there was motion, work, and movement toward assigning men, transporting them, training them, and sending them off to defend the country. Testing, testing, testing. It was the Navy way of life.

Ton had tested his skills along with other recruits, and the Navy determined his aptitude lay in becoming a signalman. He found himself on a bus headed for the Navy training center located in Farragut, Idaho, to do the initial training and learn how to send signals by flags and semaphore, a lighted, flashing signal system for ships nearby. As always the Navy was correct in their assessment of talent, and he graduated as honor man of his class. There was no time to waste so the newly vested signalmen were transported on to Treasure Island, California, where they would undergo more training and learn about life on the sea.

Ton was allowed a short leave home arriving at the grand Union Station in Omaha before being whisked away by sister Tude and her husband, Al, to Oakdale and a joyful yet cautious reunion with his parents and Nadeen. All too soon leave was over and he was back on the train bound for California and the vessel that would be his home for the next few years.

The *USS Lindsey* and Ton Eymann came into the Navy at approximately the same time. Their lives would forever be joined although neither knew it at the time. She began life as a destroyer minelayer but ended up becoming a destroyer minesweeper—a dangerous, challenging job. The small but mighty ship was laid down in San Pedro, California, launched in March of 1944 by the widow of the man the ship was named for, and did its shakedown cruise off southern California. Aboard with the three-hundred-sixty-three-man crew was Signalman Ton Eymann who stood proudly with the other sailors as she was christened that August of 1944. She immediately set off for the war raging in the Pacific.

It seemed to Ton that life on a destroyer was much like a small town, similar to Oakdale, he thought as he climbed the stairs leading from the berthing quarters below up onto the deck. The deck level resembled the Main Street of Oakdale, he mused. If you thought of the small rooms located on board as "stores," then it was like the same thing he could find on Main Street in his hometown.

There was a "bakery"—the hot, tiny room where the cook made all the meals and baked the bread the men devoured each day. The hospital on board was known as "sick bay." The doctor there only had one bed but at least it was available to the sailors if they needed it. The tools of his trade and his medicines were carefully stacked against the bulkheads and placed in the white cupboards to use when necessary. All sailors prayed those items were only going to be used for normal illnesses and not for war wounded.

The radio room was like the newspaper and telegraph station all rolled into one. It was in this dark, often times oven-like room that the messages came in and went out. This room enabled the ship to keep contact with the outside world while they were thousands of miles away at sea in the Pacific Ocean.

The fantail or rear of the ship was like the neighborhood pub where men gathered to shoot the bull, smoke, and relax after a hard day's or night's work. The ship or tin can as she was affectionately called sometimes even had a church. Services were held on the open deck on a regular basis with the ship's chaplain leading worshippers in a non-denominational service.

The steel mesh stairways connecting the decks resembled a ladder, and the sailors became very adept at their use. Ascending from one deck up to another the men held on to the steel chains to climb and pull their way up. But descending was much faster as the men faced outward, held loosely onto the chains and slid down to the next deck.

Located below deck was the "restaurant" or mess and although the food wasn't fancy, it was ready three times a day with a big coffee urn going both day and night. In the Navy Ton had gotten into the habit, just like most sailors, of having a cup of coffee before turning into his bunk for some sleep. It didn't matter if his "night" was after the 8:00 to midnight watch or the 4:00 to 8:00 a.m. watch; it was a comfort to unwind, sitting in the mess with a hot, steamy cup of java.

The "hotel" of the ship for Ton was the forward berthing compartment. This was the area allotted to the communications specialists, and it was here he bunked with other signalmen and radiomen. Within this tight under-deck section there were no windows and only a few spare feet of area in which to move around. The bunks were actually metal frames stacked three high. The lockers for their belongings were under the bottom bunk.

Every sailor quickly staked out his territory judiciously with the slowest man ending up with the bottom bunk. The bottom bunk was to be avoided at all costs because as each duty shift changed and the sailors came and went, it was necessary to get into their lockers for personal items and clothing.

Whoever designed these destroyer minesweepers missed something important, Ton decided, because whenever anyone opened his locker, the lid hit the sailor on the bottom bunk and pushed him over. Bottom man on the totem pole took on a whole new meaning when a sailor had to sleep (or try to sleep) in that bunk.

Necessity is the mother of invention and the sailors not only used their bunks for sleeping but also for laundry purposes. The men would spread their clean clothing out under their thin mattresses and the weight of their bodies would "press" the clothing in lieu of an iron.

At first, Ton had a difficult time sleeping in the stale air and claustrophobic atmosphere of the berth, but after time, with the work load and exhaustion, it became easy to drop off to sleep no matter what. That is, if you didn't think too much about the fact that your sleeping quarters were directly over the magazine of the vessel—the compartment that stored all of the ship's ammunition.

Slightly forward of this sleeping berth were the officers' quarters, and to Ton's eye these rooms looked pretty swanky. Only two men shared bunk beds and desks and they even had small closets. The officers' mess was also coveted by the enlisted men although Ton never saw much of this area.

But, far and above, the most envied benefit for the officers were the bathrooms. Enlisted men were forced to share their bathroom with a couple hundred other men. The four sinks, four toilets, and two showers did not go very far when their use was required by so many men at the same time.

"Main Street" on the USS Lindsey continued below deck with the "Dry Goods Store." Ton knew this just had to be the most popular place on the ship. The "store" sold cigarettes, candy, razors, and items for the personal needs of the sailors. Everything was dirt cheap. There was method in this madness because at home this store would never have made a profit, but here nothing was sold to make money. The "store" and its items helped bolster the morale of the sailors and made them feel a bit closer to home.

Way out in the Pacific Ocean they could still buy the Bazooka bubble gum and Marlboro cigarettes they were used to buying in the USA. A barber shop was tucked into this floating Main Street. Although the tin can contained a designated room to cut hair, there was no barber assigned to the ship. Never at a loss, the sailors held tryouts for whichever sailor did the best job of cutting hair. There were some nasty haircuts before the winning barber was discovered!

Ton tried his best to align his ship with his hometown but like so many sailors he was often homesick and anxious for letters from home. However, Ton came to understand when you live in close quarters with men for extended periods of time, you get close to them so the men of the ship were like "neighbors" in Ton's hometown comparison.

He was indeed grateful for the friendships he formed on board. He tended to gravitate toward farm boys like himself so it was no surprise that he and Merle became best buddies. They had a lot in common since Merle hailed from a Kansas farm. Ton and Merle spent many companionable moments talking to each other about memories of the farm life they shared.

Life on the ship could get monotonous, just like in a small town, but it could never be described as dull. The sailors were always busy doing something, but all work and no play makes for no fun! The men were inventive about their shipboard amusements.

The main deck area was the location of morning calisthenics but Captain Chambers was also smart enough to allow the men to hold boxing matches. Sailors crowded around to see who would win and to place their bets on their favorite pugilist. Gambling was a large part of ship life. Men loved to play poker and make exorbitant bets. When a sailor would find himself overextended in a hot poker game yet sure his luck was about to change, he would seek out Joe. Joe, being a Christian man, never played poker, yet he was the money lender on board and he made the guys the very best deal.

He would bargain with them saying, "I will loan the money to you to change your luck and if you win, you pay me back right away. But if you lose, I will come and get you for Sunday church services on deck." The sailor would readily agree to such an easy deal, being absolutely certain he would win big and pay off his debt that very night.

But, as luck would have it, the sailors inevitable hit a dry streak at poker, staying up and playing until the wee hours, thinking that Joe would forget about his promise, only to be awakened early the next Sunday morning for a church service. Joe never forgot! Ton laughed to himself remembering the groans and swearing from an unlucky sailor as he trailed Joe to "church," because to renege on a promise was the lowest thing a sailor on board could do.

Then, of course, there were the truly creative sailors who, lacking any alcohol, created "torpedo juice." These daring, ingenious men would "borrow" some orange juice from the galley and mix it with torpedo fluid to concoct a potent alcoholic cocktail. No doubt the next day brought a hangover to end all hangovers. It was most assuredly a miracle none of them fell overboard.

There was other more tame entertainment such as movies that Ton enjoyed as did most sailors. Yet the most important Main Street store was the "Post Office." Mail call was by far the most upbeat time aboard ship and all sailors lived for the long-awaited letters from home. Those letters could describe the most mundane days in the States, tell of the town gossip, or even give the sorrowful news about the passing of an elderly relative. It did not matter in the least what the letter said. The life blood that kept morale flowing high was the mail because it alone reminded the sailors of why they were fighting and just whom they were fighting for.

If the *USS Lindsey* was a small amphibious town, then Captain Chambers was the town mayor. He was, in large part, why the morale on board was so positive. Captain Chambers was a quiet, calm leader, always in charge but he was never aloof or placed himself above the enlisted sailors. He would walk the deck and come across some of the men who, after their duty hours, were sunning themselves with their shirts off. The rules stated that all men were required to wear dungarees, chambray work shirts with the sleeves rolled down, white hats, and black socks per regulation.

The men would see Captain Chambers and jump to attention, salute, and hope for the best. He would wave them off with a shake of his wrist and tell them, "Relax boys. I don't need you to salute me. Rest while you can." And then he would turn and continue his walking tour of the deck. The men, on the whole, loved and respected Captain Chambers for his kind, yet firm command of the vessel.

The ship even had its town "school." It was called Identification School and was held every day in the enlisted men's mess area. Each day the school instructed the men who were not on watch, and all sailors were required to attend. The men sat and were shown slide after slide of Japanese aircraft. They were taught about the capabilities of each plane and were drilled on how to identify each and every one of them. The sailors were quizzed on how fast the plane flew and the maneuvers the plane could make as every detail was noted.

The men could all see why the gunners needed to be sharp with the identification process. Their rapid identification could mean more precise shooting and very well might save their lives. Yet they had to wonder if all sailors needed to know this information.

Ton said to Merle, "I always liked school but this endless repetition and drill of those slides is going to drive me out of my mind!"

Still, they listened and learned because they knew they might be the one called upon to describe to a gunner the type of aircraft coming at them. Their knowledge might save many lives.

The marine village also had the equivalent of the "corner vegetable market." It was common knowledge among the sailors the cooks kept potatoes in the food lockers on board. However, these potato lockers were never actually locked the way the food lockers were. Most of the time, the cooks and stewards on ship were African American. They were not allowed to serve in other capacities. Those cooks were clever. They looked the other way as sailors would grab a raw potato now and again to use as a snack. It was well known among the crew that raw potatoes helped ward off seasickness, and more than one sailor had gobbled a potato in order to not lose his lunch while the ship pitched and rolled on the high seas.

The captain and the cooks knew the sailors were always hungry. Good, readily available food on board was as important to the morale of the crew as anything. Potato snitching was not considered a serious crime.

However, some crimes were serious. Continuing with his analysis of his ship as a town Ton thought about the "jail" located on the fantail. Rule infractions earned a sailor time in the on-board brig. This brig included a guard to watch over him at all times. Ton wondered just why. Where was a "criminal" going to escape to when the ship was hundreds of miles from the nearest shore? Ton was tickled with his comparison of life aboard a ship to his hometown. It occurred to him to write about it in his next letter home. His mom would be happy to hear how well they were taking care of her son. But now, it was time to get to work.

He left his berthing compartment and headed for the first set of ladders leading up to the deck. By now, he was used to the metal steps and chain strips and could take several steps at a time. Although he was only five feet ten inches tall, he had to duck his head. Again Ton was bemused by the design of the boat. The "ceiling" was made for a man six feet tall but that did not take into account the steam pipes that spanned the length of the ship. Experienced sailors were well practiced in where and when to duck.

The first set of stairs he scaled led to the main deck. From there he rounded the corner, passing the entrance to the radio room, and made his way to the next set of stairs that led up to the bridge. The pilot house was located there.

This area was the "mayor's office" of the floating town. Captain Chambers commanded the entire ship from this room and the ship was steered from here. The captain's brown padded chair rose up in the corner and looked out over the bow of the ship. Captain Chambers was the only man on board with his own cabin. He not only had one cabin, he, in fact, had two. Below deck, his cabin had a bed, closet, and his own bathroom. But it was the other cabin that was highly important. It was located to the rear of the pilot house and was as compact as a closet with only a bunk and a sink. The captain often used this room when things heated up and he needed to stay close to the command center in order to oversee the operation of the ship.

Ton poked his face in to see what was going on but then headed directly to the side and rear of the pilot house. Here was his duty station. In the outside air on the bridge level was his flag bag and his semaphore. The long, narrow canvas enclosure contained all of the flags he needed to do his work as a signalman. In the daytime a blue pennant with a stripe of the American flag flew to show that the *USS Lindsey* was a commissioned American ship. By night, a flag of white stars on a deep blue background flew.

The flags of letters and sets he needed in order to message other ships were all folded and contained in the flag bag with the rigging to hang them close by. Several of the flag lines now flapped in the stiff wind. Ton would hoist the flags as needed. These means of communication were crucial to the safety and security of the vessel, especially when no radio communication was allowed, and in war situations that was often.

He checked his semaphore. This metal structure contained a crank that turned the metal slats and sent out bursts of light. Ton was able to send light signals in Morse code to nearby ships. In tough situations this proved an excellent, quick way to communicate. He was in constant motion during his watches. He sent, received, and scribed messages constantly. He perused his area of the bridge. His bulkhead or wall, protecting him from the outside, was only a partial one, about half the height of a regular bulkhead. Ton had it in his mind if and when they encountered enemy aircraft he meant to put this bulkhead and as many as he could between him and any attacking plane.

Ton set about his daily duties and compared just how much life on the *USS Lindsey* was like his own small town. Although given the choice he would readily go home at a moment's notice, any day, any time. He was satisfied that he was, nonetheless, in a town where he felt he belonged.

Ton with semaphore aboard the USS Lindsey.

24

Mailbag, Summer 1944

D ear Mom and Dad,
I am writing to tell you that after a year in Hawaii I have applied to be a pilot. I know you will be shocked and probably angry with me after learning this. You already know this has been a very easy, enjoyable duty but I feel I must do more to help the war effort. I am capable of so much more than driving a jeep! Hawaii has indeed been a wonderful experience for me and I realize the work at the hospital ship is important. However, I am such a small part of that. I want to be a part of a something bigger! I want to learn to fly an airplane. It would be fun to chase the Japanese or Germans around.

I am bound for a program at Oklahoma A and M. I already got my three letters of recommendation from George Hunter, Al Bates, and Harold Allen. These three letters really helped me get into the pilot program and I am forever grateful to these men. Be sure to thank them for me when you see them as I don't know when I will next be home. I am tickled pink with this duty and I can't wait to start learning how to fly gas-propelled planes.

I understand this will be hard for you to accept but it is my choice of what I want to do. Hawaii has been a good start for me but I long for more action. I know I will be in dangerous situations but it is what I must do. I hope you will accept and support my decision and that you will be proud of me.

Your loving son, Chub

Dear Sis,

God damn Army! After only one month here in Oklahoma the Army is scrapping the pilot program. The explanation was that they need men for other things with the way the war is going now. They told me, "You are going back into the infantry." This time I was tickled sour!

I am now in Gainesville, Texas, for three months of Army training. We will ship out to France when we are finished. Please do a favor for me and tell Mom and Dad. I don't have the right words to let them know where I am headed and what will be in store for me. I am being assigned to the 102nd Medical Battalion. I have been told my duty will be to drive for some big-wig over there.

Well, I miss the farm and everyone there. Kiss everyone for me and take care of Mom and Dad.

Your brother, Chub

Chub in pilot program in Oklahoma, 1944.

Part IV

Radioman/bombardier Turk stands next to his TBM Avenger on the USS Sangamon.

Danger and Duty

25

Taffy One, October 1944

The pre-dawn hours were punctuated by spells of rain pelting the ship in the pitch-black darkness of October in the Pacific. Occasionally the rain squalls gave way to some clearing and a spectacular view of the star-packed sky. Among the ships of the American force located there was the *USS Sangamon*. Hans and Turk had both been assigned to the *USS Sangamon* and together they had spent the last months in action.

Life began for the *Sangamon* as an oiler. But as the war raged in the Pacific, and it became crystal clear that planes and more planes were needed, the vessel had hastily been converted from an oiler to an escort aircraft carrier or a CVE.

While the ship was undergoing its transformation at the shipyard, a flight deck, hangar deck, and aircraft catapult were added, along with a few other innovations. The ship stretched out to five hundred fifty-three feet while the deck alone was five hundred and two feet of that. Indeed, the ship had an odd look about it, as if someone had glued a flight deck meant for something much larger to the insignificant ship beneath it, but the CVE was efficient and produced results.

Hans knew the crews of the big-boy carriers mockingly referred to the CVEs as jeep carriers or baby flattops yet they always got the job done. Although the crew of the *Sangamon* was proud of their efforts to win the war, they too joked about the ship by saying CVE stood for Combustible, Vulnerable, and Expendable.

Hans and Turk had both been assigned to the ship as radiomen/ bombardiers in TBM Avengers. The Avengers were torpedo bomber airplanes capable of delivering destruction to enemy ships. The Avenger was a flying workhorse and was considered to be the hardest working bomber of the Pacific. As radiomen aboard Avengers they had both logged hundreds of hours of flight time. Some of the hours had been spent in battle, some dropping bombs on land-based targets, and some searching for lost crewmen. Although the entire ship and the Avenger crews had been on high alert and were battle ready, as Hans climbed up the metal ladder to the deck, he considered his current location in the Leyte Gulf, Philippines, to the places, sights, smells, and sounds he had seen and heard in the last year.

As a radioman on an Avenger, he had been through some of the most horrific and brutal battles in the Pacific. He pondered the meaning of the word *Pacific*. One of the guys told him that it meant peaceful, but that meaning had nothing to do with what he had seen and done at Tarawa, Saipan, Tinian, and Morotai, to name just a few of the small islands in the South Pacific where battles had taken place.

Hans stood on the gray and darkened deck of the baby flat top that had taken him to all of those places. He decided he would never have seen such beauty, the white sands of crisp clean beaches, the green palm trees amidst the lush jungles of tropical islands, and the blue, curling waves that lapped over them if he had not joined the Navy.

At the same moment, he recoiled at how those beaches looked during the fierce combat he had taken part in and witnessed. Tarawa, with the bodies of Marines stacked one upon the other, bodies caught in the wire barriers erected by the Japanese at the beach, dismembered bodies floating on waves and being tossed about before being dragged in and out with the tide like broken seashells.

He could still hear the voice in his headset commanding his Avenger crew as they landed on the tiny atoll, "Look forward, don't look back!" Yet, he had already seen for himself the death and complete devastation the war had brought to the island and to the men who fought and perished there.

At this point in the war he was just glad to be alive for another day. General Douglas MacArthur was the reason he was here in the waters near the Philippine Islands. The corn-cob–pipe smoking Field Marshall had vowed to return to the Philippines after losing the island to the Japanese in 1942. Return he did that October of 1944 and along with him all the destroyers, carriers, and cruisers that would support the landing force. The task forces of the U.S. Navy all lay in positions just off the islands of Samar, Leyte, and Mindanao in the Philippine Sea. The *Sangamon* was part of Task Force One or Taffy One as they were called, the southernmost force, while Taffy Two was just north of them, and Taffy Three the most northern force.

All three Taffy forces were sending bombers to support MacArthur's landing by striking at the Japanese-held airfields, ammunition sites, enemy targets on the ground, and even dropping leaflets heralding the return of the Americans out of their bomb bays. Hans and Turk had both flown many bombing missions since arriving in the waters of the Philippines.

Now, everyone had been put on high alert. Hans was aware the task force was preparing for the most important battle of the war and that his Avenger crew would be part of it. But, right now, the Americans were playing a game of cat and mouse with the Japanese, waiting to see where and how they would strike and then strike back at the most opportune moment with the best planes, pilots, and ships that the U.S. Navy had to give.

The sailors and aviators were aware that Admiral Bull Halsey of Task Force Thirty-Four was positioned at the mouth of the San Bernardino Strait and would intercept and be the first group to take on the Japanese Center Force. With its massive battleships and huge entourage of accompanying ships, the servicemen were sure Bull could handle anything the Japanese had to throw at them and keep the Taffys safe to continue their work.

Hans offered up a small prayer that after a year of constant combat he and Turk would make it through another battle together but he wondered, *Was this the one where their luck would run out?* He was not sure of the answer. "How long can a guy's luck hold out?" he muttered to himself.

With almost seven hundred hours of flight time logged to his credit, he had seen it all. Some of the most frightening times were not the ones in the heat of battle but instead happened right on the deck of the ship. He had seen planes catapulted into the air from the deck only to lose altitude and fall into the sea. He had witnessed pilots and planes careen over the edge of the ship on takeoff, crashing into the choppy waves below. He saw pilots who had missed their "catch" to stop their aircraft and make a safe landing and so instead continued their path falling into the ocean waves and certain death. He had even seen one pilot decapitated while trying to land, failing to hook the wire, crashing on deck, and wrecking both himself and the plane.

Hans had also experienced several close calls including the day a wheel had blown out on takeoff. There had been nothing else to do but fly the mission without thinking too much about how they would be able to land the plane. Hans admired and respected the skill of his pilot, Lt. Stouffer, on that day because, sure enough, on that rolling airstrip called a deck, he was able to land the plane on one wheel.

But one brush with death, in particular, scared Hans. He had been sitting in his plane, waiting in line for their turn to take off. He felt an unusual vibration in the plane and sensed something was not right. Looking out his tiny window he could see deck hands running toward his plane, shouting and waving their arms in a frenzy. An acrid, metallic smell penetrated through his radio position at the rear of the plane. He could smell burning metal when he heard someone shout, "Get out, get out!"

Hans was no fool and he immediately slithered through the small door of his plane only to look back and see the tail being chewed off by the propeller of the plane behind him. This chewed up section was only inches away from where, only seconds before, he had been sitting. Hans felt a huge rush of relief wash over him after being saved from that near miss.

There was no sense in dwelling on the past though, and he swiftly switched gears. Hans was a man of action, not prone to overthink any situation but rather to solve problems and then take matters into his own hands and do something. He was ready, willing, and able to do whatever was asked of him to end this war and get everyone home quickly. In reality, this was the bottom line that every man on board was fighting for.

The days of tension and waiting continued for the *Sangamon*. From the instant General MacArthur had set foot back on Philippine soil, the ships and planes of Taffy One, Two, and Three were working hard to support the landing of troops in Leyte Gulf. They were now poised to retake the land that had cost so dearly in American lives.

With clockwork-like precision the aviators and aircraft of the Task Forces had launched continual and regular flights against enemy positions on the islands. The Avengers had also flown cover for the landing forces. Since October 20 the work had been nonstop, and Hans and Turk had flown many hours of bombing runs. The flight crews were exhausted. Now everyone was on edge and vigilant for the confrontation with the Japanese surface force they knew was coming sooner or later. For the aviators and sailors who had been continually fighting and at sea for over a year now, much more was soon to be asked.

Hans returned below deck to look for Turk. He had not seen him since they returned from their last bombing mission. His search ended when he found his brother below deck in the mess.

"Eating as usual, I shoulda known where to look for you first!" Hans called out to Turk who was seated at a table chowing down.

Without missing a beat or a bite Turk glanced up at Hans and said, "Hey, Hans, I haven't seen you in a while but it's good to see your ugly mug!" Hans sat down and the boys bantered back and forth, regaling each other with their latest mission stories. For a while they joked and laughed together until the talk turned to home. Speaking of home forced them to both pause and consider just what was at stake—the true reason they were in the Pacific and just how much they would lose if they did not return from the missions ahead of them. Neither one could bring himself to talk much about the farm, their parents, or their siblings so they glazed quickly over the news they had each received from pals in Oakdale.

Finally Turk said, "Now Hans, you be careful out there. You know I promised the folks I would bring you home safe and sound. You know that Dad will beat me black and blue if I damned well don't do it. You always were the hothead of the family so take it easy. Don't be a hero. Keep control of that temper of yours before you go up, ya hear? Watch out for yourself and don't feel you have to defeat the whole Japanese Navy by yourself, got it?"

Hans looked up from his chow into the face that looked so much like his own. He sensed his brother's mood had turned serious. There were no words he could say or at least not the right words to give in response to Turk's plea. Hans's gaze did not falter as he stared back into Turk's eyes. Both of them clearly understood the importance of the exchange.

RRRRRRROOOOO. RRRROOOOOO. The klaxon sounded General Quarters. The voice over the loud speaker shouted, "Battle stations! Pilots be alert and ready." Startled by the noise the boys jumped up from the table, pulling their gear on as they ran.

Zekes, the Japanese carrier-based fighter bombers, screamed and buzzed through the sky overhead like furious wasps. Turk and Hans ran to the planes stacked up like playing cards on the exposed gun-metal expanse of the deck. All around them men headed toward their planes. As Hans inserted himself into the miniscule compartment and took his place on the tiny bench, he recalled the look in Turk's eyes. He was grateful he had been given the chance to talk to him one last time because looking up at the hoard of roaming Japanese planes directly overhead, he was not at all certain whether he would return and talk to Turk ever again.

Queen for a Day, 1944

Mick's feet hurt as he trudged down the dirt road toward the farm, his younger sisters trailing behind him. He had passed yet another long and tedious day at school. For a fourteen-year-old boy, sitting in a desk the entire day was more than he could bear, especially since he was aware of all the work that awaited him at home. But, more than that, he longed for the freedom of the fresh outdoor air, the sounds of the animals who needed his care, and the camaraderie of being with his father, whether that was milking cows or cutting hay. He wished he could be at the farm with his dad more often since, at times now, his dad seemed far away and unreachable. Maybe if he were there, things would be better for his dad.

His thoughts turned to his brothers—four of them gone now, away fighting a war. Mick missed them more than he would ever admit and wondered if he too would soon be following them. The only redeeming thing about school, he mused to himself, was the girls. Mick smiled as he recalled walking hand in hand with Mary at lunch recess today. For sure, Mick was never without a girlfriend with his chocolate brown eyes, tawny skin that glowed in the sunlight, and best of all his quick wit and ability to make anyone smile, except maybe the teacher.

Mick's senses were on high alert as the three children neared the house. Lately, Mick could never be sure in what state he would find his father. Would he be working in the fields or barn as normal or would he be sitting silently alone in the house? A ripple of trepidation coursed through Mick as he realized there were more of the brooding, unspeaking days now than there used to be before his brothers left home.

He always tried his best jokes and pranks to pull his father out of the shadowy funk that overtook him from time to time, but nothing seemed to work anymore.

Mick recognized and understood his role in the family had changed. He now had to be the responsible man of the house when his father looked to be incapable. His brothers were gone, serving in the war, his sisters were too young to help, and the older girls were gone, taking care of their own families at this point in time. Willingly, Mick milked the cows, picked the corn, and helped his father maintain the farm in any way he could. But Mick lived every day with unease about his father and even more with anxiety for his mother.

Hattie would ask him, "Mick, why is he like this?" But there was no answer to that question and no comfort for the worry and fear that inhabited their minds. Some days Chriss was normal as pie and other days he was gone from them, unreachable in his own world, impervious to their pleas.

As Mick walked through the door, he knew today was one of the black days. His father was nowhere to be seen, and Hattie seemed frantic to tend to the work there was to accomplish yet today.

She called to him immediately, "Son, I need to get some things from the store and I need your help to get there." Hattie had never learned to drive and, even if she had, the old Model T was temperamental.

"Sure, Mom," Mick replied quickly but then instantaneously remembered checking the car over last weekend. He realized they had a problem. The tread on the front tires was threadbare at best and was just barely hanging onto the wheel rims. The back

Mick Eymann back home on the farm. School photo.

tires were only minimally in better shape and Mick had been wondering just how they were going to baby those tires along and make them last. With wartime rationing Mick knew tires were impossible to get now and even if they were available, they had no money to buy them. They desperately needed to keep the car going and spare cash was nowhere in sight.

What to do? Mick thought the situation over carefully. He sure loved his mom and would never do anything that might hurt her in any way, but Hattie Mae was definitely on the plump side. She had been full figured as a young girl and after giving birth to eleven babies she tended to the fleshy, rounded side now. At her height of five feet, she carried quite a bit of extra weight. If she sat in the front seat with Mick those tires just might blow, leaving them with no transportation at all.

Mick, on the other hand, was a tall string bean who had to stand twice to make a shadow. Suddenly an idea and a plan jumped into his head.

"Hey, Mom," Mick offered as he opened the back door of the car for Hattie, "you sit in the back, okay? It is much more comfortable and you can stretch your legs out and rest a bit while I drive you to town. Kind of like those limousines with chauffeurs we saw in the movies. You know … big city stuff."

Hattie turned to look at Mick and she smiled wearily but happily, "Oh, Mick, you are such a good son, always thinking of me and worrying for me. Yes, I do believe I will take you up on that offer, I will just sit back here and take a quick rest."

Mick heaved a huge sigh of relief. Catastrophe avoided. The front tires were safe for another day and they just might last longer if he could keep talking Hattie into riding in the back while he drove her around. With a warm smile for his mother, he closed her door and hopped into the car, and they set off for town. Son in front, mother in back, feeling like a queen.

We're Hit Back Here!
October 1944

" Holy shit, this area is hot," Hans said as the plane flew from the *Sangamon* and into the fray taking place overhead. With a 2,000-pound torpedo loaded in the bomb bay, their mission today was vastly different from their usual bombing missions on the island. Hans and his Avenger crew were on their way to assist Task Force Three or Taffy Three and to attack the Japanese Surface Force. But first they had to evade the marauding Zekes who were intent on stopping them.

From the minute the plane catapulted off the deck there was never a moment in the radio compartment of the Avenger when Hans was not busy doing something. He pulled his light flight suit tighter around him with his leather-gloved hands. His leather bombardier jacket felt warm and he was grateful for the heat because the temperature plummeted as the plane gained altitude. After months of constant wear and tear the jacket felt as smooth as a baby's behind. Headphones covered his ears as he monitored the greenish cathode tubes of his radio set in front of him.

Hans wondered if he had been chosen for radioman duty because of his scores and abilities or because of his size. If he were an inch or two taller, legs a bit longer, or even weighed a few more pounds, he would never have fit in the radioman's seat. Being a radioman/bombardier wasn't for anyone who had claustrophobia either. Cramped in between the small seat that folded up and down, the radio equipment, and the fuselage, there sure wasn't any extra space. It often felt to him as if he had been shut up in a closet. The one redeeming feature was a modest-sized window. Although it was next to impossible to see out of it, the window brought in some light.

He was too busy with his work to look out much though. Hans knew his job was important and he liked doing it. He recalled the sign he had read once on board the ship: Fighters Make Movies, Bombers Made History.

Truer words were never said. With those words in mind he put himself back to work. Although their primary mission had been to bomb the island and support the landing forces on Leyte as much as possible, in the eyes of the crew the first and most important job for the Avengers now was to seek out and destroy or disable Japanese battleships. Without the all-powerful behemoths the Japanese Navy would be dead in the water.

Every Avenger crew scanned the horizon for a pagoda-like structure atop a ship. Only the leviathans of the Japanese Imperial Navy contained these floating towers. Some of the *Sangamon*'s Avenger crews carried out their missions of strafing and bombing the main island, but each one was continually searching for the prize: the Japanese fleet and its source of might, the battleships.

Seated in the belly of the plane, Hans could sense the 2,000-pound aerial torpedo mounted and waiting in the bay underneath the aircraft as he continued to watch and monitor from his radioman position. About fifty some miles north, just off of Samar Island, the ships, planes, and men of Taffy Three were being attacked by the full force of the Japanese Navy. Taffy Three was a small force of escort carriers and destroyers and was being mercilously pummeled by the mighty Imperial Navy.

This situation was never meant to take place because Bull Halsey was supposed to intercept the Japanese at San Bernardino Strait. To the horror of Taffy Three, Bull Halsey had been duped into leaving the strait unguarded. The Japanese knew Halsey would always seek a confrontation with an aircraft carrier, so they positioned and were ready to sacrifice a portion of their forces as a decoy, drawing Halsey to the north and away from the battle.

Taffy Three was in deep trouble as they valiantly fought against the fiercest battleships the Japanese Navy possessed. It was a little like throwing pebbles at a gun, but fight on they did, never backing down. The call had gone up for any and all aviators to rescue and aide Taffy Three. The action they had all anticipated, feared, and yet sought was finally here and it was do or die now.

Turk was equally as caught up and busy in his aircraft with the same responsibilities and duties of a radioman. Lt. Katz was his pilot and they had flown many hours together. Turk had all the confidence in the world in Katz's skills as a pilot. They had won the Distinguished Flying Cross for their bravery in the battles of the Pacific. Although Turk's primary mission was the strafing and bombing of Leyte, he fervently hoped they would score a hit on a battleship, the most prized kind of hit, within the next few hours. Time would tell as the Avengers made their way through the Philippine skies toward their meeting with destiny.

Clouds gathered and discharged intermittent periods of rain over the battle zone. As quickly as the clouds gathered, they also moved on. And so in these periods of clouds and rain the ships of Taffy Three tried to hide whenever possible. Stretching out on the horizon the aviators could see the small ships of Taffy Three assembled and fighting mightily. There were areas of gray-black smoke screening the destroyers while the Japanese ships lobbed shells at them. The red, blue, and orange shells landed all around the force creating a scene that appeared to have been painted on the horizon. At times the colored shells did their job of placing the ship and zeroing in to make a kill. With ear-shattering whistles and explosions, the shells found their mark, blowing metal, men, and ammunition into oblivion.

The planes droned on toward the battle and hoped they would be in time to rescue at least some of Taffy Three. Soon enough Lt. Stouffer announced, "Dead ahead I have in sight a convoy of light and heavy carriers, destroyers, and, holy cow, it looks like we got us some battleships! Let's get 'em boys!" he crowed and began to take the plane lower.

Outside orange balls and puffs of smoke from the Japanese antiaircraft artillery known as AA or ack-ack, crackled and zipped around the plane. Hans listened to the pings of AA fire erupt all around the plane. He was sure some of the pings hit the plane but there was no major damage. Yet Lt. Stouffer's crew had the reputation for flying in the lowest in order to do the most damage. So far, luck had been with them because they had always made it back even though the plane had been hit many times. Hans and the crew had seen plenty of AA fire but they had a job to do. Low and slow ... the motto of the Avenger ... it gets the job done. Hans mapped the coordinates of the battleship as the plane continued its drop toward the Japanese armada.

Stouffer shouted, excitement evident in his voice, "We got us one, boys. There she is! A perfect Nip battleship and she's ours for the taking!"

The force of American planes swarmed the Japanese convoy, destroyers, cruisers, and the prize, the magnificent battleships. They appeared like fireflies around the ships, zigging and zagging to avoid the lightning-fast Zekes who were protecting the convoy. Rising and falling, the planes positioned themselves to get the perfect aim and score their hits.

The effort of this monumental sea battle took all of their concentration and ability. Hans was not surprised when he felt the plane drop down for him to get a better read on the ship and position the torpedo drop. Lt. Stouffer had been able to elude the Zekes and now he saw his opening. He made a large swoop and veered straight toward the battleship. As Hans looked through the open weapon bay directly underneath him, he coordinated the timing and sighted the ship. Hans relayed the information to Stouffer, and, in what they hoped would be the ideal moment, the torpedo was released.

The Avenger began to climb out of the dive. As the plane lifted, the crew waited to see what would happen. Although it had been only seconds since the beginning of the attack, it felt like an eternity had passed as their plane gained altitude and the crew anticipated the result. Suddenly, the aircraft gave a mechanical shudder as they felt rather than saw their torpedo hit its mark. Rising in the air and circling back around they could see fire, smoke, water, and oil spouting from the deck of the gashed battleship. The three-man crew cheered! Hans let out a huge whoop of satisfaction. Stouffer dove the plane down toward the battleship to strafe the monstrous ship.

The next sounds they heard however were not from the wounded ship. Thud, ping, bam, clang, zing. The predatory Avenger had escaped the Zekes but had not escaped the AA fire this time. Low and slow was the way to hit the mark, but it was also the most dangerous way to fly. This time the Avenger had caught intense enemy fire. They did not have much time to celebrate as Stouffer's slightly panicked voice came through the headset, "The plane has taken a hit and we are losing altitude. We may be going down. Get ready!"

In the rear of the plane Hans did not need to be told. He could smell the smoke and burning metal of the plane. From the damaged underbelly of the aircraft he yelled to Stouffer, "We're hit back here."

Stouffer fought with his controls. "There must be a hole in the tail," he screamed. "Hang on!" The plane began to pitch and yaw wildly. The controls in Stouffer's hands were not responding to anything he tried. The jubilant mood in the plane was replaced by sheer terror as the plane began to lose altitude rapidly and spin toward the unfriendly sea.

Hans's knees hit the fuselage hard and his elbows pounded against the radio gauges in front of him. Hans desperately wished he could help Stouffer gain control of the spinning, swirling plane as it fell through the Philippine sky. But there was no direct route through the fuselage of the damaged and wounded Avenger. There was no way for Hans to reach the pilot.

Through the open weapons bay Hans could see the puffs of AA fire still striking the disabled aircraft. Hans sat trapped in the bilge surrounded tightly by the tubes, wires, and gauges of his compartment. Helpless, he prayed, "Lord, help us get outta this and forgive me for all the things I ever done wrong!"

He struggled to maintain some sense of equilibrium as the plane careened wildly through the skies over the waters of the Philippine Sea and toward its cold, dark, and menacing depths.

Amazingly, in seconds Hans felt the plane slow its descent, right itself slightly, and regain a bit of balance as Stouffer fought the controls to take back the plane. At least they were no longer swirling and banking precariously from side to side. Hans quickly began to test his equipment.

He heard Stouffer's thick voice through the headphones, "Everyone okay? Looks like we limped out of that fight. That battleship may have punched us once or twice but we're not down yet. Hang on tight!"

The crippled plane steered a course toward the island of Leyte. The tense crew held their breath as they neared Tacloban airbase. Hans could see that the landing strip there was actually nothing more than a muddy path, pockmarked by bomb craters and covered with wrecked machinery. The Americans had repaired the airstrip as best they could by filling it with crushed coral, but takeoffs and landings there were precarious at best.

After the rough, rocky landing the crew collectively let out a sigh of relief. As Hans disembarked he overheard an Army major declare, "There's nothing for you Navy guys here. There's a war to fight on Leyte ya know."

Without missing a beat Lt. Stouffer shot back, "Listen, buddy, Taffy Three has been supporting you guys for days and right now they are under attack from a big-ass Japanese surface force including battleships. Now we just torpedoed that monster out there belching black smoke, and I sure hope it is sinking, but we need fuel, bombs, and ammo to get back into the fight. So patch up that hole in the tail, give us what we need, and get us back up in the air pronto. I promise you, if you don't help us repair and rearm then pretty soon the only bombs you are going to see will be Japanese and they will be falling directly on this airfield!"

A message from Captain Whitehead, the Seventh Fleet's Commander of Support Aircraft sealed the deal. He "invited" all orphaned CVE pilots to land at Tacloban and reform groups to continue the battle. The Army airbase workers got busy, and the Avenger was hastily repaired, refueled, and rearmed. Hans looked at the tail section and prayed the patch job would hold together as the Avenger crew got back on their plane and headed back to the battle.

Stouffer wasted no time getting into the thick of things. However, this time there was no torpedo. The plane's bomb bay was loaded. Hans worked ferverishly to plot coordinates as the plane approached the Japanese ships. Again and again Stouffer dove down toward the battleship to release his bombs and do the most damage possible.

Hans heard the cracks and pings of AA fire again hitting the plane. Lord only knew how much more the plane could take. Suddenly, Hans felt the aircraft tremble and quake. Immediately the plane began to lose altitude and shimmy wildly.

All became quiet among the crew for a few agonizing seconds. Finally, Stouffer's voice could be heard again. In a matter-of-fact voice, he explained, "Boys, I am guessing this time the tail has been shredded by that AA fire. Our balance is precarious and we got a nose heavy plane here. I think I can keep 'er gliding for a while unless we get hit again. But we definitely need to get this bird landed soon. There is no way we are gonna make it back to the *Sangamon*. But I am gonna do everything I can to land us on one of Taffy Three's escort carriers before we have to ditch. Get yourself ready. It might be a rough, wet landing."

Hans had been expecting these words but they still sent a chill up his spine. He swallowed hard. "Dad gum it, I hate to swim," Hans moaned but he checked his life jacket harness one more time, pulled it tight, and braced himself for whatever was to come next. The plane shuddered and bumped along in its downward flight path. Everyone on board worked quickly and as hard as they could to prepare. But each tick of the clock brought the murky, cold, terrifying water closer and closer to the plane. The crew sat mute, fear gripping their bellies for what lay ahead of them.

28

Letters from France, Fall 1944

Dear Betty,

    I am writing to you as I sit and wait to board the ship that will take me to France. Standing in this long line of soldiers I have only a few minutes to scratch out a line or two to you. Would you please fill everyone else in on what is going on here with me because I do not have time to write to all.

    I couldn't believe it when I looked down the long row of soldiers waiting here at the dock. It turns out we are boarding the same damn transport ship that took me to Hawaii! If that don't beat all because now it's hauling me over to France! I can't say that I'm not disappointed about the pilot training being cancelled but there is nothing I can do about that now. It's funny though, I am on my way to France to do exactly what Dad feared and I know I could possibly be fighting against my very own relatives. But I don't have much time to dwell on that either because I already have my new orders. I am getting ready to be the driver for the company commander when I get to France. Seems like I have had enough experience with that anyway! But I doubt it will be anything like driving in Hawaii. Guess I will be finding out soon enough. Take care and tell everyone hello from me!

    Your brother, Chub

October, 1944

Dear Mom and Dad,

Here is your son writing to you from France after a long miserable trip over in that huge transport ship. The food was just as terrible as the first time I was transported by that damn ship. The sleeping berths went on forever and we were stacked three or four guys high so you had barely enough room for your body to slip into your bunk without hitting the guy above you. The rows of bunks just went on and on forever … it looked like it took up an area the size of a football field!

I miss home and France seems even farther away from Oakdale than Hawaii did. I sure don't see any palm trees or warm sandy beaches here! The city looks drab and worn out. I am sure the people and the land here have been through quite a bit with the Nazi invasion and the fighting that went on here. How is the harvest going this year, Dad? Sure wish I could be there to help you and I am hoping to make it home for spring planting. I am eager to get going, win this war, and get back to the farm.

Well, the sergeant is yelling at us to get our gear and get moving so I need to sign off. It seems we are to march into France and they tell us we will bivouac at the radio station the Americans have set up just inland from here. When I think about it I have to laugh … I have been from one side of the world to the other. Not bad for a small town, farm boy from Nebraska.

Your loving son, Chub

October, 1944 – Western Union Telegram

Mr. and Mrs. Chriss Eymann

Regret to inform you that your son, George Eymann, was this October wounded in the performance of duty and service of his country. To prevent possible aid to our enemies we cannot divulge more information at this time. You will be advised as reports of condition are received.

The Adjutant General

Chub Eymann, Army photo, 1944.

29

Anguish Aboard the *USS Sangamon*, October 1944

The American and Japanese forces traded punches with each other throughout this day of appalling battle—each one counting both many hits and an equal amount of losses. The sea around the battle area was a mass of oil with some of the spots burning here and there, releasing acrid black smoke. Portions of ships floated within this slippery sea, and here and there the bobbing heads of American sailors could be seen. The Philippine Sea was a ghastly sight of death and destruction.

Adding to the eerie atmosphere were the colored splashes laid in the water by Japanese shells seeking their targets. The smell of cordite, burned flesh, and blood was everywhere. The scene was a biblical hell indeed. The noise in the area was unworldly and unlike anything previously heard by the sailors as the Japanese battleships unleashed their payloads against the small vessels of Taffy Three. It was David versus Goliath, the force of Taffy Three was fighting against unbelievable odds ... and they were hanging on ... but just by a thread.

The planes of the *Sangamon* had joined the battle to aide Taffy Three but now, hours later, they began to straggle back to the ship, short on fuel, ammunition, and energy. They had dropped their torpedoes and bombs on the Japanese Imperial Navy, attempting to help Taffy Three in any way they could, but out of fuel had returned to their ship to regroup. The landing signal officer brought the planes in by their normal counter-clockwise circle pattern. General quarters was still on but as the battle-worn pilots landed, the crews went below to get some food, a stiff drink, a cigarette, and a bit of rest before they reentered the fray, while the crews prepared their battered planes for more action.

Turk and his crew disembarked from the Avenger and started to file below deck like the others. Turk stopped and gazed over the planes and crews, searching for Hans as he did after every mission.

Lt. Katz noticed his concern and he knew why. He said, "C'mon, Turk, let's get some chow while the plane is readied. Hans will be back soon."

Turk shook his head and responded, "I'm gonna wait here for a while and talk to some of the crews. I want to find out if any of them saw Hans's plane. I'll feel better if I know he is on his way back and someone may have seen him."

Katz turned to continue below deck but stopped to try one more time, "Suit yourself, Turk, but you know Hans will find you when he gets back." Turk just shook his head slowly again. Katz knew that when the quiet, stubborn farm boy made up his mind, no one would be able to change it.

Turk scanned the skies watching plane after plane land on deck. Minutes ticked by slowly as he kept watch. Minutes turned into hours as the crews resumed flights and missions. The day wore on, the battle continued. Turk's crew flew another mission and landed on board yet again.

There was anticipatory chatter among the deck crews. "We heard rumors that the Japanese force has turned tail and sailed back north. Guess Taffy Three was more than they could take. Only too bad they didn't meet Halsey and the big boys!"

Turk didn't know what to believe but he did know he needed to see and talk to Hans. He began to question the arriving crews about anything they had seen or heard of Hans. Finally, one of the pilots recently returned in the last wave stepped up to address Turk, "I can't be certain and I sure as hell hope I am wrong, but I saw Stouffer's plane drop low over what looked like a mountain of a Japanese battleship. I did see them gain altitude but then it looked like the tail took some flak. It appeared to have at least one hole in it, bout a yard wide but it was still flying when I last saw it. It was right after that all hell broke loose from that damn battleship—fire, smoke, explosions—and we got the hell out of there."

Turk fell silent. He was aware that Hans's pilot was one determined SOB. They usually came the closest to any ship they attacked, but he was just not ready to accept or believe what he had just heard. They had taken flak before and had come back to tell about it. He managed to mumble "thanks" but any other words got stuck in his throat and he felt sick. Hans was his brother. He was responsible for getting him back to Oakdale safely and for taking care of him just like he had taken care of all of his brothers his entire life. They had gotten through seven hundred hours of flying time together on the same ship. It was not possible; it was unthinkable that something had happened to Hans now.

Turk sat down, numbed by the news he had just received. Memories of his brother flooded his mind. All he could see was that scrawny kid with huge blue eyes wearing patched and worn overalls at least two sizes too big for him. No shoes on his feet.

Turk recalled the day the boys decided to steal some watermelons from Roy Emerson. The four of them walked one mile north of their farm, crossed the river and then hopped over his fence. They crept quietly into the garden to "borrow" the sweet treat. Sitting smack dab in the middle of the garden, they devoured as much as their stomachs would hold, throwing the green rinds over their shoulders. Satiated, they stuffed some melons down the bibs of their overalls for later.

Turk remembers ordering, "Hurry, Hans, grab those melons over there and I'll get these."

As the boys gathered the melons a harsh voice rang out, "What in the hell are you all doing in my garden?" It was Roy!

"Put a move on it and let's get outta here," Chub chimed up.

Turk replied, "Okay, okay," as he grabbed up the last melon. Chub, Ton, and Hans tore off weighed down with melons in their overalls but running still. Just as Turk stuffed the last melon in his overalls a shot rang out.

"Damn that old man Emerson if he didn't go and get his gun!" Turk mumbled as he scrambled to get out the garden, leaking melon parts behind him as his three brothers laughed at him from down the road a bit. "Damn you all to hell, don't just stand there and laugh, help me!" Turk ordered them as he heard more shots.

Hans yelled back, "Drop 'em Turk and run for the hills, you idiot!" Finally, back in the safety of their own barn, the boys hurriedly ate the evidence, seeds and juice spurting everywhere. Hans chided Turk, "Good thing old man Emerson can't run with his arthritis or you'd be a goner, Turk," all the while his blue eyes sparkled merrily at Turk's expense.

The memories of that day faded as Turk waited on the deck of the ship for his brother who did not return.

30

The First Casualty, October 1944

Marseilles, France
Dear Mom and Dad,

Well, I bet you have been worried sick and wondering why I have not written for so long. I am sorry if I have caused you even one minute of concern. As you know, because I am writing this letter, I am fine but I have a story to tell you. Get comfy because this is a doozy!

It took our unit several hours to walk to the radio station where we were to bivouac once we disembarked in Marseilles. We were all tired and ready for a rest. Once we made it to the station we got to work setting up our tents. Ours went up fast so while I waited I watched soldiers working on the long wires connected to the radio towers. It made me think of my brothers and all the stuff we made out of spare parts around the farm. I thought to myself, Ton would love to be here to see this. I know he would say, "Think of all the stuff we could make with those tools and wire!" That gave me a chuckle.

But pretty quick after that they came to me with papers for my duty assignment. I had been assigned as the driver for a jeep carrying an anti-tank gun. Wow, did that ever make me nervous! I have heard stories from soldiers stationed here about the German snipers who hid up in the trees and picked off soldiers one by one as they drove past on the road. I could not imagine an easier target than the driver of an anti-tank jeep and I figured I would be the prime bull's eye for the German bullets. But I had to do what I had to do. No sense dwelling on what I could not change, so the rest of that evening was spent chowing down on some C rations, getting our tents in order, and settling in for the night. I went to sleep quickly that night, being tired from the day's march and duties.

Middle of the night, sound asleep, I am awakened by a strange noise. I hear "ping," "bam." Instantly, I could feel something crawling on my legs and I was certain someone was walking over my ankles. I pulled my leg out from under the blanket to shake him off and pushed my leg over the side of the bed to get up and find out just what was going on. But, again, I heard weird noises and now it felt like something was pinning my leg down to the bed. I heard the guy in the bed next to me make an "ughh" sound and then I got real worried about what was happening.

I just stayed put in that bed, silent and not moving a muscle, because I was not sure of what was going on in that tent. Maybe an enemy raid? Suddenly, all hell breaks loose around me. I heard loud screams, shouts, and the noise of tent poles falling to the ground. I looked over at the soldier in the cot next to me because our cots were so close together you could hear your neighbor breathe. I got chills up and down my spine at the sight I saw that night. I still have nightmares about it!

The corporal's eyes were open but he was not moving. A stake that held the tent down was stuck in his throat and there were wires laying all over him. Blood was everywhere! Immediately several guys surrounded the cot. They were trying to get the wires off of the corporal and get him some help.

One guy looked at me and yelled, "Eymann, Eymann, don't move, we will get help for you!" I wondered what in tarnation he was talking about because there was nothing wrong with me! Then, I looked down to check out what was going on. It was at that moment the pain started. My right leg was sprawled out at a very odd angle … not the direction any leg should go! I couldn't move my right leg, but my left leg, which I had pulled out from under the bed covers, seemed to be just fine. Well, not much else I could do but lie there and keep quiet because all the action was taking place next to me.

It turns out the problem was when they put up the tents they stretched some of the wires too taut and then attached them to the stakes. During the night the wires gave way causing the stake to be pulled out of the ground and the wire to snap with it. This was the stake that was now sticking out of my neighbor's throat. It was too late. He was dead. There was nothing else they could do to help him. Finally, they gave up trying, covered him with a sheet, and took him away. It was then they came over to me, gave me a styrette of morphine, and asked me, "Why didn't you yell and tell us how badly you were injured?" All I could say before I lost consciousness was, "Because I didn't know!"

They put me in a full length cast that went clear up to the top of my thigh and I lay in that hospital bed for the next six weeks. I was so disgusted I could barely talk. The nurse came in the room one day and said, "That is the luckiest broken leg ever … they are sending you home to the States to recover."

I was not happy and I told her, "If I'm here, I just as well be going with everybody else to fight the Nazis."

She just laughed and said, "Now, Private Eymann, how would you do that with a bright, white cast around your leg? No sir, you are on your way home."

A few days later the officer in charge of my company paid me a visit. I was proud when he told me, "Eymann, your display of courage was outstanding. You remained calm and did not complain even though you were injured. Your display of courage and self-control was an inspiration to the men and you provided leadership while we suffered our first casualty. Good luck with your recovery and our best wishes go with you. We'll be up at the front kicking the hell out of the Nazis."

I thanked the officer for coming to see me and I told him I sure wish I was going with you because I know you need a good driver but I'm not much good with this broken leg. But I'll be back as soon as I recover.

Within the next week they will put me on a hospital ship headed for the States. Not sure yet where I will be for my recuperation but as soon as I know I will write and tell you. Please don't worry I really am doing fine and will be back to normal soon.

Your loving son, Chub

December, 1944

Dear Mom and Dad,

I can't believe nearly two months have passed since I was injured. I am still in this stateside hospital but they tell me I should be able to get home to Oakdale for a visit very soon. I can't wait to be back on the farm and I am sure hoping to make it in time for Christmas this year. I got some very sad news yesterday. My unit went into what they are calling The Battle of the Bulge shortly after I left France for the States. Over half of my unit was killed in action. I feel badly that I was not there to help them. I can still see the faces of the guys in my unit and I wonder which ones did not make it.

Your loving son, Chub

31

The Most Sorrowful Task, October 1944

The battle was over. After the intense fighting and attacks subsided, the *Sangamon* was to set off for Seeadler Harbor in Manus, New Guinea. Four days had passed since the operation known as the Second Battle of the Philippines and still no word from Hans.

Turk sat on his bunk staring at a blank sheet of paper in front of him. He had decided that it was time to write the letter to his parents. He could not put the sorrowful task off any longer. Without a doubt it was the worst and hardest thing he had ever had to do.

The days had passed with crews arriving back to the *Sangamon* but Hans did not make it back. For four days now Turk had prayed, wished, both cursed and pleaded with God and made promises about all the things he would do if only his brother to come back alive. But Turk realized now that he was not coming back, indeed, they may never know what actually happened to Hans, and he should not postpone the inevitable any longer. He must be the one to write the letter to his parents telling them about Hans. His fingers gripped the pencil and he strained to make them write words on the paper. Turk simply could not comprehend that he had lost Hans to a watery grave. In the end, despite all he resolved to do, Turk was powerless to keep his brother safe.

Those memories of his brother and the simple farm life they left behind crept upon him without warning. He recalled the cave they dug out with their bare hands in the bank of the Cedar Creek. Turk smiled as he recalled their rebellious moments. It had been Hans's idea to dry corn silks until they were brown and crisp. The boys then mulched them up, rolled them in thin tree bark, and tried to smoke them. Turk could still taste the smoke that filled his mouth. It had tasted akin to drinking acid but, still, they continued to experiment with all kinds of dried tree leaves and dead wood. Some of these homemade cigarettes had been so potent they couldn't get any air through them and their lips puckered up for several minutes before unsticking them. He could see the comical faces his brothers had made and the smell of the bitter homemade cigarettes.

These sweet, naïve memories gave Turk a brief period of respite. But reality reared its ugly head and he remembered what he had to do. How will his parents live through this news that Turk must write to them? Why did Hans have to be the one to die? Turk would absolutely give a million dollars to trade places with him now and bring Hans back but that was not the fate they had been dealt.

Unable to answer any of these questions, Turk brushed away the tears that fell down his cheeks. He put the paper and pencil on the bunk. Right now, it was just too much for him. He swung his feet over the bunk and slipped to the floor to go up on deck for a walk. He must clear his head or maybe just hide the tears.

32

Confusion Reigns, October 1944

The piercing wind whizzed through the open weapons bay and ripped over Hans. The pings and puffs of AA fire drilled the water around them as they continued to lose altitude despite the best efforts of Lt. Stouffer. The sprays of water rose like miniature volcanoes in the open sea. Each crew member was braced in as snuggly as possible anticipating the impact of the aircraft with the water.

Suddenly, Stouffer's excited voice interrupted their calamity. "Well, gee whiz, boys, if that ain't a pretty sight. Looks to me like an American escort carrier just waiting over there for us! I'm gonna try to land this bird on that ship so I'm gonna let 'em know we're comin' in. They best get ready for an unexpected guest. I'll be sure to mention to them we got a damaged tail so get ready for a bit of trouble."

Hans checked his instruments to occupy his mind and braced for what he hoped would be, if not a smooth landing, then at least a dry one.

It didn't take long for Stouffer to line up with the deck of the unfamiliar carrier; they were close and had scant time to spare as the plane continued its unabated descent to the ocean. Hans peered out of the tiny window next to his seat, low in the belly of the plane. He looked out on the ocean and the sight of the ships of Taffy Three. They were sure a welcome sight but he also knew the battle was still raging. He could only hope and pray the Nip planes and the AA fire would stay clear of the Avenger and allow them to land.

The yaw of the plane was getting worse by the second as they glided down toward the escort carrier *USS Kitkun Bay*. Although he trusted in Stouffer's flying ability, his hands were sweating and his throat was dry. Suddenly, Hans's body lurched forward as the plane slammed onto the deck of the *Kitkun Bay*. It screeched down the deck of the carrier until it was caught by the flight hook and reeled back from the edge, just like a fishing pole reels in a fish.

"There ya are, boys," Stouffer said matter of factly, "just like always. We might not have made it back to the *Sangamon* but we made it to the *Kitkun Bay* nonetheless. That's good enough in my book."

On shaking legs and with weary heads the crew climbed out of the plane. They were welcomed by an unfamiliar crew but welcomed just the same. It was at that moment all three men looked over the horizon and saw the monumental plume of black smoke. They could still see planes buzzing and hear the big guns of the ships.

The deck chief strode up to the three aviators and said, "I gotta shake your hands! It appears you boys made a direct hit on that Nip battleship over there that's belching out smoke and oil. That monster's been giving us fits all day! Congratulations and thanks for coming to help us out. We owe you and I am proud to shake your hand and make your acquaintance. Although I'd love to stay here and chat we better get you three down under. There's a war going on here!"

Hans and Stouffer looked at each other and broke into huge smiles but the smiles did not last long. The men took one look at the tail section of their plane and Hans exclaimed, "Hot damn! What in the hell happened to our tail?"

The tail or what was left of it was nothing more than a mass of tattered metal. The initial damage patched together at Tacloban had been torn apart and expanded by the second hits of AA. As the crew peered inside the hole made by the AA fire, Hans stated out loud what they were all thinking, "I can't believe we made it. We got here just in time. How this aircraft stayed in the air I will never know!"

The deck chief grinned. "Never fear boys, we seen worse. We will have this plane patched up and flying before you know it. You're gonna be flying missions for us and believe me we need you!"

Although no one on the Avenger crew truly believed him, they were too exhausted to argue the point. They followed the chief below deck to get some coffee, chow, and they hoped a drink of bourbon to calm their nerves—as the battle continued to rage on around them.

Hans's log book entry, October 1944.

Amazing Grace,
USS Sangamon, October 1944

T hings on the *USS Sangamon* were getting back to normal five days after the Battle for Leyte Gulf. That was if normal included a damaged flight deck, injured and dead sailors, and the after effects of the fiercest sea battle ever fought.

The *Sangamon* had been strafed relentlessly during the battle and had experienced a piece of the first Kamikaze attack. The crew was spent physically and emotionally, yet spiritually the American forces had achieved a great victory, sinking some of the Japanese ships, chasing the Japanese Imperial Navy from the Gulf, and sending them packing back to Japan. The flight crews had returned and the aviators were attempting to regroup as best they could.

Turk strode across the massive gray deck as he did every day and lifted his eyes out over the Philippine Sea. He understood it was an exercise in futility to search the horizon for Hans every day, yet he was bound to his obligation to keep looking for him. Each day he sat down to write the dreaded letter home and each day found him unable to complete his task. He was not ready yet to give up hope. But, now, five days after the battle and no word of Hans, Turk admitted the obvious … Hans was gone.

Turk proudly told anyone who would listen, "I know it was Han's crew who took down that Japanese battleship." Turk tuned in to all of the accounts of the returning pilots, gathering as much information about what happened as he could. No one story could be proven because in the heat of battle, with the flak, smoke, fire, and chaos of the struggle, accounts differed. Yet he was sure Hans and his crew dove down, released their torpedo, and then had been hit. After that, no one knew, no word, no sightings, nothing.

Now, after these five days had passed Turk was forced to give up hope. Each time Turk looked into the face of other Avenger pilots he knew they were thinking of Hans, his crew, and what had happened and that they were hurting for Turk too.

The ship was put on Condition Two, and there was no hint of battle, so Turk finished smoking his cigarette and turned back toward the hatch and the ladder that would take him below deck. As he turned his back to the sea he could hear the hum of a plane engine approaching the CVE. That was nothing out of the ordinary here. Missions and planes were always coming and going for one purpose or another.

For some reason he halted and took an extra moment to watch the plane catch the wire and make a safe landing. It seemed more important to him now to make sure as many Avenger crews as possible came back safe and sound. He wanted to spare other families the pain of loss he felt. Turk noticed the tail section of this plane in particular. It had obviously sustained terrific damage and had been patched up. The aircraft jerked to a halt after catching the hook.

Turk resumed his walk to the hatch secure in the knowledge the plane had landed safely when suddenly he heard a familiar voice call out, "Hey, you old dog! Come back here! Aren't you glad to see me?"

Turk's head pivoted toward the recently landed plane. There, climbing out from the rear door stood Hans! Overcome with emotions of relief, love, anxiety, and happiness he ran to his brother, grabbed him by the neck, and threw him to the deck. As he pummeled him with his fists Turk yelled, "You son of a bitch, where in the hell have you been?"

Hans laughed as he rolled on the deck dodging Turk's fists. "Get the hell off of me, you punk," Hans called as he got to his feet but as he said these words he grabbed his older brother into a huge hug. The boys stood locked together in this truly glorious moment of awe and wonder at the miracle of life.

Pushing Turk away Hans said, "Well, if you get off of me for a minute I'll tell you what happened. Ya see when we dove down on that battleship we released our torpedo and then circled back around to do some strafing. Going in low we took quite a hit to the tail section. It was pretty dicey for a while as Stouffer fought to keep the plane under control. We were prepared for a wet landing there in the middle of all of those Japs, but somehow we made it back to Tacloban. The Army guys there patched us up and got us back out into the fight. We went in low to drop our bombs and gosh darn if we didn't take some more AA. This time we were in real trouble until, low and behold, Lt. Stouffer spotted the *Kitkun Bay* close by and we were able to land there."

He continued the story, "We were lucky they had room for us because we couldn't have flown much longer. Although the *Kitkun Bay* was smack dab in the middle of the battle, we sure were glad to set that plane down on her deck. There were so many planes and crews that got mixed up that day. Half the guys that landed on the *Kitkun* that afternoon were not from the ship. Some of their crews did not make it back so it seems they were mighty short of flyers. They patched us up and told us we were staying put and flying from their ship for a while. They needed us. I sure wasn't gonna argue with them because things were pretty rough out there and we did what we were told. When the Japanese fleet hightailed it out of there and the dust settled a bit they let us go. Here I am standing in front of you today as living proof."

Turk listened to the words but hardly comprehended the story. But one fact remained: his baby brother was back and alive. He was in total shock and felt weak. He slid to the deck and landed directly on his butt. Hans looked down at him in surprise. Here was his older brother, tough as nails, at a loss for words.

In a split second to spare him any further embarrassment, Hans reached for his arm and pulled him to his feet. "Turk, I told you I would not do anything stupid and that I would be okay. Here I am, back with you, and more than ready to get this war over with. C'mon, let's go get some chow. I'm hungry. Turk threw his arm around Hans's shoulder and the two boys walked over to the hatch and down the ladder to finish their war together.

Hans Eymann receives the Distinguished Flying Cross for his exploits during the Second Battle of the Philippines, 1944.

Part V

Turk's wedding, December 1944. Turk (from left), Chub, and Hans at the Methodist church in Oakdale.

Love and War

34

Sailor Boy on Wheels, Bremerton, November 1944

T he *USS Sangamon* had docked in Bremerton, Washington, after fourteen months at sea. With the Second Battle of the Philippines behind him and a Distinguished Flying Cross pinned to his chest, Hans was ready for dry land and some rest and recovery.

Turk hightailed it to California as soon as he could. He and Kay had spent every minute together while he was training there and they had rekindled their love affair. With memories of fierce battles still on his mind and his own Distinguished Flying Cross pinned to his chest, he couldn't wait to get back to her.

Hans only knew he was happy his feet were on dry land, the sun was shining, and he was ready for some fun. He left the naval base where the ship was docked. Right now he did not know what his new orders would be but that was the last thing on his mind.

At home, Hans loved to roller skate and jitterbug. Since it was the middle of the afternoon he decided his best bet was the roller skating rink. He knew it was a great place to meet local girls. He always entertained the girls and drew attention to himself with his fancy skating, which he had perfected back in Nebraska. It was high time to test his skills and see if they were still there. With a few of his buddies in tow, they strolled into the rink, girls on their minds.

Hans peered over to the opposite side of the rink as he laced his skates on his feet. There was a group of five or so girls preparing to skate, hunched over their lacings and giggling together. Immediately he spotted a beautiful blonde girl.

"I am going to make sure I meet her tonight!" he mumbled under his breath. He finished his lacing job and set out on the rink. *Yep, I've still got it*, he decided as he leisurely made a few laps. His mind wandered as he skated. He passed a gaggle of off-duty servicemen and the girls just off of their work shifts who were looking to have some fun and forget the world for a while. They just wanted to be young. He scrutinized the crowd as he skated though, always on the lookout for the blonde girl. His plan was to skate as close as possible to her and strike up a conversation.

The plan worked but not in the way he had expected. As he rounded a corner he saw her fall flat on her butt in front of him. He quickly skated over, leaned down to give his assistance, and asked, "Are you hurt? Can I help you up?"

She seemed flustered and embarrassed but responded, "Sure and thanks!" Hans took her arm and helped her to her wobbly feet. He skated over to the waiting area with her and helped her make her way to a bench so she could catch her breath.

Hans bravely began a conversation, "My name is Hans Eymann, what's yours?"

She answered, "Ann, just Ann for now. Do you think you could get some water for me? I am afraid I am not a very good skater and I could use a drink."

Hans was quick to reply, "I can do better than that. How about a soda? You're not so bad at skating, you just need some practice."

"That would be great and thanks so much for the encouragement. You are sure sweet to stop and help me out," she said gratefully.

Hans returned with the drinks for both of them and suggested they take a break, take their skates off, and sit at the tables for a while. Ann was more than happy to agree with his request because during her fall she twisted her ankle and it was throbbing a bit.

She needed a break. Hans grabbed both sodas and linked his arm with her arms to help her to a table.

"Where are you from? I can tell by the way you talk you are not from around here. So many soldiers here and it seems everyone is from some different state. I am learning my geography due to this war!" Ann explained to him.

"I am from Nebraska, a small town farm boy. How about you? Were you born here?" Han asked her in response.

She shook her head, "Oh no, I just moved here. Bremerton is abuzz with work and activity with the naval yard so close. There are so many jobs and so much life here. I wanted to be a part of the war effort, have fun, and make some money. This is a great place to do all three!"

Without realizing it, the night had passed away while Hans and Ann sat at the table together. Ann's friend called to her, "Time to go home."

She turned to Hans and said, "I have to go now but I sure enjoyed talking to you! I would love to see you again. Here is my number. Give me a call, okay?" She limped off to join her friends.

Hans could not quite get used to the change in girls since he went away. Who would have thought a girl would give him her phone number? He sat a while at the table after she left and enjoyed the simple pleasure of sitting and talking to a girl. It was the small joys of life like the companionship of a nice girl that he missed while at sea. However, the human connection he had just made caused him to long for home even more. He was downright homesick for Oakdale, his family, the small town streets, his mother's cooking, and all of the friends.

But, nonetheless, Ann brought some joy to his life. He hoped he could see her again. With that thought in his mind he got up and walked home, happy for a few hours.

While Hans remained in Bremerton waiting for the ship's overhaul, Turk had jumped on a train and sped to California.

The time spent apart from Kay made Turk even more serious about her than before. He was more mature and had seen way more than he ever wanted to see. He wanted to surprise her so he showed up outside her apartment building unannounced one bright and sunny afternoon.

After Turk and Kay had run into each other in San Diego months earlier, they had spent every minute together. The old flame was certainly still there. If it was possible they were more in love now than as teenagers and the relationship was progressing rapidly.

Then Turk had shipped out. He missed Kay more than he wanted to admit and he just hoped she missed him as much. He thought she did because her letters came on a regular basis. So it was no surprise that Turk could not get back to San Diego fast enough when the ship reached the shores of the mainland. He wanted to spend as much of his leave with Kay as possible.

Outside her apartment, Kay was definitely surprised and happy to see him waiting. She hugged and kissed him and took his hand to lead him up to her place.

Kay had recently rented a small apartment by herself in the months Turk was gone. She no longer shared her space with a roommate. Although it was actually no more than a small room, it was hers alone. The room itself was narrow and tiny. Kay had covered the chairs with fabrics in deep, rich and warm colors and the white walls were covered with pictures of friends and family from Oakdale. The room radiated a cheerfulness that was a part of Kay. A small, rectangular window allowed a small amount of breeze into the room. The salty, fresh sea air permeated the room making the tiny space even more pleasant. The clean, bright room in combination with the sea air smelled deliciously welcoming to Turk just like Kay did.

Turk was captivated by so many aspects of Kay's personality and her being. The perfume she wore was not so noticeable when she was present; rather, it was an aspect of her essence as real as her soft skin or green eyes. Oddly, her perfume was most noticeable to him in her absence, like the sight of a favorite sunset or the warmth of the sun's rays, intangible yet powerful. The subtle waves of aroma that surrounded Kay and wafted gently over anyone close to her were, indeed, a part of her essence, a part of the elegance, beauty, and peace that accompanied her and defined her.

Turk stood in the doorway for a moment, hesitating before he entered into Kay's private domain. His masculine presence seemed to take up all the space in the feminine room he was about to enter and he was not sure there was enough room for him there.

Kay motioned him forward, using her cheerful, brisk manner to get her point across, as she directed him, "Sit over there on that chair, the only chair, while I fire up the hot plate to make us some coffee."

Kay breezed over efficiently to the small sink and placed the enamel pot on the hot plate. Turk watched, amused by this intricate ballet of space and motion. Kay deftly maneuvered her trim body around the tiny space she occupied, with no wasted motion, for there was no room for that. After finishing her tasks and hearing the pot start to percolate, she turned back to Turk, walked over to the other piece of furniture, a narrow bed, and sat down.

Turk smiled. When she sat down on the bed he looked into her dark, intelligent eyes and asked her, "Why did we ever break up?" He honestly could not remember the exact reason. There had been some fight or disagreement and now, after all of this time, it really didn't matter to him.

"Turk," Kay began to speak tentatively, "I have missed you so much! I have thought a lot about the past between us. I want to apologize to you for leaving Oakdale so abruptly and not even taking the time to at least come by your folks' house to say goodbye before I left. We just never ...," her words trailed off as Turk cut her off by placing his fingers on her lips.

"Kay, it doesn't matter. We're here together now so let's just allow the past to be just that, the past. It amazes me that we found each other here in California. Let's think about the future and not look back."

Turk and Kay sat together and chatted for a few minutes about friends and family from home, her work, and his missions. Soon her hand was in his as they continued to speak. Suddenly, Kay remembered the long forgotten coffee. She moved to get a cup for Turk and as she got up and walked in front of Turk his muscular arms encircled her tiny waist.

She paused, looked down, and as her eyes met his, he said firmly, "Not now, Kay, I just want you to sit with me." She bent over a bit in order to sit back down, her face close to Turk's. His hand caressed her cheek, turned her face to his, and he kissed her gently on the check, and then on the mouth.

The days, months, and years they had been apart fell away as they kissed in their familiar way, more deeply now, holding each other close. Turk's hands moved up and down Kay's bare legs.

"I have always loved your legs, Kay," Turk said to her. Kay smiled but kept kissing him as he bent down to tenderly take off her shoes, placing more kisses on her ankles. His hands moved continually over her legs, caressing them as he kissed his way up to her thighs. Kay gave a sigh, happy to have Turk back. Turk grasped her hips and they both lay back on her bed, body to body, hands intertwined, as they kissed away the time spent apart.

When Turk kissed Kay he tasted home, the sweet, clean air of spring on the Elkhorn River, the spicy taste of apples in the fall, the dry autumn scent of fallen leaves carried on the wind, and the pungent, sweet smell of alfalfa ripening in the summer fields. The tastes and smells of home!

Kay smiled again, took Turk's face in between her hands as she said, "I love you, I have always loved you, and I will always love you." Pleasure shone in Turk's eyes as the coffee pot bubbled away somewhere in the distance.

35

The Surprise Guest, December 1944

The days of Turk's leave passed rapidly. Kay and Turk spent every minute possible together in California since his return. They both knew it would end and Turk would be thrown back into the war full force. Every minute together was poignant and sweet and the two were closer than they had ever been.

Kay was the instigator. She began to talk about their future and making a life together. At first, Turk was a bit taken aback. It seemed to be too close to his experiences in Leyte Gulf to talk about the future. For him, the future may be only days or weeks and it was inconceivable to discuss months or years down the road. Yet Kay seemed to be in such a hurry. She justified her obsession to Turk by explaining to him that she wanted to be a permanent part of his life no matter what the future brought because he was the most important thing to her.

Since Turk was also hungering to get back to Oakdale and his family, Kay agreed to go with him—but only if they could get married while they were in Nebraska. Turk finally consented and the two took the train to Omaha. They were picked up in Omaha by Kay's parents and deposited at the Eymann farm to plan a quick wedding.

Short engagements were nothing new during the war and no one thought anything about it. They were too busy planning a

Hans, Kay, and Betty choose a
Christmas Tree, December 1944.

Christmas ceremony for the bride and groom. Hans had made his way home to Nebraska as soon as he could. He wanted to hunt and breathe in the crisp air of the late Nebraska fall, which was rapidly turning to winter. He was already at the farm when Kay and Turk arrived. The house bustled with excitement of the season and the wedding. Hans thought they might be hurrying the wedding a bit but he was proud to take his place as best man.

The late afternoon shadows of December were falling as the toot of a car horn sounded in front of the farmhouse. Hattie was cooking the wedding "feast" of roast chicken and had just finished putting the last touches on the small wedding cake when she heard the horn. Who could that be? There was no time for visitors now as they had to be at the church soon.

Hattie pushed back the kitchen curtains to see what was going on and a huge smile spread over her round face. She opened the door and ran toward the car. It was Al and Tude in from

Omaha but as the back door opened, a white-casted leg swung out, followed by a pair of crutches and the uniformed body of Chub. He was home!

He had been released from the hospital finally after weeks of recuperation. Tude had planned the entire surprise, and they had brought Chub home just in time for the wedding. Hattie screamed and clutched her hands to her mouth at the sight of her son. The smile on Chub's face was radiant and in the matter of a few minutes he was engulfed by Jix, his sisters, and his mother.

Hugs and kisses and oohs and aaahs ensued. Chub nearly fell over from the embraces. He pushed the crutches under his arms and looked up at the house. Standing in the doorway were Turk and Hans. The two boys jumped down from the porch as Chub made his way up toward the house. All three boys grabbed each other tightly. No words were needed. The only thing missing in this reunion was Ton who was now somewhere on his ship in the Pacific.

Chub arrives in Oakdale for Turk's
wedding, December 1944.

Hattie said, "I hate to interrupt, boys, but we got a wedding to attend. It is perfect now that you are here, Chub. The three boys walked into the house with their arms tightly drawn around each other.

Chub Eymann in Oakdale still in the cast, 1944.

36

A Wedding Made of Tinsel, December 1944

Turk looked devastatingly handsome and very happy through the candlelight of the church. The boys were dressed in their uniforms for the ceremony. They were polished up so brightly that everything on them shone.

Turk needed a minute to catch his breath and have a cigarette. He snuck quietly outside to the back of the church leaving his brothers for a few minutes. He needed to be alone to think for a while before he took the step that would change his life forever. Turk had not shared this information with anyone yet, but Kay had told him that she thought she was pregnant. Turk was bursting with pride and love. He was both thrilled and ready to become a father. Most of Turk's friends had already married. He had gotten a late start.

The real truth was that all Turk had ever wanted was a home and a family; he just did not want to admit it to anyone. Now that wife, home, and family were all coming together at the same time, he was content with life. He was not sure what the future would bring with the war but he was certain of what he had here in Oakdale.

Turk stood out back of the church in the semi-darkness smoking to calm his nerves a bit. Suddenly, he heard the sound of footsteps on the snowy sidewalk. He looked up to see Kay's sister Bernita.

He smiled at her as he said, "Bernita, you better get inside quickly. It is bitter cold out here!" Turk stopped short as he noticed a strange look on her face. "What's wrong, has something happened to Kay?" he questioned her anxiously.

"No," Bernita replied slowly all the while keeping her eyes glued to her shoes, "nothing is wrong with her. I just wanted to talk to you for a few minutes before the wedding."

Turk was alarmed by the severity of her tone and he listened to her intently. "Whatever you have to say, Bernita, just say it."

Bernita was not able to raise her face to look Turk in the eyes because she was afraid she would lose her nerve but she continued, "Turk, this wedding is all wrong, it is simply wrong," she finally blurted out the words she came to say.

Turk melted just a bit. He felt he was responsible for this statement and he knew Bernita was trying to protect her sister. He reassured her, "Bernita, I know you may think I am not good for Kay. When we were younger, here in Oakdale, I may not have treated her the way I should have. But everything has changed now. I am older and more mature. I realize Kay is the only girl for me. I want to treat her right, take care of her, and have a family with her. We may have had our arguments and problems but those days are behind us now. We are ready to get married and I want to be with her forever. I promise I will be the best husband possible for her."

Bernita looked up startled by Turk's response. Her eyes searched Turk's face as he paused. She started to speak, "Turk that is not what I ..." but her voice trailed off and she didn't finish her thought because they both heard the sound of the heavy wooden church door open and then a familiar voice.

"Turk," Kay called from behind the doorway, "are you going to marry me tonight or not? You know it is bad luck for the bride and groom to see each other before the ceremony, so give me a second to get in the sanctuary and then get in here!"

Turk laughed, put out his cigarette, turned, opened the door, and motioned for Bernita to go in as he reassured her again, "Don't worry now, Bernita, it will all be okay. Bernita lowered her head but said nothing as she walked with Turk into the church, the glow of candles lighting their way.

37

I Suggest You Pray,
Late March 1945

The seas had been very rough for the last few days as the destroyer *USS Lindsey* steamed away from the horrors of Iwo Jima toward the unknown. At times, water washed over the bridge in the roiling seas. The days and weeks of high alerts, general quarters, and the pounding of guns releasing their killer salvos had taken its toll on everyone. The ship had done its duty of sweeping mines, firing at small boats on the reefs, and supporting the ground attack at Iwo.

However, by far one of the most difficult jobs for the crew was picking up survivors from ships that had struck mines or were hit. The doctor on board the *Lindsey* did all he could to aid the wounded sailors, giving plasma and anything else he could to keep them alive. Some did not make it. The final nightmare was burying men at sea. All of the sailors on board the *Lindsey* hated these moments.

Ton watched as the deceased were sewn up in canvas with weights. They were buried with full military honors and as much dignity as could be mustered in the middle of a war. He watched and saluted with the other sailors as their comrades' bodies were dropped over the side of the ship. Each sailor thought of the families who would never see their loved ones again nor have the closure of receiving their bodies for burial. Ton shuddered. This solemn ceremony was the hardest to handle.

Leaving the killing zone of Iwo Jima to head to another was nerve wracking for everyone, but the voyage did provide a bit of a break from the frenetic pace of the previous month. The sailors took advantage of this small piece of down time to shoot the breeze together on the fantail of the ship. Others played poker clustered in small groups around the ship while others took the opportunity to write some long-neglected letters home. For some sailors this was the first opportunity in several days to clean up and shower. However, when they heard the captain's voice come over the ship's intercom to address them everyone paid close attention.

Captain Chambers's voice was strong and clear. As he spoke to the exhausted crew of the *Lindsey*, his voice never wavered or hesitated.

"Men," he began strongly, leaving little doubt as to what type of information he was about to share with them, "we are sailing into a dangerous situation. There will be tough times ahead for all of us. Now some of you may choose to use this time before trouble arrives to play poker, some may choose to tell jokes, and some of you may choose to pray. Gentlemen, I suggest strongly that you pray."

And with that Captain Chambers finished addressing the men who were suddenly absolutely quiet.

Love Lost, Winter 1945

T urk felt settled into his new life and in his new role as husband. Although they had been married only a few weeks, Kay had always been the love of his life. It seemed natural and inevitable to him that they should be together. Still, it amazed him to realize the odds of their meeting again in California were small and it had truly been a miracle they reconnected.

Every day was a gift for Turk. He knew he would soon be returning to the war, but he pushed that from his mind. It was confirmed now. Kay was pregnant. Turk couldn't believe he was going to be a father. When he returned from the war for his next leave, the baby would probably already be born.

It boggled his mind but Turk had lived a thousand lifetimes during the last year and a half. He felt older than the rest of the world and was ready to settle down. In just a few days he would return to the *Sangamon* to finish his tour of duty. But there was one big difference: Hans would not be with him.

Since the five Sullivan brothers had served and died on the same ship, the Navy had cracked down on the unwritten rule that brothers did not serve together or, at least, that is what Turk thought. Hans would not be boarding that ship with him but was instead remaining in Bremerton, Washington, and from there who knew? Turk would miss his brother, but maybe it was for the best. There was still some major fighting left in this war, and Turk knew the *Sangamon* would be in the middle of it. Possibly Hans would be sent somewhere safer—or so he hoped.

Kay's parents were coming to California to stay with her when Turk left. It put his mind at ease to know they would help with the baby. "War babies" they called them. With all the hubbub of war no one had the time or energy to worry or wonder how long a couple with a baby on the way had been married. There were weddings and babies every day, each couple in a hurry to tie the knot before the husband shipped out. With the future so unknown it seemed foolish to waste even a precious minute.

The days passed uneventfully. Kay's pregnancy had made her moody and short with Turk but he tried to understand. She seemed to always be on edge. She seemed preoccupied and nervous but Turk imagined that was just what happened to a pregnant woman.

Her parents had arrived in anticipation of Turk's imminent departure. They were staying in the tiny apartment with the couple. Turk had also noticed that Kay's father seemed more agitated than usual. He thought back to the odd, incomplete conversation he shared with Kay's sister Bernita just before the wedding, and he wondered if her father was also worried about how he would treat Kay. Maybe they wanted Kay to move back to Oakdale until the war was over and he was back. At times it seemed her father wanted to say something to Turk and maybe it was about the move.

This was definitely not what Turk wanted because if he got some leave time, it would be much more difficult to get back to Oakdale to spend time with her. One thing he did know was that when he got out of the Navy he was moving Kay and the baby back to Oakdale. Maybe they would be able to buy some farm land with the money he hoped to save, settle down, and become a happy family. Turk didn't push her father to talk. In fact, he tried to avoid it so he could keep Kay in California. But he knew the older man would speak in his own time so he let things stand as they were between them.

Then it happened. One night after dinner Kay's father turned to Turk and asked him, "Turk, come outside with me. I want to stretch my legs a bit and I sure don't want to get lost here in this big city!"

Turk replied quickly, "Sure, whatever you say." He followed the older man outside. He was sure he knew the direction the conversation would take. He had his arguments and reasons prepared as to why Kay should remain in California.

Kay's father turned to Turk on the porch of the apartment building. He took his time and chose his words carefully, "Turk, you are a good man. I respect you and I admire your courage. I know you have seen and fought in the toughest situations known to mankind. I know you are a strong person, but I need to say something to you that is almost more than I can bear. I fear for how you will handle it but I need to be honest with you."

Turk was now feeling unsettled with the direction the conversation had taken. This was not at all what he expected to hear, and he sensed he was about to listen to something unexpected and unwelcomed. But, for the life of him, he could not begin to imagine what it was. "Go on," Turk said directly.

"Turk, I love my daughter with all of my heart. But my conscience is screaming at me to do the right thing here. I cannot let her go on lying to you. That baby she is carrying … is not your baby. When you were gone all those months, Kay was lonely. She met a sailor who was lonely too. She made a bad decision about this guy while you were in the Pacific. She got pregnant. When she told the sailor about the baby, he left and she never heard from him again. Then you came back, more in love with Kay than before. She does love you and at the same time she saw her way out of trouble. She knew you were an honorable man who would always do the right thing. She was scared and felt alone. Kay has always loved you in her own way so she saw the chance to make a family for the three of you. But it is just not right that you should go on believing this baby is yours."

Turk felt as if someone had punched him in the gut. He struggled to breathe in and out. It took a few minutes but Turk drew himself up and handled things in the way he always handled things.

He looked back at the heartbroken man standing before him and said, "I appreciate what you just did. I know it must have been very hard for you. I thank you and I wish you only the best." And with that Turk walked off the porch, down the street, and over to the base.

A few days later Turk boarded the *USS Sangamon* bound for the war still raging in the Pacific. He did not speak to Kay again in person but only through the divorce papers he had prepared before he shipped out. He just wanted to forget the past few months.

To everyone who saw him, he showed no emotion. But inside, his heart was truly broken, even if he did not allow himself to admit it. He had lost the only woman he thought he could trust and love. But he also had lost the child he dearly wanted and the family he dreamed of having. It would take a long, long time to get over this hurt of his pride and his emotions. Through strong effort he willed his mind to think only now of his duty, his ship, his brothers and sisters. He just wanted to get through the war alive and get back to the farm.

Part VI

On leave in 1944, Ton and Jix at the farm.

Danger in the Pacific

Operation Iceberg, March 23–April 6, 1945

From his vantage point on the bridge, Ton was able to look out over the immense surface force of ships gathered near the coast of the Japanese island of Okinawa. Rough and rolling seas had made the trip from Iwo Jima to Okinawa difficult at best. To make the journey even more dangerous, two days from their destination the USS *Lindsey* began to encounter floating mines.

The *Lindsey* and its battle-hardened crew had a job to do near the beaches of Okinawa in order for the assault troops to land and fight for control of the Japanese-held island. Sweeping mines was a tedious job and, at times, dangerous as the mines exploded, but that task was preferable to being out in the ocean on patrol or picket duty.

The sailors called this patrol line of destroyers The Ping Line. The Japanese launched well-planned attacks against the small destroyers guarding the outer perimeter of the island. The sailors called this duty "Torpedo Junction" or "Suicide Patrol," and it was here they were attacked by various types of Japanese aircraft—all hell bent on demolishing as many American ships as they could, in any way they could.

Ton had seen his share. On picket duty a Japanese Judy dive bomber had zoomed by the ship at three hundred yards. To Ton, it looked as big as a house. The gunners of the ship were continually firing at one aircraft or another, and so far none of them had done any major damage to the ship.

At dawn the *Lindsey* approached the beach with the transports. A plane with the red, rising sun circled past the ship and suddenly dove for the destroyers closest to them. All ships began firing with everything they had. The pilot had miscalculated and he missed the tin can floating beside the *Lindsey*. Realizing his error he turned sharply across the stern and headed directly for the *Lindsey*.

But by then the plane was being hit by fire constantly. The aircraft barely missed the *Lindsey*'s fantail, hit the water, and exploded a mere fifty yards off the starboard.

Yet another aircraft had sped near the ship, the *Lindsey*'s guns blazing away at the plane. This time the pilot went through the gun house as he hit and there was nothing left of him or the plane after the explosion. Shrapnel and pieces of the plane littered the *Lindsey* but with no serious injuries to the crew or damage to the ship. The crew was more than ready to leave the area as soon as their work was completed, but no one knew when that would be.

Like the other vessels, everyone on the *Lindsey* had been pleasantly surprised by the lack of resistance from the Japanese forces on the island. The transport ships landed with no difficulty. They had not even been fired on and, at times, the beach was jammed with American soldiers. Many had been able to land that day on Okinawa. The first goal was to take the airfields. The strategists had allotted four days to achieve this goal; instead, it was accomplished in a matter of hours. So rapid was the change in ownership of the airfield, Ton had heard a pilot of a Zero had landed on the now American-held field, stepped out, and was promptly shot, never realizing the Japanese were no longer in control of the airstrip.

Ton watched as Japanese Betties, land-based bombers, attacked nearby ships who, in turn, retaliated with withering AA fire. But it was the Navy fighters who swooped in and hit the Betty like a whirlwind to keep the ship safe. He had also seen ships strike mines and be blown apart. Part of the task of the *USS Lindsey* was to recover the survivors, most of whom were blown clear of the ship. The majority of the time they were recovering dead bodies and picking up severely injured sailors. Not many survived.

With the near constant gun fire, burning fires on the island, and huge plumes of smoke everywhere, a pall of dust hung over the beach. Planes attacked day and night. All the while the myriad of ships near the shore sent in round after round of shells, artillery fire, and bombs to the island. It seemed the Americans held tight control over the area close to the beach. But where were the thousands of Japanese who were purported to be defending the island? The Japanese planes that attacked the American ships close to the beach were, for the most part, shot down before reaching them, but what was to happen when the *Lindsey* was sent back to picket duty, alone and vulnerable out in the ocean?

Ton wrote in his diary that life in the Navy can certainly make a guy nervous. His last entry was, "What is coming up now for us?"

40

The Ping Line, Okinawa, April 12, 1945

The past few days had been a blur to the sailors on the USS *Lindsey*. Since arriving at Okinawa on March 23 the destroyer–mine sweeper had been busy with a multitude of tasks. In addition to their work they had to fight off the barrage of planes the Japanese threw at them at an alarming new rate of speed. General quarters was the norm now, not the exception. Men who were accustomed to working in four-hour shifts had been pushed to their physical limits by the constant need to man battle stations. If a sailor got a couple hours of sleep it was considered to be a good rest. Nerves were frayed and everyone was on edge, unsure of what each day would bring.

The *Lindsey* was back on picket duty, near the island of Aguni Shima, just off the coast of Okinawa. Separated from the somewhat safer surface force, the destroyers were open to attack. The life expectancy of a destroyer on picket duty was a short one indeed. The sky was just beginning to turn from night to dawn. The stars blinked their white light into the Pacific sky. The plethora of stars in the wide open sky was an ominous sign. The improvement in the weather conditions meant only one thing for the sailors: more Japanese planes.

The klaxon loudly announced yet another general quarters as Merle and Ton prepared to man their stations. Merle, a Kansas farm boy, and Ton, a Nebraska farm boy, had become friends easily, talking about their shared backgrounds and interests. Merle was assigned to the radio room directly under the bridge. It was here he sent and received messages within this dark and busy hole.

Ton, on the other hand, was a signalman and his station was on that very bridge. His "tools of the trade" the flags and the semaphore he operated were located to the rear of the pilot house on the bridge. From his location in the open air, he had as good a look as anyone over the vast ocean.

Merle and Ton were seasoned shellbacks aboard the *Lindsey*. They had both been with the ship since it sailed from San Francisco that late November day in 1944. They had passed over the equator together and had endured the comical, entertaining, but humiliating "crossing the line" ceremony.

The days of horsing around and innocent fun were gone. However, it was the combination of the boyish pranks endured by all, and the real strain and stress of war that cemented the vital relationships of the men on the ship. The men had formed friendships by the test of battles including Iwo Jima. They had been severely tried and tested and they had proven their worth. Each was bound to the other and their fates rested with each other. It was unthinkable to let your fellow shipmate down if it could be prevented. They were in this together and together they would get out of it.

Scared? They were all scared to the core and as Ton contemplated the next wave of attacks he intended to place as many bulkheads as he could between himself and any plane. They had all tasted their share of the war.

As the klaxon continued to bellow, Ton rolled himself out of his bunk in the tightly packed berthing quarters and into a standing position. He pulled on his dungarees and long-sleeved chambray shirt. He flipped his hat to the back of his head, tucked his shirt in, and rolled up his long sleeves. He was ready for work. His hands grasped the metal chains as he climbed the ladders up to his station on the bridge.

With daylight breaking through, the day was on its way to becoming clear, unlike the previous few days. There were a few puffy white clouds in the sky. The temperature this Thursday might hit sixty degrees, Ton thought. March had proven to be a cold and rainy month in the Pacific. Sailors hated the cold rain as it made their life on outside watches miserable. But as the morning wore on, Ton could see blue sky and white clouds with no rain in sight for today. The thought of what the clear day could bring sent a chill up his spine.

Time passed with no attacks. General quarters was lifted and high alert posted. Ton had time to go below and grab some food and coffee. The Navy was well aware that one way to keep morale up was food. Food was vitally important to the men on the ship so it was stocked with the best they could offer, even at times with real butter.

For a scrawny one-hundred-twenty-pound kid Ton could eat more than most and he was always hungry. Merle also went below to grab a bite. Ton commented to him, "I sure am glad for that bit of clearing in the skies this morning. It will be one of the first days I don't get wet!"

Merle replied, "Thanks for the weather report, buddy. You know the only thing I can see in the radio room is equipment. There is not one ounce of daylight in there. I envy you the sunshine!"

But with those words both men fell silent. The improved weather brought the increased threat of Japanese suicide planes. The Navy censors had kept the reports of the crazy suicide attacks on U.S. ships hidden from the people back home. But all of the sailors on the ships surrounding Okinawa were painfully aware of the brutal attacks. Most of the crews had experienced, at least, a brush or two with a plane intent on crashing into their ship. All men feared the attacks greatly. The crews of the destroyers knew their job was to form a radar picket line, the first defense, against the attacks in order to protect the carriers nestled closer to shore. But enough was enough. They were simply sitting ducks out on the water and each day more men died in the hideous attacks.

Ton questioned Merle, "Do you know whose idea it was to make the destroyers form this picket line? I bet it was one of the muckety-mucks up high who designed this crazy plan!"

Merle laughed and answered, "Of course, you know it, brother! I heard it was ole John McCain himself who thought this one up: a picket line to protect his carriers and men on shore. Now that's a great plan for them but it sure makes us easy targets out here. What were they thinking? Not about us that's for sure! It seems like the destroyers and every man aboard them are expendable."

"Yep, appears those Jap planes are using us for target practice these days," Ton responded. He thought about all of the rumors he had heard. Most of them were not funny but one courageous, clever sailor had painted a large arrow on the deck of his ship and had written a message for the Japanese pilots:

Carriers That Way→

Ton also recalled an odd word he heard lately bandied about the ship, Kamikaze. On board the ship was a Japanese American, a Nisei. He was American born and bred and was proud to be serving his country on the ship. He was also able to translate for the crew and he told them the Japanese character for Kamikaze means "divine wind." Why in the hell they call themselves the divine wind Ton did not understand and what's more, he did not care. He only wanted them to go away. But the sailor went on to explain the story to them.

In the year 1281 the Mongols set sail for Japan with the intent to invade the islands. Before accomplishing their goal, they were hit by a devastating windstorm. The entire fleet was demolished. The Japanese people believed that the Son of Heaven had intervened on their behalf and saved them by sending a divine wind or Kamikaze. He went on to explain the dive bombers were the 1945 version of a divine wind sent to save Japan from the Allied invaders.

The boys prepared to return to duty, wondering how long they would be kept at their stations with no break. It looked to be a tension-filled day so they both anticipated long hours. Merle said, "Any duty we have to do is better than picking up and transporting those Yard Mine Sweepers and Patrol Gunboat Motor survivors. Doc Burgess sure did a great job of helping those poor guys. Some of them were pretty bad off. I feel even worse for the guys who were blown clean off the ship. Those poor fools will never be found."

Ton and Merle grew silent again as they remembered the action of the past few weeks. The worst days were the ones when the sailors gathered on deck to drop the canvas-bagged bodies of dead sailors into the ocean. This terrible task made the men take stock of their own chances of survival. It was demoralizing to see a shell casing placed as a weight between the knees of the deceased sailor and then sewn into a bag before being dropped into the ocean. No matter how respectful the ceremony for these dead sailors was, it gave the men a chill to think their final resting place was at the bottom of the ocean.

Although the flag that was draped over the bodies would be removed and sent to the next of kin, it was no substitute for recovering the body of their loved one. It was a rough pill to swallow, but they all had to get on with their duties and put it out of their minds.

Perhaps in an effort to reassure himself of the might of the destroyer Ton recalled, "Remember, our gunners brought down that twin engine bomber with no problem. Those Japs didn't even know what hit 'em. Not only that but a couple hours later we got ourselves that Zeke. I couldn't believe my eyes when that ole Zeke changed course and swooped down on us. Damn, if those gunners, crazy fools, didn't open up with the twenty-millimeter and forty-millimeter fire to bring him down quick as a wink!"

Merle caught the tone and intent of Ton's conversation and followed up with his own perspective of the most positive aspects of that day. Recounting past achievements was the best way to face the danger of the daily life they led, so Merle went on, "Captain Chambers is one smart guy, I tell you. He just ordered the ship's speed up to twenty-five knots. That Zeke tried to wing over, but with our speed up he just passed our stern and crashed smack dab into the ocean. He only cleared our deck by twenty-five yards starboard but we got him for sure. That's what I call a very close shave!"

Merle and Ton finished their break and hustled back to their duty stations: Merle to the dark radio room and Ton to the bright sun of the open-air bridge.

Despite the ever-present danger, Ton delighted in his station on the bridge. The sky had turned a silky blue and the sun was warming things up a bit from the dreary past few days. He possessed a 180-degree view of the horizon. As he prepared his flags, he gazed out from the bridge over the starboard bow toward Aguni Shima, a small outlying island, and from there farther on toward the main island of Okinawa, or the Great Loochoo as the sailors called it.

The first, smaller island was only about six miles from the ship. The main island a bit farther, but from the viewpoint of the ship they might as well have been a million miles away. The islands appeared lush, tranquil, and even beautiful with looming green mountains. However, since the American invasion the reality was vastly different. The lush and tranquil island was not a paradise but now a battlefield where brutal hand-to-hand combat was taking place.

The sailors aboard the destroyers worried daily for their safety, but Ton had heard about the fierce fighting taking place on the island from the Marines they had transported and aided. Japanese soldiers refused to surrender. Caves and tunnels had been dug into the mountains with the Japanese Army entrenched inside, refusing to leave. Americans had been forced to flush them out using grenades and flame throwers. It was neither tranquil nor beautiful any more.

Often times the island was covered by a film of smoke and dust with the screaming sound of shells shattering the air. It was a savage and barbarous combat location, not a Pacific paradise that met Ton's gaze from the bridge.

Near Ton's station the lookout on duty laughed as he watched Ton's meticulous preparation. "Flags, you certainly are persnickety!"

Ton smiled and said, "I just gotta have everything in the right place and ready to go. Quick communication means safety to me, I guess."

The officer of watch scrutinized both men silently as they all went about their business. They were all acutely aware their lives depended on each sailor doing his job rapidly and efficiently. Things seemed to be heating up and the bridge was quickly awash in activity. Ton decoded many messages about the activity on the island and the ships in the area of the beach. Most of these messages were sent via semaphore. The blinkers of flashing lights clicked off the Morse code used to communicate among the surrounding ships. The situation was tense as Ton took this message:

```
X Latest Japanese secret weapon is one man
depth charge boat X Purpose to attack convoys
approaching beach X A boat head for transport
at top speed and as soon as in position to
strike hull of ship makes an about turn
dropping depth charges over stern X
```

"Great," he commented to no one in particular on the bridge, "the Japs have thought of one more way to attack American ships as if the Kamikaze attacks are not enough! We are truly target practice for those Jap attack forces."

Below in the radio room Merle was frantically busy. The radiomen took the messages and passed them on to the officers. With the good weather it appeared a second wave of attackers was on the way. Quickly the message was sent from the radio room, by the officer in charge, to the bridge and pilot house through the communications tube. Everyone was on high alert for incoming planes. None had been spotted yet by either the lookouts or radar.

Merle was beyond anxious. There were no windows in the radio room and although he knew exactly what was going on from the messages they received, he could see nothing. It seemed as if he were living a reality in which he had no part to play but rather must simply endure. All of the equipment in the radio room was bolted down tight so as not to fall during the rough seas, including the seats.

Merle always felt like he was in prison once he was seated at his desk. He could barely move and he knew, no matter what happened, he was there for the duration. He choked back the feeling of claustrophobia that enveloped him. The activity in the room was at a fever pitch with messages flying in and out. Merle's work was constant; he had little time to think or worry about himself.

Up on the bridge Ton received the message everyone knew was coming but all had been dreading. He distributed it quickly to the officer in charge:

```
X USS Jeffers under heavy attack X Proceed to
aid X
```

Within seconds of the arrival of that message Captain Chambers gave the order and the *Lindsey* steamed rapidly to the *Jeffers's* location, ready to provide any help needed, just as it had done for so many other ships in the past months. A few minutes after noon, Ton decoded the next message. This one came from the Force Flight Director.

Anything that came from the Force Director did not bode well for what was coming next. This message was the most feared of all, and it put a chill in Ton's spine as he quickly relayed it.

```
X Heavy attack force of planes in the area X
Vals in area X
```

Despite the new information, orders were orders and the *Lindsey* plugged along on her way to assist the beleaguered *Jeffers*. Everyone, especially those on the bridge, was on pins and needles and each man scanned the horizon constantly looking for attacking planes.

The Identification School training now seemed vitally important rather than boring and all sailors aboard were looking for any signs of bogies, Japanese aircraft of any kind. Even though the warning was somber the *Lindsey* was equipped with radar, pinging away on the ship. So far, no signs had appeared on the scope to indicate incoming bogies on the screen. Everyone hoped the lack of action on the radar screen indicated the bogies had been splashed or better yet turned back by the American fighter aircraft.

Despite the reliance and faith in technology to intercept the planes and allow the men time to prepare their defenses, advance warning was not to be. At 14:45 the look out's frantic voice from his position rang out, "Look over starboard bow. Bogies incoming!" He had sighted the mass Kamikaze attack force headed straight at the *Lindsey*.

Low on the horizon, so low it was difficult to separate the planes from the waves of the ocean, the sailors on the bridge could clearly see an attack force of Kamikaze planes coming straight at their ship. General quarters blared over the vessel as all men raced to their battle stations.

This was not the first Kamikaze attack they had experienced. They had been in the situation before and knew what to do. As Ton watched the approaching planes, the fear in the pit of his stomach gnawed at him and threatened to overtake his ability to respond. He looked on from the bridge in both terror and fascination unable to tear his eyes from the sight of what could be the death of his ship. Today, in their attempt to help a fellow ship, the *USS Lindsey* had run smack into Kikusui Number Two, the second mass Kamikaze attack to be thrown at the forces defending Okinawa.

Someone screamed, "Those bastards snuck over the island of Aguni Shima so low our radar could not pick them up. They don't care if they have enough fuel to make it back or not because those are suicide planes!"

The panic was evident in his voice. Everyone knew there was nothing they could do to prevent the attack except to hope the gunners would be able to shoot them all down. But there were scores of Japanese planes zooming over the American fleet, and the likelihood they would all be shot down was next to none.

Ton now had a front row seat to this life or death show. Like it or not he watched in alarm as three suicide planes closed in on the *Lindsey*'s starboard bow. He gasped in shock and apprehension as four Vals appeared out of nowhere on the horizon. The Japanese had mastered the trick of flying extremely low over land in order to evade the American radar on the ships on The Ping Line. Instead of diving at the ships from high altitude, they skimmed the waves in their low altitude pattern as they zoomed toward the bridge of the *Lindsey*.

The gunners of the *Lindsey* opened fire at the Vals with everything they had. The noise was thunderous. At times their guns were pointed straight up toward the sky in order to hit the planes.

Captain Chambers yelled out orders from the pilot house near Ton's position, "Pivot starboard!" The ship responded to his order rapidly in order to keep the gunners in the best position to fire at the roaring planes as they clustered around the ship.

But the Japanese planes split up. One Val crossed the ship's bow and the other three Vals headed astern. The difficulty of the gunners' job had increased a thousand-fold. Instead, they tried to fire directly into the water, which caused water spouts to form and shoot up from the ocean, blocking the view and, hopefully, confusing the low flying pilots.

The sailors watched for tell-tale ocean splashes of a disorientated pilot crashing into the waves instead of the ship. But their best efforts proved to be useless. The starboard guns fired absolutely everything they had at the Val as he neared the ship. He was only three hundred feet above the ocean. The water spouts did not faze him at all. He set a course and bored intently in, heading right for the bridge. He was so close Ton could see the tail of the white scarf he wore around his head as it fluttered in the wind.

"We got him, we got him!" yelled a starboard gunner. They had, in fact, hit the Val. There was jubilation on the bridge. Ton cheered wildly with relief.

They could see their shells had hit the fuselage of the plane and it was now just a twisted mess of metal, fire, and dark smoke. The plane, which minutes before had been in perfect shape, was now disintegrating as it flew through the air, held together by scraps of metal. Ton could hear the cheers of the sailors on the lower deck as the plane spiraled into a death dive.

But the gunners had underestimated the determination and desire of the Japanese pilot to carry out his mission to crash into the ship. Their cheering died quickly as the determined pilot of the flaming, speeding mass of burning metal gained control over his aircraft and took dead aim at the starboard bow of the Lindsey. There was no doubt he would hit the ship instead of dropping harmlessly into the water as they had hoped.

At 14:47 the racing, fiery plane turned itself into a flying bomb hurtling itself into the ship and exploding at the base of the bridge structure directly under the location where Ton was standing, powerless to intervene in his fate.

Meanwhile, the radio room where Merle and others were feverishly working remained dark. They had taken enough messages to know things in the sky near the ship were not good yet they remained quiet and efficient. The atmosphere in the radio room was uneasy. The fear was palpable. The continuous firing of the gunners rocked the room. The roar of the guns was ear splitting. The acrid smell from the ammunition seeped into the sealed room.

The men held their collective breath. They could hear the cheers go up and smiles spread across their faces. Although they did not know exactly what was happening, Merle knew the cheering voices were a good sign the gunners had been successful.

Suddenly, BOOM.

An unearthly noise erupted right beside the radio room bringing a sensation of heat and motion and the smell of cordite and smoke. The sailors in the radio room looked at each other. Some began to rise from their seats, both curious and afraid of what was happening right outside their door. They heard shouts now and smelled the fire and smoke that billowed from the deck. Fear was raw and rampant throughout the dark hole.

The officer in charge cleared his throat loudly and pulled back his jacket to reveal a gun in a holster around his waist. He calmly told the men, "Stay at your stations, you hear. If anyone gets up, I will shoot you dead!"

The men dropped back into their chairs, unsure of the reason for the chaos outside their door but unwilling to die trying to find out. They all knew the situation was dire, but the men sat obediently, not knowing if they would be rescued or if they would burn to death within this confined area.

Ton, on the other hand, could see it all unfold. When he realized the plane was not going down into the water but was instead headed for the bridge, he dove down to take cover. As the plane hit and exploded, the men on the bridge were thrown in all directions. Shrapnel spread over the bridge. Burning, billowing black smoke rose from below the bridge.

Ton pulled himself up to his feet and peered down on the scene below him. Gasoline, aviation fuel, oil, and flames were everywhere. Fire was leaping, rolling, and taking everyone and everything along with it. The Kamikaze plane had pierced the deck of the ship and rammed directly into the galley where, only hours before, Merle and Ton had sat.

Any sailors who had been in the galley never knew what happened because they were instantly incinerated by the heat, mowed over by the flying, scalding hot shrapnel, or died choking on the black, acrid smoke that filled the area below deck within seconds of impact. The forward sleeping berths of the sailors were demolished along with any sailor not fortunate enough to make it to battle stations before the plane hit.

Some of the blazing ruins of the plane and ship were tossed onto the superstructure deck, just ahead of the bridge. Body parts flew up into the air in front of Ton's eyes, landing on the upper deck. Although horrified, Ton could not take his eyes away from the hellish scene unfolding before him. Absolute chaos and horror continued with seemingly no end. Logically he knew in order to save his life he must get under something and behind a bulkhead.

Oddly, at that moment, he was not thinking about what he must do to save himself. His mind was on Nadeen, Oakdale, the farm, his siblings, and his parents who would mourn him when they found out he was gone.

He willed himself to move and get to the floor behind the bulkhead and under some object that might protect him. He looked up at the sky. Although only two minutes had passed since the attack began, he had already forgotten there were not one but four Vals striking at the *Lindsey*. He peered up and saw the other three Japanese planes. Hell on earth was not yet over.

Ton and Nadeen, 1944.

41

The Divine Wind,
April 12, 1945

" Get down, get down," the officer on watch shouted to the other sailors on the bridge. As an officer he was responsible, but at this moment as chaos erupted around them, it was every man for himself.

Ton hit the floor hard. He could feel the searing heat rising from the wreckage of the first plane on the deck below them. He struggled to open his eyes. His eyes felt as if they were on fire, and he had trouble focusing in the murky haze of smoke that now surrounded the ship. Through his blurry eyes he spotted the ledge. He grabbed onto it to try to pull himself up but quickly retracted his hands now burned from the hot metal that was everywhere, burning and spewing smoke above the ship.

Ton quickly decided that if he had any chance to live he must get up and get off the bridge. He pulled himself all the way to standing and looked out over the bridge. Fire was everywhere as he searched for an escape route. Through the pall of smoke Ton blinked his eyes. He could not believe what he saw.

On the deck below him was an inferno of shrapnel, fire, smoke, bodies, and blood. There were arms and legs lying disconnected from any human body. Men in zombie-like trances were struggling to walk. Some had horrendous burns on their smoldering bodies.

Ton could see the remains of the Kamikaze plane. Miraculously the bomb attached to the bottom of the Val was still intact. It had not exploded on impact but Ton wondered just how long before something set it off. He could see the mangled body of the pilot lying awkwardly out of the ruins of his plane. There was not much left of the body, and Ton would not have even recognized it as being a human if not for the shreds of clothing still wrapped around it. The body, or what was left of it, was also smoldering, but Ton could still make out the remnants of the white cloth he saw flying behind the pilot as he rammed into the ship. Shreds of the white scarf with the red sun were yet visible around the head of the dead pilot.

It was strange that he should notice something as small as this piece of cloth while a scene of catastrophic devastation was taking place around him. Yet it was as if time had slowed down. He could vaguely hear the terrified screams of injured sailors, the pleas for help, and the roar of the raging fire. The reality of yesterday was gone, replaced by this unimaginable world he now inhabited. He was certain this was the end of him and of his ship.

"We are gonna die up here!" the lookout shrieked to the wind. The explosion of the plane hitting the ship had torn into the bridge spewing flaming shrapnel onto the bridge and pilot house. The wounds Ton saw on his fellow bridge mates from this fiery shrapnel were ghastly and gruesome.

He did not know if he had been hit or not because he could not feel a thing. The smell overpowered him: burned metal combined with the repulsive aroma of scorched and melting skin. The smell of blood and death was everywhere. Hot metal, fire, shrapnel, and flaming debris bored into the wardroom just underneath the deck giving the sailors there no chance of escape and immediate death. The three brave gunners of the twenty-millimeter guns had no chance of survival nor did the two men from the nearby gun crew. There was absolutely nothing left.

"Eymann, Eymann, are you still alive? Are you hurt? Have you been hit?" a sailor's voice could be heard among the screams, moans, and bedlam of the bridge. The men who were able to stand and move had already begun to assess the damage in the few seconds following the attack.

Ton touched his head with his hands. Raw pain flashed through his body and everything hurt. He struggled to his feet and fought to maintain his balance. He could vaguely hear the forty-millimeter guns port side firing away. His head felt as if he were inside of a metal building with sound reverberating like the dull beat of a drum. Everything sounded a bit tinny, and there was an unfamiliar ringing in his ears. His head was fuzzy and his reactions slow.

A steady stream of black smoke billowed skyward and formed a gigantic column that rose above the ship. Meanwhile underneath the smoke a growing line of flames was quickly engulfing the ship. The entire destroyer was in danger of sinking to the bottom of the ocean.

As Ton strained to regain his equilibrium, his eyes were drawn to the open, blue sky. As he peered forward from the bridge into the sky, his blurry eyes spotted the most terrifying sight he could possibly see.

A second Val had come around and was headed back toward the ship. He stared into the cockpit of the plane as it whizzed toward him. One wing of the plane had been shot off, the pilot appeared to be dead, and the plane was on fire.

"Dear Jesus in heaven," Ton prayed, "Send that plane into the sea." But his request was not to be granted. As soon as the words left his mouth the ship was rocked by an even bigger explosion than the one caused by the first plane. This detonation sent the men on the bridge flying into the air. Men were hurled back to the floor while others were blown off the ship.

At impact this second Val sliced through the thin skin of the *Lindsey*'s deck between the main deck area and the water line close to the gun mounts. The 550-pound bomb attached to the bottom of the plane blended with the smokeless gunpowder stored in the forward magazine of the ship. This combination of fire, bomb, aviation fuel, shrapnel, and gunpowder created death. This time everything exploded in one gigantic blast. Nothing was left of the sailors who seconds before were at their battle stations on the port side of the ship. They had simply disintegrated. The combustion was immense. The sound was ear splitting. No one on board had ever heard such an explosion.

With the detonation of the bomb the entire ship was lifted out of the water. The men on the bridge were thrown turbulently in every direction. Shrapnel, metal, guns, bedding, food, and bodies were strewn over the entire front area of the ship. The deck of the ship was now on top of the bridge and the bow had been torn completely away from the vessel. The ship slammed back down on the waves.

Inside the radio room of the *USS Lindsey* there was no power, no light, nothing at all. The men stationed there braced themselves. Merle did not know what to expect. Yet even with this heightened awareness that something terrible was happening outside their door, no one was prepared for the vicious lurch of the ship as she was blown up out of the water. Men were sent sprawling in every direction. Mass confusion and chaos ensued as they now fought the panic and terror. They realized that they might be torched to death or drowned inside this dark room. Merle was sure the ship was going down. He knew he would never leave this room or see daylight again in this life. He heard praying above the crying and screaming, "Our father who art in heaven ..."

At the instant Ton saw the second Val headed for the ship, he ducked under debris left by the first explosion. Some cover was better than no cover, and there was no time to do anything else. Then came the bomb blast. Ton's body was lifted and hurled through the air as if he were a weightless insignificant doll. He had no control over his body. Hot metal, shrapnel, fire, and smoke formed a curtain around him. He felt something fiery hot hit his head.

He was sure the ship was sinking and that he was already dead. He fell back to the deck of the bridge, bleeding and unconscious.

42

A New Life Together, April 1945

The train carrying Hans back to Bremerton from Oakdale chugged over new terrain—land that Hans had never seen before. He never tired of looking at the ocean as the train moved along the coast.

Nearing Bremerton he was amazed at the amount of trees and the cold, damp weather. The small towns that dotted the journey of the train caused Hans to miss Oakdale and his family. He knew it was crazy to take this train back to Bremerton but he had to take the chance. Turk had ridden him hard about being too involved with a girl he hardly knew. His enlistment was up and this month he would receive his separation papers. Hans was resolved to see Ann and be with her again. Letters had flown between them the last few weeks. It seemed to Hans that Ann had missed him as much as he missed her. So right or wrong, good or bad, he was on the train and on his way to find out exactly how Ann did feel about him.

Hans peered out of the window anxious as the train stopped in Bremerton. Ann was there waiting for him wearing a red dress with a red hat to match. In her last letter she had told Hans she would be there with red on, just for him. He rose from his seat and practically dove over everyone in his way to get to the exit.

"Hey, doll," he hollered from the doorway.

Ann turned to look at him smiling widely. They hugged each other and kissed in the station. He told her, "You look swell!" They made their way to the car Ann had borrowed from a friend and drove off together.

Ann was introducing Hans to her family today. They were welcoming and kind but the young couple was anxious to be alone. They simply wanted to spend the day together around Bremerton. It really didn't matter to Hans where they were because he was happy just to be with her.

Impulsively, Hans grabbed her hands, swung her around so they were face to face and said, "Ann, I love you. Let's get married."

She laughed and then looked into his eyes to see if he really meant it or if he was simply teasing her the way he loved to do. His eyes and face were absolutely serious. She could tell it took all of his courage to say the words out loud. She searched his face but she was not certain exactly what she was looking for. She hesitated with an answer.

Hans went on, "I mean, we haven't known each other very long but I feel so comfortable with you. My separation papers came this month and I need to make a decision about my future. I want to be with you. What do you say?"

Ann asked, "Oh, Hans, are you sure?" But she had already abandoned her hesitation and jumped into his arms. "Yes, Hans, yes, yes, I will marry you."

"I don't want to wait," Hans continued. "Let's go home and tell your parents and start planning for a wedding. I need to start looking for work and we need a place to live so we better get busy."

The arrangements were made. At this point in the war there had been so many quick weddings it was nothing out of the ordinary. The wedding was held on a beautiful spring day. Hans, Ann, her parents, and family went to city hall for a simple wedding in front of the justice of the peace. Hans had not even had time to tell his family. And so they started their new life.

43

Three Minutes to Hell,
April 12, 1945

C aptain Chambers's voice barked out a rapid order, "All back full, all back full!" The wounded ship reversed direction. With this order the captain saved the incredibly damaged ship from sinking.

This backward motion prevented the in-rushing water caused by the horrific explosion from collapsing the fire room bulkhead. As the *USS Lindsey* went all back full with everything it had, the water displaced from the explosion of the second plane shot up into the air and poured over the flaming bridge. The Captain had not only saved the bulkhead to preserve the ship, his order had also extinguished the fire caused by the first Val. In a day filled with misfortune this was one piece of extraordinary good luck. Without Captain Chambers's quick action, the ship would have been inundated with water and sunk within minutes.

On the bridge was an eerie, uneasy stillness. For the first few seconds after the ship came back to rest in the water there was no movement or commotion. Then the men still alive began to stir. Ton's blood-soaked hands pushed off the debris that covered his aching body as he looked around to take stock of his situation.

Ink-like smoke poured from the site where the second plane imploded. Men were running in all directions. The chaos and noise were unbelievable. Ton looked out over the bow ... there was no bow! It had been torn from the ship and was sticking straight up in the air over the bridge. The area where the fire control equipment was kept was gone, blown to bits in the first attack.

Ton was exhausted from the immense effort of raising himself up to standing. His legs crumpled beneath him and he was, once again, on the deck of the bridge. He could feel an abnormal cold creep through his entire body and he felt tired. So tired. Blood was pouring from his head wound and formed pools under his body. He sat up, was immediately overcome with dizziness, and quickly vomited from the amount of smoke and aviation fuel fumes he had inhaled.

He realized he must move or die. He got to his feet. He saw dead sailors lying at odd angles here and there on the bridge. He called out as he searched for other survivors, "Anyone here? Anyone left alive?" Through the dusty air he spotted the lookout standing upright on the bridge. He was quietly and methodically taking off his shoes and socks.

Ton's throat was dry and painful. It took some effort to speak but he managed to spit out the words, "What in the hell are you doing? Get down. There may be more planes coming. This is not over yet. Take cover!"

But he did not answer. He simply looked at Ton with eyes that registered fear, confusion, and anguish. He did not seem to be seriously hurt and was able to complete his task with no difficulty. He placed his shoes and socks neatly under the debris of the bridge, walked calmly over to the side, and before Ton could react, he jumped into the ocean.

Ton screamed, "Stop, stop!"

But it was too late. He was gone. Ton rushed over to the edge of the bridge and looked out over a scene directly from hell. There was a mass of dead bodies floating in the water, their lifeless eyes open to the blue sky. Amid the bodies, metal, shrapnel, and the bobbing heads of sailors floated among the burning pools of aviation fuel and oil leaked from the first plane.

Ton searched the waters and called out again in this muddle of humanity and carnage but his shipmate was nowhere to be seen.

"Jesus Christ," Ton cursed. He guided his damaged body closer to the edge to get a better look. He looked up at the clear blue sky where he could see the other two Vals veering away from the *Lindsey*. He knew those planes were convinced the ship was in the throes of death and was sinking so they headed off to look for fresh targets.

Damage, death, smoke, fire, and destruction were all that remained of his ship. Above the mangled deck, debris flew everywhere in the wind. Paper, clothing, provisions from the galley were strewn all over. The twisted deck plates and steel of the ship were now mixed with hamburger and butter from the galley refrigerator and the AA ammunition from the forward magazine.

Ton looked again to the sky searching fearfully for more planes. In the rigging of the ship he could see bedding, linen, and clothing. Thankfully no planes were on the horizon so he turned his attention to the deck. The metal plating of the ship had melted and gray droplets dripped into the ocean like solder from a welder's gun. Amid the ruins of the deck he could see body parts, blood, and injured seamen begging for help everywhere. Some men were burned beyond recognition while others sat dazed and bleeding oblivious of their severe injuries and in shock.

Ton watched as a sailor reached into the water to assist another and pull him back out of the burning water. But, to Ton's horror, the sailor's burned skin melted from his body and the sailor on deck was left holding only the skin of the now drowning sailor. The smell of scorched flesh was in the air along with the odor of hot metal, smoke, and the distinct aroma of aviation fuel. Ton knew he would never be able to get that smell out of his mind.

He looked out again over the horizon at the Vals retreating into the distance. He decided to leave the bridge.

Ton inched his way through the wrecked equipment, paper, wires, and debris of the bridge over to the communication area. He pushed aside the shrapnel but it was still hot and burned his hands. He needed to try out the systems to see if there was any power and communication capability on the ship. They needed help now. He must send a flag signal for help. There was no lighting, no telephone, and no power at all. Ton found three other sailors alive on the bridge.

One panicked sailor asked, "Can we fire if any other planes come in?"

"Hell, no, we can't fire," came the gruff reply from the officer of watch. "Them bastards blew our Number Two gun mount clean up to the bridge. Don't you see it hanging in the rigging?"

He continued, "We need to get a message out to the other ships for immediate help. If we are sinking, we need them to come and pick up survivors. If we manage to stay afloat, we are sitting ducks for any other Jap who wants to dive on us. We have no forward guns and no power." The crew members knew communication was their only chance for survival.

But another sailor voiced his doubt, "We gotta get out of here pronto. This ship could still blow and there may be more Vals coming in. If they see us still afloat, they will attack and we are dead in the water."

The officer disagreed, "If you jump in that water and we do sink, you will be pulled down with it. The ship may blow but it may not, so your best chance is to stay put."

He ordered Ton, "Send a signal out for help—ASAP."

Ton heard the words being said but his vision was locked on the surreal scene taking place on the deck below them. He could see a sailor cradling the head of a shipmate who was burned and bleeding profusely. The sailor was speaking calmly and the wounded sailor offered a weak reply from time to time. It was clear that he was dying. Then he gently released the sailor's head to rest back on the deck and clasped his two hands together in front of him in a posture of thoughtful prayer. He made the sign of the cross as life ebbed out of the sailor. While all around him disorder, pandemonium, and bedlam ensued, one sailor was graciously and lovingly praying for his shipmate.

Ton responded to the scene, "This cannot actually be happening. What kind of people send planes into ships and kill themselves on purpose?" The fires burned, the smoke billowed, as he sat numbly waiting and pondering his next move. Any decision or action he should take weighed like a five-ton weight on his shoulders. He was incapable of making either one.

As sailors now scurried to try to save themselves or to help their fellow shipmates, one sailor stopped on the deck directly below the bridge. The remains of the first Japanese plane were littered there. Ton watched him bend down toward the wreckage of the plane and take a pocket knife from his dungarees. He calmly scraped at something on the deck with his knife. Ton could not imagine in his wildest dreams what could be so important to save in the midst of this chaos. He watched more closely now and he saw what the sailor was after. He had peeled what appeared to be the thumb of the Japanese pilot from the melted deck and wreckage. He put the thumb in his pocket and quietly and quickly walked away.

Through the chaos of the besieged ship now covered by the suffering of men, oil, smoke, fire, and burning metal, Ton looked up to see the ship's clock in the pilot's house. It had been jerked from the bulkhead and was dangling precariously over the captain's chair. He saw the hands frozen now, never to move again, stilled at 14:48. Three minutes, Ton thought, three minutes was all it took to change the world forever for the men of the *Lindsey*.

USS Lindsey, *official Navy photo, 1943.*

USS Lindsey *after the Kamikaze attack at Okinawa, April 12 1945.*

44

Modern Life, Bremerton, 1945

Since the wedding Hans had spent his time these last few months in Bremerton with Ann. Just before the wedding he completed his separation from the Navy and was honorably discharged. Turk had also received his separation papers.

Hans was pained when he considered Turk and the fiasco with Kay and the divorce. Turk had since gone home to Oakdale. He was driving a truck and doing farm work, but Mom wrote that Turk never left the farm. His heart had been broken and all he wanted to do was work and stay home. Hans wished he could be there to help, but now he had a wife to support. He had never been the sort to sit back and wait for life to happen to him so he was making the rounds of businesses, factories, and anywhere else he felt he might be able to put his skills to good use and make money. He would get a good job soon, he was sure.

But despite his happiness in Bremerton his mind often drifted back to the farm on the banks of the Elkhorn in Nebraska. Maybe he should head home and take his young bride with him. He was young and strong. He could get work as a farm hand, drive a truck, or work at the cement factory. He wanted a job where he could be out in the fresh air and feel free. He never wanted to feel the claustrophobia of the cramped radioman compartment of an Avenger again, or anything that resembled it.

Hans had a plan. He would go home to Oakdale for a visit, look for work, and then convince Ann to join him. The plan was great but he was worried about how Ann would feel about it. He vowed to say nothing to her of his plan yet or she would throw a fit for sure.

She loved being closer to her family in Bremerton but, most of all, to her friends. As she explained to Hans she had grown very close to them during the war. They worked together and played together. They were inseparable.

He wasn't at all sure, if push came to shove, whether he would win the battle if he gave her the choice of staying here or going to Nebraska with him. In fact, Hans worried a great deal about the way Ann would "meet" her friends after she finished her shift. When he voiced his displeasure and cautioned her about the amount of time she spent with friends having drinks, she would sigh and say, "Oh, Hans, don't be so old fashioned! You know us girls helped the war effort. Shoot, some of my friends even learned how to weld to build those ships for your boys. Times have changed. It is perfectly fine for girls to go to work and just like you boys we need some time to relax after those long hours of hard work. I need to see and talk with my friends. We just joke around and shoot the breeze. Don't you worry now!"

Hans tried to reason with her, "Why can't you have your friends over here at the apartment? Why do you have to meet them at the bar? You know there are lots of sailors hanging around down there just looking for girls!"

Ann rolled her eyes and crossed her arms tightly over her chest as she lectured Hans, "Because it is close to work and easy for us to walk there for a couple of drinks before we come on home. Hans, this is 1945 and you just gotta adjust to the modern woman. I am not your momma."

She went on, "I am young and alive and I am not gonna hide myself away and work myself to the bone at the factory and then come home and do housework here too without having a little bit of fun. Just let me live a little, will ya? I don't bellar and whine when you have a few beers with the guys. Let's not argue about this anymore, okay? Let's move on to bigger and better things."

And with that Hans let it go for now. He knew there was no use in arguing with Ann once her mind was made up. She was as stubborn as they came.

Ann was an enigma to Hans. It was as if an artist had pencil drawn the outline of a person and neglected to fill her in. So it was with Ann's interior. The inside of her lines was sketched in by whomever she was with or whatever situation she encountered. When she was home with Hans, Ann was the dutiful wife, cleaning, cooking, sewing, quiet and neat. At her job she was a faithful and loyal worker. She came to work every day and did whatever was necessary for the war effort. To her parents she was obedient and kind.

Yet when she was with her friends, she took on their character, a character that, to Hans, was totally foreign. Her lines then filled in with drinking, laughing, and ribald jokes. Swear words came from her mouth that Hans only heard from other sailors.

They had met and married in such a hurry he now realized he did not really know who Ann was. The situation would bear watching and he worried plenty about it.

But Hans did bring up another subject with her. "Ann, I need to go home for a while and help my folks. Chub and Turk are both home helping out but Ton is still in the Pacific. I am gonna take the train home for a couple weeks."

Not wanting to antagonize him further than she already had, Ann nodded her head. She understood the need for family. "Sure, Hans. We can scrape some money together. Go home for a visit."

Several days later Hans boarded the train for the long ride to Nebraska leaving Ann to her modern life.

45

The Harsh Truth of Liberty, Lincoln, Nebraska, June 1945

Lincoln, Nebraska, was the perfect spot for Nadeen and her mom to make their wartime home. There were plenty of job opportunities for both of them, and the apartment they shared was cozy and warm. Nadeen enjoyed the time she spent alone with her mom. It kept her worry about Ton at bay to have her mom close. Work was the perfect antidote to worry, so she worked as much as possible.

Nadeen worked at Egger's Market while her mom worked her shift at Ben Simons. In addition to her job at the store Nadeen often babysat for Colonel Smith and his wife in the big white house on Huntington Street. She was able to protect her mom now and keep her safe.

This sunny Sunday afternoon she had a break with nowhere to go and no work to do so she decided to walk outside. She was not sure where Ton was right now. The last word she had from him contained a coded message. But the strange-sounding name meant little to her—Iwo Jima—until the news reports began to filter in. To her utter horror she heard the stories of the American loss of life and the bloody battle that took place there. But that was months ago. She had not received word from Ton in weeks, and worry was as much a part of her daily life as eating and sleeping.

Egger's Market, University Place, Lincoln, Nebraska, 1945.

The spring weather in Nebraska had turned toward summer with the sun beating down a warm eighty degrees. Nadeen made a list in her head as she walked to occupy her mind. She listed the chores to do at home, the errands for tomorrow, and the work schedule for the week. As she turned the corner in University Place, she passed the small store selling candy, soft drinks, and magazines to the students from the nearby college.

In the window was a sign: "Latest Liberty Magazine on Sale Today." She didn't have much spare money but decided she would like to have something to read this afternoon plus she would be getting paid extra tonight for babysitting. In addition to the colonel's kids, their friends were bringing their two children for her to watch. She purchased the magazine, chatted about the weather with the clerk, and then left the store.

Nadeen leafed through the magazine, looking at the photos as she continued her walk back to the apartment. Suddenly, Nadeen felt as if all of the air was being squeezed out of her body. She dropped to her knees on the sidewalk. There in the middle of the magazine was a picture of Ton's ship, the *USS Lindsey*, and a short caption. What she saw in the picture was not really a ship at all but a mass of twisted steel and mangled metal. As she read the caption, fear swelled up in her throat and she could barely breathe.

"The ship," she read, "had been hit by two Kamikaze planes." She quickly scanned the page for more information. The short article gave no details of how many men were killed or wounded. Of course, those facts would be kept from the public as they would surely damage the morale of the soldiers and the families waiting at home if they knew the full truth. It simply stated the ship was being repaired at Kerama Retto. One look at the state of the damage told her that many sailors lost their lives on that ship.

Nadeen struggled to function. She must get home as quickly as possible; surely someone has had word from him! He could not have died in that inferno of a ship. She looked up now at the people passing by seeking assurance in their faces that Ton was not dead.

A kindly couple stopped to help her up thinking she had tripped and fallen, but when they saw her face and the picture from the magazine gripped tightly in her hands, they knew it had nothing to do with the uneven sidewalk or carelessness. They had seen that look on other faces during this war.

Nadeen stumbled blindly home, gripping the magazine still in her hand but unaware of its existence. The picture was starting to blur as the sweat pouring from her hand ran into the magazine. Maybe if she gripped it tightly enough she would stall the bad news she was expecting. She must find out if Ton had made it through the attack.

She pushed all thoughts of catastrophe from her mind and focused on what she must do at home. First, she must tell her mother. Next she should write Ton's family. Maybe they had received word of the attack and of his fate. She prayed she would not have to be the one to break the news to Ton's mother and father of the attack on the *Lindsey* with the probability their son might be dead.

Ton and Nadeen during Ton's last leave, 1944.

46

Hothead Heartbreak, Bremerton, 1945

Hans had been sitting on that blasted train for hours but it seemed more like days to him. He was hot, sweaty, hungry, and thirsty. On the bright side, though, he was on his way back to Bremerton after a visit home.

Fortunately, Tude and Al had been able to take him to the train station in Omaha, but they could only take him if he could leave on Thursday. His original plan had been to head back the following Saturday, but he could not turn down a free ride to Union Station. He considered sending a Western Union telegram to Ann to let her know he would arrive early but decided against it due to the extra cost. She knew he was coming home in a few days anyway, and he could certainly walk from the train station.

He made up his mind to surprise her with his early homecoming. He bought her a heart-shaped necklace. He was hoping the early arrival and necklace just might offset the proposal he had for her: he wanted to move back to Oakdale and take her with him. He knew it would be a battle but he also knew it was the right thing to do.

During his days in Oakdale, Hans spent time roaming the farm, taking the dogs to the river for walks and swims, drinking beers, and catching up with his old buddies who had also enlisted and served just as he had. Chub and Turk delighted in having him back, even for a short time, and they quickly put him to work.

Hans's gruff exterior crumpled just a bit when he realized Ton was not there. No one knew for sure where he was. Things were so hush-hush with the war. There had been no word from Ton in quite a long while, and Hans could see the toll it was taking on his parents, especially Chriss. Hans shuddered as he thought of how close he, Turk, and Chub had come to not making it back home in one piece. He worried for his younger brother still in the Pacific because the odds were stacked against him. He pushed the thought from his mind.

It was somber at times to be with friends at home and to see a hole in the group where three of them were missing. These were the unlucky ones who had died in the fierce fighting and were gone forever. Oakdale, like the rest of the country, was not exempt from the loss of life so many families had suffered. Driving through Oakdale and Tilden, Hans saw the houses with the Gold Stars hanging in the windows. He shook his head sorrowfully to think of the mothers and fathers who had lost a son to the war and the agony they had to endure, knowing their son would never come home. The Gold Star in the window was the only reminder left.

But by far the hardest thing to see had been his father. Hans had not laid eyes on Chriss for months. Chriss could have walked past Hans on the street and he would not have known his own father.

Chriss was gaunt and haggard as if he were a sailor who had been forced overboard and left stranded on an island for months. His arms were as thin as the handle of a rake and his legs were no better.

Despite his ravaged appearance Chriss never seemed to tire. In fact, he now worked more hours than before. There were dark circles under his eyes. His brown eyes had a blank, frightening stare, and when he looked at Hans, it seemed as if he was just looking through him, not really seeing him at all. He was a hollow shell of the man he had been when Hans had left Oakdale for the Navy.

So Hans tried, oh how he tried, to reach Chriss. He went out to the fields with him daily to help and to try to draw him into conversation about the weather, the crops, anything. He tried to eat dinner with Chriss but inevitably Chriss would disappear into the night. No one could find him. They were never sure where he went, but Jix seemed to be his ever-present shadow accompanying him on his nightly rounds. Hans hoped Jix could keep Chriss safe. Try as he might Hans could not seem to reach into Chriss's veiled reality and pull him back. Still, he tried every day. In exasperation Hans turned to his mother for advice.

Hattie declared, "If only you boys would all come home, then I think things would be better. Chriss could see you every day and he would realize you are all okay. Mostly, right now, we just need to hear from Ton. We all need to know he is safe and alive. Then your dad's mind could be at peace."

But as the family listened each night to the radio and the news turned to the war, they lived with fear in their hearts. The battle for Okinawa raged and they knew, without a doubt, that Ton was there. The reports of causalities from Okinawa were staggering and they choked back sobs as they listened. Chriss had long ago quit listening to the radio news reports. Hans was glad for this now because he knew it would only make things worse.

Chriss was nowhere to be found when Al and Tude arrived to pick up Hans. He could not bring himself to say goodbye to Hans. For his part, Hans was not even sure his father understood that he was going back to Bremerton, not to the Pacific, although he had tried to explain it to his dad many times.

Instead, Hans stood with Hattie before entering the car and vowed to his mother he would return as soon as possible to help out on the farm. He never mentioned his new wife to his family. It didn't seem like the right time to tell them. Hans didn't think of how he would break the news to Ann about moving home either. He simply pretended that part of his life did not exist. Chriss and

Hattie had enough to worry about, and he would not add fuel to that fire. He would deal with it himself in his own way, but he would return to help his family.

The train plugged along and Hans dozed from time to time. He listened to the conversations of the other passengers while trying to keep his mind occupied and off the terrible situation at home. He was anxious to reunite with Ann as soon as he could, so when the train finally stopped at the Bremerton station he grabbed his satchel and jumped off the train.

He felt energized to be back and to being so close to seeing his wife. He loved her and was sure he could somehow convince her to move with him back to Oakdale, if even just for a while, to help his family. With his newly found energy he walked back to their apartment through the damp evening air. He felt to make sure the box with the necklace was safely tucked into his pocket.

He bounded through the door of the building and ran up the flights of stairs to their apartment. The building was quiet with only the common evening sounds of radios and the smells of recently cooked dinners lingering in the air.

The apartment was totally silent as he unlocked the door. He walked through the tiny flat and called her name but no response. That is odd he thought; she should be home by now. But Hans knew Ann and he thought there was a good chance with him being gone she had stopped for a drink with her friends after work. With the satchel still slung over his shoulder, he decided to go to the pub and surprise her there. He walked the few blocks to her favorite bar.

Hans pulled open the door of the crowded establishment. He wove his way through throngs of people looking for Ann or any of her friends. The first one he saw was Mary and the look on her face when she saw him was anything but happy.

"Hans, what are you doing here? You are supposed to be in Nebraska," she stated, taking his arm and leading him to the front of the bar.

Hans shook off her arm and said, "Have you seen Ann? I want to surprise her so I came home early. Is she here?" Hans turned to walk through the bar but Mary stepped in front of him again.

"Hey, Hans, tell me about home," she stalled. Then the crowd moved just enough for Hans to get a view of the dark back part of the bar. There was Ann, sitting on the lap of a soldier in uniform, her arms tightly wound around his neck and kissing him passionately as he ran his hands up and down her thighs and back!

Hans's anger shot out white hot. He ran toward the table, pulled Ann off the surprised soldier, and punched him squarely in the mouth. The soldier's chair tumbled over backward, and he scrambled to get up and away from this madman. Hans continued to pelt him with blows as several men grabbed his arms and legs and attempted to pull him away.

Ann screamed, "Hans, knock it off. Stop. Stop! I can explain!"

Sputtering with anger, and being held back by unfamiliar men, Hans turned to face her. For a split second he was not sure what he would do. Then he made a brash decision.

He pulled the gift box out of his pocket and threw it at Ann, "There, there is the gift I wanted to surprise you with but instead you surprised me! How many times have you done this before? How many other soldiers were there? There is no explanation here. There is nothing here between us at all. I wash my hands of you. Don't talk to me, don't call me, and don't contact me in any way ever again. I'm going home for good!"

With those words Hans adjusted his rumpled clothing, secured his satchel of belongings, and walked out the door leaving a crying, flustered Ann in a heap on the floor. He walked straight back to the train station, bought a ticket back to Nebraska and out of Bremerton. He never wanted to come back. He was certain he had the answer to his question about his future. Where did his future lie? Back in Oakdale. He was going home and never looking back. Never!

47

The Boneyard, Kerama Retto, April 12, 1945

❝ If there is a place worse than hell then I am in it." Ton's high school history teacher had explained to them that Abraham Lincoln had used these words to describe his anguish over the Civil War. Those words seemed appropriate to describe what Ton saw.

Kerama Retto was one of the smallest islands in the Ryukyus and lay only a dozen or so miles south of Okinawa. When the invasion of Okinawa was planned, it was decided to first target Kerama in order to use the island as a staging area for the coming assault. Kerama provided anchorage for the American ships and an ideal location for supplying and maintaining the forces needed to invade Okinawa. The island was taken easily on March 26, 1945.

But no one could have predicted that one of the main uses of the island would be as the destination for the ships devastated by Kamikaze attacks. Now it was the *USS Lindsey*'s turn to be hauled stern first into the anchorage of Kerama. Ton's eyes gazed over the docks where he could see ship after ship that lay anchored with their decks blown apart or some other horrendous damage visible.

The twisted steel and mangled metal of the ships was not the worst sight by a long way. Ton gazed at the docks lined with gauzy white sheets fluttering in the breeze. Under these sheets he could see the outline of the sailors who had perished in the attacks on their ships. They were waiting on the docks to be identified and accounted for before burial.

The sadness and finality of the view bothered Ton. He averted his gaze from them toward the living, moving sailors. Yet this vista brought no relief for these were the walking wounded of the attacks. He saw sailors with indescribable burns over their arms, legs, faces, or for some their entire bodies. One of the worst injuries but unfortunately the most common in the Kamikaze attacks were the burns and Ton could not get the sight or the smell out of his mind.

His hand moved up to his head to feel the bandage. He gave a prayer of gratitude that when the bleeding was finally stopped all that remained was a gash caused by the shrapnel. He was not even hurt that badly, and when he looked around at the other wounded sailors he forgot there was anything wrong with him at all. He had been blessed by God and spared while so many others had not.

Ton heard a shuffling noise approach him as the ship drifted deeper into Kerama. Merle came and stood quietly beside him. For a few minutes they stood together that way, lost in thoughts, and glad to be alive.

Merle told Ton about the instant the door to the radio room was opened. He stepped out and was shocked and immediately felt dizzy to find the bow of the ship missing. Merle was unscathed physically in the attack but emotionally it was a different story. He had been unable to see the Kamikaze attacks entombed as he was in the dark and isolated radio room. He was mortified as he emerged into the light of day to see the causalities and the wounded lying everywhere.

The dead and dying were all around him, yet he had not a scratch anywhere on his body. How could that happen? Immense devastation took place, yet a few feet from where he stood no one was injured. It was the luck of the draw he guessed,

Heavily damaged, the USS Lindsey was towed into port at Kerama Retto after a Kamikaze attack.

but that did not make it any easier to bear. Somehow his mind just could not wrap itself around what had just happened to his ship and his buddies.

Finally Merle spoke, "Do you think they will be able to repair the ship or will she have to be scuttled?"

When Ton replied, even he was shocked to hear the other worldly quality of his voice. Life as he knew it changed forever that day and it registered in his words. "Merle, Captain Chambers saved our ship for a purpose. She didn't sink so I think she can be repaired somehow, some way. It is going to be a major job but these guys can do it. Look around. You can see they are working on the other ships to get them back out there and help our guys at Okinawa."

Merle's voice wavered a bit with emotion as he continued, "I had no idea what had happened while we were in the radio room. I sure am glad to see you alive. How badly were you hurt? You know you will get a Purple Heart for this, right?"

Ton's eyes flashed and he sighed deeply as he responded, "Ya, Merle, I am okay. Just a scratch really. But I swear on the bible I will not put in for a Purple Heart! Look around Merle. These guys were hurt much worse than me. I could not live with it if I put myself on their level. They are the ones who deserve the Purple Heart, not me by a long shot."

The men grew silent again. The ship was making its way to Wiseman's Cove, the repair facility of Kerama Retto. It was lined with ships waiting their turn. But now it was the *Lindsey's* turn to dock, remove the dead and wounded, and take stock of their situation.

Within days the surviving sailors of the *Lindsey* would be asked to perform some of the most gruesome, demanding tasks of the war. When the time came a few days later to send men into the lacerated bow to recover the bodies of the sailors trapped under the deck, Ton volunteered. Six days after the Kamikazes hit the ship, it was both his grim duty and his distinct honor to carefully extract his fellow sailors from the ship where they gave their lives.

In the next few days news of the outside world filtered in to the men of the *Lindsey*. In an ironic twist of fate the Kamikaze attacks had not been the only devastating blow to the Americans on April 12, 1945. The men learned that their Commander-in-Chief, President Franklin Delano Roosevelt, had died on the same date.

There was no time to mourn or grieve. The war was still on and Kerama Retto was as much a target as Okinawa. Ton resolved to do his part to help in whatever way he could to get his ship back into fighting shape and do his duty.

Part VII

Up home on the Eymann family farm, Oakdale, Nebraska.

Homefront

48

Along the Banks of the Elkhorn, Fall 1946

The war was over. Peace had finally settled over Europe and the Pacific. Life was slowly returning to normal. The Eymann boys had all returned to Oakdale except for Ton. With several months remaining in his enlistment he had been sent to Guantanamo Bay, Cuba, with his ship, the *Lindsey*. His letters home now were full of stories of sightseeing and playing golf. Navy duty there held little danger and the family was more at ease with his situation.

Turk worked constantly either helping at the farm or driving trucks. He had met a beautiful bank teller named Marian during the summer. They met while swimming with friends at the river. They would hold their cigarettes over their heads while they swam out to a sandbar to bask in the sun. Turk was seeing her from time to time, but a shadow of sorrow still surrounded him and he preferred to spend most of his time alone, working on the farm.

Chub returned home from the service and had been back the longest. He was also working on the farm. While in town one day he met a pretty store clerk named Bonnie. Hans told him, "If you don't ask her out I will." Chub asked her out immediately! Chub and Bonnie were in love and planning to marry soon.

Ton Eymann, Guantanamo Bay, Cuba, 1945.

Ton on leave, 1945. From left, Betty, Nadeen, Ton, and Turk.

Turk at the Eymann farm, 1945.

Hans did not waste time pining away over Ann. He had already met Lucile who was the exact opposite of everything Ann had been. She was attractive, hard-working, wise, and kind. Hans was head over heels in love with her and planned to ask her to marry him, but he had yet to tell her he had been married before. He was waiting for the perfect moment to break the news and was a little bit scared.

The only cloud on the horizon was Chriss. Hattie had asked all of the boys to keep a good eye on him during the days of working on the farm. She was worried. To those outside of the family nothing seemed amiss. Chriss worked harder than ever and put in long, grueling days in the fields and taking care of the animals. There were times when he loved company, especially when Lucile came to the farm. He would talk to her about the boys and their exploits in school, sports, and the war.

But then there were those days when Chriss disappeared both physically and mentally. There were the times of blue funk when he just sat, staring straight ahead, saying nothing and recognizing no one. Sometimes he went to the cellar to be alone. Other times, when Hattie looked out of her window she would see his silhouette drifting through the shelter belt of trees. The Elkhorn River seemed to hold a fascination for him, and they would find him walking the banks staring into the cold waters.

No matter where he went Jix was always with him. If he set out for the fields to work, Jix was there. When Chriss did his chores, Jix went with him. If he walked the river, Jix trailed a bit behind. Hattie observed, "Jix is the best friend Chriss has. He watches over him constantly."

The boys just knew their dad had a lot on his mind. He never spoke of his worries or concerns, but when he set out alone they knew he was lost in a gloom they could not penetrate.

Back home, Hans, 1946.

Eymann family portrait taken during Ton's leave in the fall of 1946. From left: Betty, Mick, Hattie Mae, Ton with hand on Wella, Chriss, Chub, and Deets.

Early spring 1945. Chub stands with Chriss and Hattie. His injured leg is still in the cast.

49

The Tribulation and the Sorrow, January 13, 1947

The cold Nebraska wind whipped up the powdery snow that lightly covered the ground near the farmhouse. Inside, the boys and Hattie were gathered around the kitchen table. Hattie began to speak in a worried voice, "Turk, Dad did not come in for dinner today. I am worried and I have a bad feeling this time."

The war was over and the boys were all home now. Chub, Hans, and Turk worked at the farms around Oakdale and helped Chriss with his farm work too. Ton received his separation papers at the end of September and was now living in Lincoln attending Wesleyan University and working. The cruel days of drought and war were behind them, and the family looked toward the future. Life was returning to the normal work of the seasons for everyone except Chriss.

It seemed things were getting progressively worse with him. It was not unusual now for him to disappear for hours or even days without anyone knowing where he was. Turk looked up at his mother and then over to Hans and Mick who were seated at the table.

"Ma, you know he doesn't want to be bothered. You know those moods he gets into. Even if we went to look for him, there is no guarantee he would even take notice of us. Just let him be. He'll come back when he is ready. I am tired of taking

Chriss and Hattie Mae, Fall 1946.

care of him! Mick, Hans, and I need to get some hay out to the cattle today. There is more snow coming and we need to be ready. I already got lots to worry about, I'm not gonna borrow trouble today."

Hans nodded in agreement but Mick just watched them silently with his big brown eyes. At seventeen years of age he should have been in school but lately he skipped days to stay home more, watch over his mother, and help her. More often than not these days his father was not even capable of taking care of himself. His mother needed help with the farm, the house, and his little sisters.

"No, boys," Hattie set her foot down, "this feels different to me. I need all of you to go and look for your dad and bring him back to the house. I certainly don't want him to freeze to death if he is having one of his spells outside. Please go and find him," she begged the boys.

Hans was the first one up, "C'mon, let's go, the sooner we bring him back the sooner we get our work done." The three boys slipped on their coveralls, boots, coats, and hats and set out the door.

They began to look for Chriss's footprints in the snow but the gusting wind had erased any signs and none were to be found. The boys walked the tree line of the shelter belt scanning for him but no sign of Chriss at all or even that he had been there. Chriss often liked to walk the river bank. It made sense for the boys to separate and look for him in different locations along the river, but a feeling of dread that had possessed Hattie now had overtaken the boys and they stayed together in their search.

Abruptly, a high-pitched, moan floated on the wind. At first Turk thought it was only a gust blowing through the crevices in the hen house or barn, but he then realized it was much too loud and insistent for that. Silently, Turk turned toward the barn with Hans and Mick following. The noise was coming from there, he was sure. The barn door was slightly ajar and had caught in the frozen, muddy rut in front of it. Hans and Mick backed Turk up as he strode toward the door. The noise was louder now and was animalistic in nature. Turk was sure some animal was sick or dying. He entered the door and walked cautiously to the far end of the barn with Mick and Hans close behind.

There, on the straw-covered floor, lay Jix, moaning and crying. Turk looked up. His throat caught as he saw his father dangling from the end of a rope tied to the beam of the hayloft.

"Hans," he screamed, "get your knife and shimmy up there! Cut him down quickly. He might still be alive!"

Hans did as he was ordered. Although Mick's eyes were wide with fright, he followed Turk over to his father and as Hans cut the rope, Turk and Mick lowered the lifeless body to the floor.

Mick fell to his knees, feeling for his father's heartbeat but his skin was already cold and blue. As Mick knelt over him, cradling his head on his lap, his tears began to fall and he cried, "Turk, do something!"

Turk's face was white with terror and anger as he felt for his father's pulse. Nothing, no response. How long had he been hanging here? No one knew except that it had been too long. He was gone.

Hans scurried down the ladder to assist his brothers, prepared to take any action necessary. He dropped to his knees alongside Mick as they frantically tried to revive their father. Turk stared at the rope still in his hands.

Finally, he straightened himself, threw the rope to the ground in disgust and stated, "Nothing left to do. He is dead. We have to take him back to ma."

Turk, Hans, and Mick lifted the lifeless body of their father. He had worn only his overalls. His shirt was worn through at the elbows and his skin poked through the disintegrating fabric. His cuffs were frayed with the years of wear and work. Several buttons were missing from his shirt. He was as light as a feather as the boys carried him from the barn up to the house. Their only thought now was of their mother.

"Hans, go in and set Mom down at the table," Turk suggested. "Tell her that we found Dad and are bringing him home. Tell her he is hurt but don't tell her the truth, got it?"

Turk's intentions were good but Hattie already knew. Her instincts were right. She had been sure that something terrible had happened. Hattie was already crying, sobbing, and screaming as they entered the house with his body.

"Why, why, why? Chriss, why now? Why did he do this now? All of the boys are home. They are all safe. Why, Chriss?" She rocked herself back and forth in the kitchen chair in a feeble attempt to regain normalcy and comfort but it was not to be.

"Ma," Mick said as he hugged her tightly in his arms, "Ma, it's not his fault. Ma, the war did him in. It just plain did him in!" Mick bravely tried to explain this new reality to his mother.

"God damn it, God damn it," Turk cursed under his breath.

Hans sat with his head in his hands, shaking his head back and forth in disbelief. The next half hour passed quickly as the boys sought to comfort their mother as well as console each other.

Finally it was Turk who pulled himself together and took charge. He directed, "Today, everything has changed. This is what is going to happen. Mick, you will stay here with Mom. We will go and tell Chub to pick the little girls up from school and keep them. Hans, bring up the car. We will put Dad in and take him to the mortuary. You and I will be the ones to make all of the arrangements together. Tonight we will call None, Tude, and Ton to come home right away. We will waste no time on this. We will have this damn funeral, get through this together, and then we will put it all behind us."

He went on, "Then, I swear on everything that is holy, I will never say his name again in my life and I never want to hear it said by any of you. We will have our sorrow and our grieving and then it is done. After that, we will take care of everything just the way we have been taking care of everything. He is gone, and he is never to be mentioned again. Now let's get moving and get this done."

News Vultures, January 1947

B etty held the crumpled newspaper tightly in her hands. Although recently married, Betty was staying at the farm for a few extra days to help her mother. Her knuckles were white from the effort it took to rip the paper into shreds and roll it into a compact orb, unreadable and unrecognizable to anyone. She wanted no one else to read the words written in the obituary about her father. Tears flowed freely and her cheeks burned a bright red. By the time she placed the ball of paper on the table her sadness had catapulted into hot anger.

"I am not going to let them get away with this!" she cried out loud. Without stopping to grab her gloves or a hat, she threw on the first coat she saw hanging in the closet and shot out of the house. She had no intention of asking anyone to drive with her into town. She knew if she asked Mick to drive her, he would only try to stop her from what she was planning to do. Her determination was like steel and her anger poured over her like molten lava as she headed down the road toward town.

She intended to walk the entire way, fueled by anger and indignation over the obituary in the paper. She needed to think of exactly what she would say.

Although it usually took thirty minutes to walk the distance, Betty made it in record time. She strode down the Main Street

Betty Eymann Rittscher, circa 1944.

sidewalk, not even feeling the cold as she arrived at the storefront that read Newspaper. Her anger flared and kept her warm as she reached for the handle and pulled open the heavy, wooden door of the newspaper office.

"May I help you?" the receptionist asked politely, but as she looked up and saw Betty's furious face she knew this was no ordinary customer.

Betty replied as evenly as possible, "Who writes the obituaries for this paper? I must see him immediately."

The receptionist could see how upset this woman was and wanted to avoid any confrontation with Betty, she led the way to a desk where a man sat at a typewriter busily working away and lost in thought, oblivious to the presence of the two women. Looking at Betty, the receptionist simply pointed at the man, gave a nod of her head, and quietly backed away, not wanting any part of what was going to happen next.

"Excuse me," Betty said loudly over the clatter of the typewriter, "do you write the obituaries?"

The man looked up, saw a very pretty young girl, and replied, "Why yes, m'am, that's me! How can I help you? I am at your service."

"It is too late for you to do anything for me," she responded tersely, "but I have something I can do for you." And with that she leaned over the desk and slapped his cheek with her cold red hand.

He drew back astounded and surprised by what had just transpired. He glared at Betty, rubbed his reddened cheek protectively, and said, "Miss, I don't think we have ever met before. Whatever could I have done to deserve that? I don't even know you!"

"Yesterday you wrote and published an obituary for your paper giving the details of the death of one Chriss Eymann. Am I correct, sir?" Betty questioned.

"Oh, yes," he replied slowly, "such a sad story of the man who took his own life. People say he was just never the same after those four boys of his left for the war. People say he was crazy after that. A sad story indeed."

"Well, how rude of me," Betty continued, "I forgot to introduce myself properly to you. My name is Betty ... Betty Eymann."

Shock registered immediately on the man's face as he realized Betty was one of the daughters he had just written about the day before. He averted his gaze from the beautiful forlorn girl standing in front of him.

"Now, I know your aim in life is to sell papers and to make money for this newspaper, but I want you to look at me. Look at my face! I want you to see with your own eyes the people you hurt when you write about private and personal tragedies. We are real, living people. My mother, my sisters, my brothers, we are all living, breathing human beings who cry, fear, and grieve. I thought I wouldn't ever be able to bear the unbelievable pain of losing my father the way we did, but together, with my family, we held up and we held together," she fired her words at the paper's editor.

But Betty was only getting started, "Then I read the words of your article and those words were like a knife that cut the fragile cords holding us together. It felt just like my father had died in front of me all over again. And then I realized I was not the only one reading those words, everyone in town was reading them too. That was just the straw that broke the camel's back, sir. How could you do this to me? How could you do this to my family? Have you no humanity, no human dignity, sympathy, or warmth in your body? Are you so callous you could knowingly and on purpose inflict more pain on others? You sit here in your office, all snug, warm, and comfortable. You think these things can never happen to you and that you and yours are safe and protected. No one gets through this life for free and your day will come too."

Betty did not wait for his response. She turned and marched out of the small office leaving him still stuttering and blinking in her wake.

She slammed out of the door into the bitter cold day, thinking her mission had been accomplished. She walked with purpose back toward the farm. Anger raged within her, but as she walked her anger turned to sorrow. Two blocks into her journey her knees gave out, she sat down on the cold snow-packed street curb, laid her head on her arms, and sobbed.

Epilogue, 1999

After leaving the cemetery I drove by the old farmstead. I took one last look at the abandoned farm and headed down the overgrown dirt road that surrounded the farmhouse. My thoughts blurred between the memories of the past and the responsibilities of the present as I approached the paved highway that would take me back into Oakdale. I needed to hurry in order to make the dinner on time. I absentmindedly listened to the rhythmic clicking of the turn signal on the car.

The drive to Oakdale's main street took only minutes, and I was soon parking my car in front of the community center in Oakdale. I was eager to see the familiar faces of cousins, aunts, and uncles. Anticipation of the warmth and love of my gigantic family tugged at my heart. I always feel both joy at seeing them all and sadness because my father is no longer waiting for me beyond these doors. I pulled the heavy wooden door open and remembered, with excitement, that I would also be meeting the newest member of my huge family.

As a child, when thinking about my grandparents, aunts, uncles, and parents, I had always viewed them as inseparable parts. Chriss and Hattie, None and Edgar, Betty and Audie, Tude and Claude, Mick and Doris, Hans and Lucile, Chub and Bonnie, Ton and Nadeen, Turk and Marian, Deets and Kenny. To me they were like snow and ice, stems and blossoms, leaves and branches. Each duo possessed its own strength and beauty, but one without the other could not survive alone. It was the combination of the two that made the end product of their union strong, vibrant, and unbreakable. It was impossible to distinguish between them, and I always thought of the two as one unit. I never realized their stories and secrets existed well before I came into the picture.

So now I remember they were once young, living through turbulent times—of Depression and hunger, of grasshoppers, of hard work on the farm, of danger, of war, of betrayal and deception in love—with passions and desires of their own.

None married Edgar well before the war and had three children. These children spent much time at the farm with Hattie and Chriss. The oldest grandchild, Russell, often times stayed for days on the farm trailing after Turk, Hans, Ton, Chub, and Mick. There were times when he was swimming with the boys in the Elkhorn that they had to pluck him out by the hair from a deep dropoff in the river. He was sure they saved him from drowning many times.

Hans returned to Oakdale heartbroken over Ann's unfaithfulness until he met Lucile. Since she was quite a bit younger, he never mentioned he had been married before. It was not until she said she would never marry someone who had already been married that Hans drank a six pack of beer and got the courage to tell her. She demanded to be taken home immediately, but after a few days decided Hans was worth the sacrifice of her principles. They were married in January 1947, the Saturday after the family tragedy. They had five children.

Turk nursed his wounds with farm work after Kay's betrayal. He worked hard for a long time until a beautiful, high-spirited bank teller named Marian enticed him to get out a bit. Her parents were wary of Turk and warned her that he had lived much more than his years. There was an aura of melancholy around him. But she kept pursuing until he kissed her firmly on the mouth on the day Hans and Lucile married. They stayed together and married shortly after this. They had two boys.

Chub met Bonnie while she was working as a clerk. With his broken leg still in the cast he courted and won her over. They married in 1946 and had four children.

In a classic case of opposites attract, Mick met Doris, a school teacher/librarian, whom he married. She kept him on the straight and narrow path when it appeared at times his fun-loving nature might have caused him to stray. They had two children. Stories of Mick are notorious in the family like when he tried to drive a Model A up the entrance steps of Oakdale High School. Mick was drafted in 1950 and served in the military in Germany.

To everyone's surprise Betty met and quickly married a B52 bomber pilot named Adolph. They farmed together between Oakdale and Tilden and had three children.

Tude divorced Al and met and married Claude, a soft-spoken man who kept her happy on the farm. Tude had one son with Al and another son with Claude.

Ton married Nadeen in January of 1946 even though he had to return to the service. Some say his Kamikaze experience aboard the *USS Lindsey* changed him. He didn't want to wait to settle down any more. Ton and Nadeen, my parents, had two children.

Deets married Kenny Smith and happily raised a large family in Norfolk.

Wella, the baby, has married several times. She drifts in and out of Eymann family life.

Through all of my life I never heard my father or any of his brothers (my uncles) say the name of Chriss Eymann. The vow Turk had made with them at the time of their father's death was not broken by the boys.

The boys moved Hattie into a pocket-sized home in the heart of Oakdale. The house had a kitchen and that is what Hattie cared about the most. After she lived there for a while the boys organized a day to install indoor plumbing for her. Everyone helped and Hattie got her first indoor bathroom. The feature I remember most about this house was the round piano bench where my cousin and I would happily spin until we were dizzy.

She passed away at age sixty-four. They found her fully dressed lying peacefully on her bed. On the kitchen counter sat a pan of cinnamon rolls, ready to take to Mick and his family.

It was not until I was in my teen years that my mother finally told me the truth about Chriss, and it has taken many years to come to terms with what happened. Some in my family have yet to make that leap of faith.

"Hi, Barb," called my cousin at the family reunion as he hugged me close. "Let's work on scanning those old pictures later, okay?"

"Sure," I replied and I untangled myself from his embrace. Next my Uncle Chub gave me a hug and a kiss and pointed in the direction of a clump of people standing around the newest member of our family. Their quiet, happy voices and occasional laughter drew me quickly over to join the group.

First, I saw my Uncle Hans. His bright sky-blue eyes twinkled happily and his mouth turned up in his own brand of smile that no one could match. He seemed to keep a perpetual smile on his face. There was no mistaking the unbounded joy he felt at this particular family reunion. His wife, Lucile, was standing beside him.

Out of nowhere my mother, Nadeen, grabbed my arm and propelled me right toward the center of the cluster of people. I could see the outline of our newest family member basking in the familial attention.

"Come and meet your new cousin," my mom ordered with a giggle in her voice.

I could already see a tall man standing in the center of the group. His bright, sky-blue eyes twinkled and his smile lit up the room, just like my Uncle Hans's.

I stretched out my hand, greeted him and introduced myself, "Hello, I am your cousin, Barb." We smiled at each other. Although I knew he was overwhelmed with this first encounter with his new boisterous family, I could see he was thrilled to finally meet all of us.

For, you see, although Steve was in his fifties, the Eymann family embraced its newest member. Only months prior to this dinner Hans had received a call from Steve with the startling news that he was a son Hans did not know about. Over the phone, in what must have been a surreal moment for my uncle, Steve told Hans that his mother in Washington had told him his father had been killed in the war.

Only recently, after his mother Ann's death, did Steve's grandmother tell him the truth that, in fact, his mother and father had divorced before he was born and that his mother never told his father that she was pregnant. Although Steve's grandmother could not quite recall the name of Steve's father, she came close with, "Eikman, I think it was and he was from Nebraska."

These words set Steve on a journey to find his biological father. Through research, the Internet, and persistence he found my cousins Ron and Carolyn. He called them and then Carolyn called her father, Hans. When she told her dad about Steve, he sat down and cried.

Through effort and work Steve and his family made it to Oakdale. It was obvious that Hans was his father. He had the same startling blue eyes and the same smile. He was the spitting image of Hans. For several months Steve and Hans had been getting to know each other and gradually the entire clan had been introduced to him.

It took some time for Hans to come to terms with the arrival of his "war baby." My Aunt Lucile was the one who made the final decision in the matter. My aunts and uncles had taken a trip together to get some winter sun in Arizona and visit Ton and Nadeen who now lived there. Lucile brought Steve's picture with them. She told Hans unequivocally, "Steve is too big to hide under a rock … you have to tell your family."

Hans responded, "Well, Lucile, you always know the right thing to do and so this must be right." With that there was no turning back. Hans broke the news to his brothers first.

So, as we gradually got to know this new cousin, I was drawn in again to the circle of my family. These people surrounded me with loyalty, faith, and unconditional love. When I looked into their faces I glimpsed the past. It cannot be changed but together we are prepared for the future.

Sources

The author consulted the following sources for background in telling her story. She conducted interviews with family members, and she referred to family photos, memorabilia, log books, scrapbooks, and family stories to provide colorful details. The photos in this book are from the Eymann Family private collection.

Books

Benedict, Ruth. *The Chrysanthemum and the Sword: Patterns of Japanese Culture.* Rutland, Vermont: Charles Tuttle, 1976.

Bix, Herbert. *Hirohito and the Making of Modern Japan.* New York: HarperCollins, 2000.

Boyne, Walter. *Clash of the Titans: World War II at Sea.* New York: Simon & Schuster, 1995.

Bradley, James. *Flags of Our Fathers.* New York: Bantam, 2000.

—. *Flyboys.* New York: Little, Brown & Company, 2003.

Brokaw, Tom. *The Greatest Generation.* New York: Random House, 1998.

Buell, Hal. *Uncommon Valor, Common Virtue.* New York: Penguin, 2006.

Christopher, Robert. *The Japanese Mind: The Goliath Explained.* New York: Linden Press, 1983.

Clagett, John. *Typhoon 1944.* New York: Julian Messner, 1970.

Cohen, Adam. *Nothing to Fear.* New York: Penguin, 2009.

Cook, Charles. *The Battle of Cape Esperance Encounter at Guadalcanal.* Binghamton, N.Y.: Vail–Ballou Press, 1968.

Cook, Haruko, and Theodore Cook. *Japan at War: An Oral History.* New York: The New Press, 1992.

Cutler, Thomas J. *The Battle of Leyte Gulf: 23–26 October 1944.* New York: HarperCollins, 1994.

Drury, Bob, and Tom Clavin. *Halsey's Typhoon: The True Story of a Fighting Admiral, An Epic Storm, and an Untold Rescue.* New York: Atlantic Monthly Press, 2007.

Egan, Timothy. *The Worst Hard Time.* New York: Houghton Mifflin Harcourt, 2007.

Erickson, Roy. *Tail End Charlies!* New York: Turner Publishing Co., 1995.

Friedman, Kenneth I. *Afternoon of the Rising Sun: The Battle of Leyte Gulf.* Novato, Calif.: Presidio Press, 2001.

Frank, Richard B. *Guadalcanal.* New York: Penguin, 1990.

Gandt, Robert. *The Twilight Warriors.* New York: Random House, 2010.

Goldberg, Harold J. *D-Day in the Pacific The Battle of Saipan.* Bloomington, Ind.: Indiana University Press, 2007.

Griffith, Samuel B., II. *The Battle for Guadalcanal.* Philadelphia: J. P. Lippincott, 1963.

Hallas, James. *Killing Ground at Okinawa.* Annapolis, Md.: Naval Institute Press, 1996.

Hillenbrand, Laura. *Unbroken.* New York: Random House, 2010.

Hornfischer, James. *Neptune's Inferno.* New York: Bantam, 2011.

—.*The Last Stand of the Tin Can Sailors.* New York: Bantam 2004.

Inoguchi, Rikihei, and Tadashi Nakajima. *The Divine Wind: Japan's Kamikaze Force in World War II.* Annapolis, Md.: Naval Institute Press, 1958.

Kawatoko, Takeshi. *The Mind of the Kamikaze.* Chiran Kagoshima Kyushu: Publishing Office, The Peace Museum for Kamikaze Pilots, 2009.

Kearns Goodwin, Doris. *No Ordinary Times.* New York: Simon & Schuster, 1994.

Leckie, Robert. *Helmet for My Pillow.* New York: Random House, 1957.

—. *Okinawa: The Last Battle of World War II.* New York: Penguin, 1995.

—. *The Battle for Iwo Jima.* New York: Random House, 1967.

—. *Challenge for the Pacific: Guadalcanal the Turning Point of the War.* New York: Random House, 1965.

Manchester, William. *Goodbye Darkness.* Boston: Little and Brown Company, 1979.

—. *American Caesar: Douglas MacArthur 1880–1964.* Boston: Little and Brown Company, 1978.

Meacham, Jon. *Franklin and Winston: An Intimate Portrait of an Epic Friendship.* New York: Random House, 2003.

Meltzer, Milton. *Brother, Can You Spare a Dime? The Great Depression 1929–1933.* New York: Alfred Knopf, 1969.

Miller, Donald L. *D-Days in the Pacific.* New York: Simon & Schuster Paperbacks, 2005.

Mrazek, Robert. *A Dawn Like Thunder: The True Story of Torpedo Squadron Eight.* New York: Back Bay Books, 2008.

Nagatsuka, Ryuji. *I Was a Kamikaze.* [Trans. Nina Rootes.] New York: Macmillan Publishing, 1972.

Naito, Hatsuho. *ThunderGods: The Kamikaze Pilots Tell Their Story.* New York: Kodansha International/Harper Row, 1989.

Newcomb, Richard. *Abandon Ship.* New York. HarperCollins, 1958.

Nihon Senbotsu Gakusei Japanese Memorial Society for Students Killed in the War Wadatsumi Society. *Listen to the Voices from the Sea.* Scranton: The University of Scranton Press, 2000.

Nitobe, Inazo. *Bushido: The Soul of Japan*. Shokabo Japan: The Leeds and Biddle Company, 1900.

Ohnuki-Tierney, Emiko. *Kamikaze, Cherry Blossoms, and Nationalisms: The Militarization of Aesthetics in Japanese History*. Chicago: The University of Chicago Press, 2002.

—.*Kamikaze Diaries: Reflections of Japanese Student Soldiers*. Chicago: The University of Chicago Press, 2006.

Prange, Gordon. *At Dawn We Slept*. New York: McGraw Hill, 1981.

Prange, Gordon, Donald Goldstein, and Katherine Dillon. *Miracle at Midway*. New York: Penguin, 1983.

Rielly, Robin L. *Kamikazis, Corsairs, and Picket Ships*. Philadelphia: Casement, 2008.

Ross, Bill. *Iwo Jima: Legacy of Valor*. New York: Vintage Books, 1985.

Rothberg, Abraham. *Eyewitness History of World War II: The Total Experience in Words and Photographs*. New York: Bantam Books, 1962.

Sears, David. *At War with the Wind*. New York: Citadel Press, 2008.

Sheftall, M.G. *Blossoms in the Wind: The Human Legacy of the Kamikaze*. New York: NAL Caliber, 2005.

Shirley, Craig. *December 1941: 31 Days That Changed America and Saved the World*. Nashville, Tenn.: Thomas Nelson, 2011.

Sledge, E.B. *With the Old Breed at Peleliu and Okinawa*. New York: Ballantine Books, 2007.

Sloan, Bill. *The Ultimate Battle: Okinawa 1945*. New York: Simon & Schuster, 2007.

—. *Brotherhood of Heroes: The Marines at Peleliu, 1944—The Bloodiest Battle of the Pacific War*. New York: Simon & Schuster, 2005.

Spector, Ronald H. *Eagle Against the Sun*. New York: Vintage Books, 1985.

Spurr, Russell. *A Glorious Way to Die: The Kamikaze Mission of the Battleship YAMATO*. New York: Newmarket Press, 1981.

Stanton, Doug. *In Harm's Way: The Sinking of the USS Indianapolis and the Extraordinary Tale of Its Survivors.* New York: St. Martin's Press, 2003.

Stinnett, Robert. *Day of Deceit.* New York: Touchstone, 2000.

Symonds, Craig L. *The Battle of Midway.* Oxford/New York: Oxford University Press, 2011.

Thomas, Evan. *Sea of Thunder.* New York: Simon &Schuster, 2006.

Tillman, Barrett. *Clash of the Carriers: The True Story of the Marianas Turkey Shoot of World War II.* New York: New American Library, 2005.

Time Life Books. *Japan at War.* Alexandria, Va.: Time Life, 1980.

—. *The Battle of the Bulge.* Alexandria, Va.: Time Life, 1979.

—. *Hard Times in the 30s.* Alexandria, Va.: Time Life, 1969.

Toland, John. *The Rising Sun: The Decline and Fall of the Japanese Empire 1936–1945.* New York: Random House, 1970.

—. *Infamy Pearl Harbor and Its Aftermath.* Doubleday, 1982.

Toll, Ian. *Pacific Crucible.* New York: W.W. Norton & Company. 2012.

Tregaskis, Richard. *Guadalcanal Diary.* New York: Random House, 1943.

Woodward C. Vann. *The Battle for Leyte Gulf: The Incredible Story of World War II's Largest Naval Battle.* Nashville, Tenn.: Skyhorse Publishing Inc., 2007.

Wukovits, John. *One Square Mile of Hell: The Battle for Tarawa.* New York: New American Library, 2006.

Youngblood, William T. *The Little Giants: U S Escort Carriers Against Japan.* Annapolis, Md.: Naval Institute Press, 1987.

Zuckhoff, Mitchell. *Lost in Shangri-La.* New York: HarperCollins, 2011.

—. *D Day June 6 1944: The Climactic Battle of World War II.* New York: Simon & Schuster, 1994.

Electronic Sources

Kamikaze Images, http://wgordon.web.wesleyan.edu/kamikaze/ stories/index.htm

World War II Database, http://www.ww2db.com

To the Blue Skies End, http://senri.warbirds.jp/08tubasa.html

Japan Center for Asia Historical Records National Archive of Japan, www.jacar.go.jp/english/index.html

The Japanese National Institute for Defense Studies, www.nids. go.jp/english/sitemap/index.html

Veterans History Project. Vernal Christianson Collection, www. lcweb2.loc.gov/diglib/vhp/bib/33687

D.L. Sears, *USS Lindsey,* www.dlsearsbooks.com/ships/dd/ Allen_M_Sumner_Class/lindsey_dd771

A Tin Can Sailor's Destroyer History, *USS Lindsey* DM 32, www.destroyers.org/nl-histories/dm32

History of Antelope County, www.casde.unl.edu/history/ counties/antelope/oakdale

Lisa's Nostalgia Café, www.nostalgiacafe.proboards.com

Wessels Living History Farm, www.livinghistoryfarm.org

Other Sources

United States Pacific Fleet and Pacific Ocean Areas Press Release No. 674 Wednesday 13 December 1944

Log Book of Hans Eymann

Log Book of Turk Eymann

Diary of Ton Eymann

Eymann Family scrapbooks

USS Sangamon CVE – 26 Pamphlet prepared for a reunion by Donald Schroeder, 2004

Interviews

K.W. "Ton" Eymann

Nadeen Eymann

Marian Eymann

Lucile Eymann

George "Chub" Eymann

Bonnie Eymann

Stanley "Mick" Eymann

Doris Eymann

Merle Martin

USS Lindsey Reunion Members

Eigo Tanaka

Russell Sharples

Fanny Retzlaf (Videotaped interview from Carolyn Eymann Nepodal)

Hans Eymann (Videotaped interview from Carolyn Eymann Nepodal)

Discussion Questions

1. Which character in this story showed the greatest courage? What did he or she do?
2. What are the most interesting facts you learned about the everyday life in the 1930s and 1940s? What things surprised you?
3. Despite the hardships they faced there were good times and examples of generosity among neighbors and townspeople. Give some examples.
4. Which character could you identify with the most?
5. Would the Eymann family consider Roosevelt (New Deal–WWII) to be a hero?
6. What role did the Philco radio play in the life of the Eymann family? Did the role change from the 1930s to the 1940s and if so how did it change?
7. Discuss how the information and communication modes differ today as opposed to WWII. Do you think the situation with Chriss would have turned out differently had he been able to communicate more regularly with his sons during the war? Do we have "too much information" about military matters today?

8. What character traits of Chriss and Hattie do you admire? What traits provided them with the strength to endure the hardships they faced? How do you think their parenting styles impacted their children?

9. What effects did WWII have on the dating and marriage aspects of our society? Give an example from the book.

10. Discuss how the concept of duty was viewed by, and affected the decisions of, the various family members. What types of duty were evidenced in this book? What do you think most motivated the Eymann brothers to enlist in the service? Did their motivation change as the war progressed?

11. How are the ways the Eymann children were brought up and your upbringing alike and how are they different?

12. The character of Chriss underwent changes throughout the story. What events caused or exacerbated these changes in Chriss? Discuss his mental outlook. How are these conditions handled today as opposed to that time— in families, the military, and society in general?

13. Which photo do you like best? Which photo do you find powerful? Which photo best represents the essence of the era?

14. The book contains many photos. Choose one photo and analyze it by answering these questions:

- If you had to write a caption for the photo, what would it say?
- What did you first notice about the photo?
- What would you like to know about these people/ places that you cannot tell from the photo?

Acknowledgments

I would like to thank my father for telling and retelling his stories even when I was too young to understand them. He patiently answered all of my questions and shared all of the rough days in his life. Thank you to my mother who has a memory like a steel trap. I could not have done this without you.

My debt of gratitude to my aunts, uncles, and cousins is immense. Thank you for sharing your time, stories, and pictures with me. Thanks to Frankie for your advice, editing, support, and for believing in me.

Thanks to the crew at Concierge Marketing: Lisa, Sandra, Ellie, Erin, Alison, and Jessica.

Thanks to the Literary Ladies of Flatrock for their support and encouragement.

Most important, thanks to Chriss and Hattie for this wonderful family and amazing story.

Index

About the Author

A box in the basement sparked Barbara Eymann Mohrman's love of history. The box contained her father's World War II memorabilia. "I used to try on my father's uniform and I would pore over the letters, pictures, and articles for hours. I was fortunate because my father patiently answered my questions and history came alive for me."

She was born and raised in Columbus, Nebraska, and currently resides in Western Nebraska.

After her high school graduation she lived and studied in Mexico. She continued her education at Nebraska Wesleyan University with the highlight of having the late Nebraska State Poet Laureate, William Kloefkorn, as a teacher. She graduated in 1976. She received a master's degree from the University of Nebraska at Kearney. She has been a lifelong educator, teaching Spanish and English as a Second Language in the public school system.

She is married, has three children, and four grandchildren. She is an avid reader and is a member of two book clubs.

Made in the USA
Lexington, KY
06 July 2014